Delia

SMITH'S

WINTER COLLECTION

Illustrations by Flo Bayley

BBC BOOKS

Conversion Tables

All these are approximate conversions, which have either been rounded up or down. In a few recipes it has been necessary to modify them very slightly. Never mix metric and imperial measures in one recipe, stick to one system or the other. All spoon measurements used throughout this book are level unless specified otherwise.

Oven temperatures

Gas Mark	°F	°C
1	275	140
2	300	150
3	325	170
4	350	180
5	375	190
6	400	200
7	425	220
8	450	230
9	475	240

Measurements

⅛ inch	3 mm
¼	5 mm
½	1 cm
¾	2
1	2.5
1¼	3
1½	4
1¾	4.5
2	5
2½	6
3	7.5
3½	9
4	10
5	13
5¼	13.5
6	15
6½	16
7	18
7½	19
8	20
9	23
9½	24
10	25.5
11	28
12	30

Weights

½ oz	10 g
¾	20
1	25
1½	40
2	50
2½	60
3	75
4	110
4½	125
5	150
6	175
7	200
8	225
9	250
10	275
12	350
1lb	450
1½	700
2	900
3	1.35 kg

VOLUME

2 fl oz	55 ml
3	75
5 (¼ pt)	150
½ pt	275
1	570
1¼	725
1¾	1 litre
2	1.2
2½	1.5
4	2.25

Introduction

Ever since I was a small child I have felt a sense of magic in the changing Seasons. For me this sense of change and the fact that nothing ever remains quite the same gives our everyday life that joyful quality of anticipation. Having said that, I can envisage nods of agreement when it comes to Spring or Summer.........but Winter? Perhaps a few furrowed brows?

The truth is that Winter has every bit as much charm as the other seasons for me: the dazzling splendour of autumnal colours and Keats' as yet unmatched description of mists and mellow fruitfulness, the stark emptiness of bare branches against the Winter skies, and always the very special pale Winter light.

Yes, there will be cold and grey days and long dark nights, but surely it is in Winter that food comes into our lives with an even sharper focus – because it's then that we all need to be warm, cosy and comforted. In Winter cooking and eating is a much more serious affair – and here on the following pages I have attempted to offer what I hope is a strong case for reviving this idea.

I have an instinct (no more), that perhaps our current preoccupation with healthy eating has eclipsed what I consider to be a very health-giving joy of more traditional cooking, of eating gathered round a table enjoying conversation, good food and good wine.

OK. excesses of anything are unhealthy. I'm not suggesting you eat Steak and Kidney pudding followed by Fallen Chocolate Soufflé every day, but what I am saying is let's not completely lose sight of our heritage: puddings steaming merrily on the stove, the smell of home baking and the evocative aroma and the sound of a joint sizzling in the oven after a long frosty walk. Then there's that glorious anticipation of something braising long and slow whilst at the same time all its wonderful flavours are being gently imparted.

I could of course go on and on, but now it's over to you – and hopefully as you read and try the recipes you too will share my enthusiasm and joy in all that Winter cooking has to offer.

Delia Smith

CHAPTER ONE

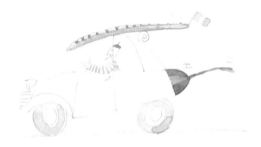

WARMING UP –
the
SOUP COLLECTION

———◇———

lthough there are some delightful summer versions, it's during the winter months that soups really come into their own. Steaming bowls of something fragrant and home-made are not just psychologically warming, they're physically warming too. Like nothing else hot soup really does give you an inner glow right down to the chilliest fingers and toes. So it's been essential for me to find and put together a very special collection of home-made winter soups to begin this book. If I'm honest I was apprehensive at the prospect of doing this as, looking back over the years, I seemed to have already made every soup in existence. But what I want people to know is that the whole subject of food and cooking never loses its fresh edge; new ideas are always popping up through travel, friends and discovering new ingredients. And the result is nine of the best soups I've ever tasted – I know you won't be disappointed!

Most of the following recipes have two dimensions. First, on their own they are good for large family meals along with good bread, cheese and salad. Secondly, with the addition of an interesting garnish, you have something a little more special for entertaining.

Stocks are now available in tubs from supermarkets, but if you need a large quantity these can be expensive. Powdered vegetable stock, gluten-free, is made by a company called Marigold and is available from health food shops – an excellent store cupboard standby. For those who do not have my other books, here's how to make vegetable stock and chicken stock – either of which can be used for the soups in this chapter – and a choice of croûtons.

———

Quick Vegetable Stock

1 stick of celery, cut in half and split lengthways	12 black peppercorns
2 small carrots, split in half lengthways	1 small bunch of parsley stalks and celery leaves
2 small onions, sliced	Salt
2 bay leaves	1–1½ pints (570–850 ml) cold water

Simply place all the ingredients in a saucepan, cover it with a lid, bring everything to the boil, and boil briskly for 30 minutes. After that strain, discarding the vegetables, and the stock is ready for use.

———————— ◊ ————————

Chicken Giblet Stock

1 set of chicken giblets (or see below)	12 black peppercorns
1 stick of celery, cut in half and split lengthways	1 small bunch of parsley stalks and celery leaves
2 small carrots, split lengthways	Salt
2 small onions, sliced	2 pints (1.2 litres) cold water
2 bay leaves	

Place the giblets and the rest of the ingredients in a saucepan, cover and bring to the boil. Boil it briskly for 1 hour, then strain, discarding the giblets and vegetables. If you can't get hold of chicken giblets, use a couple of chicken wing tips instead.

———————— ◊ ————————

Croûtons

SERVES 4

2 oz (50 g) bread cut into small cubes

1 tablespoon olive oil

Pre-heat the oven to gas mark 4, 350°F (180°C).

Just place the cubes of bread in a bowl together with the oil, and stir them around so that they get an even coating. Then arrange them on a baking sheet.

Bake them on a high shelf in the oven for 10 minutes or until they are crisp and golden. One word of warning: do use a kitchen timer for this operation because it's actually very hard to bake something for just 10 minutes without forgetting all about it. I have baked more batches of charcoal-coloured croûtons than I care to remember! Then allow them to cool, and leave them on one side until the soup is ready or store them in a screw-top jar.

———————— ◇ ————————

Garlic Croûtons

Follow the recipe above, only this time add 1 crushed clove of garlic to the bowl along with the olive oil and cubes of bread.

———————— ◇ ————————

Parmesan Croûtons

For this you place the oil and cubes of bread in a small bowl, stir them around until the oil is soaked up, then sprinkle in 1 dessertspoon of freshly grated Parmesan. Stir the cubes around to coat them in that as well, then spread them on the baking sheet and bake as above.

———————— ◇ ————————

Chickpea, Chilli and Coriander Soup

SERVES 4–6

This has decidedly Mexican overtones. It isn't too hot and spicy but the presence of the chilli does give it a nice kick, and the flavour and texture of chickpeas is perfect for soup.

8 oz (225 g) chickpeas, soaked overnight in twice their volume of cold water	**2–3 tablespoons lemon juice**
2 oz (50 g) butter	**1 x 15 g pack (or ½ oz) fresh coriander, leaves and stalks separated**
1 level tablespoon coriander seeds	**1 x 200 ml tub crème fraîche**
1 level tablespoon cumin seeds	**Salt and freshly milled black pepper**
6 fat cloves garlic, peeled and finely chopped	FOR THE GARNISH:
2 small red chillies, halved, de-seeded and chopped	**1 mild, fat red or green chilli, de-seeded and cut into very fine hair-like shreds**
1 level teaspoon ground turmeric	
Grated zest of 1 lemon	You will also need a large saucepan of 6-pint (3.5-litre) capacity.

First of all drain the chickpeas in a colander, rinse them under the cold tap then place them in the saucepan with 2½ pints (1.5 litres) of boiling unsalted water. Then bring them up to simmering point, put a lid on and cook them very gently for about 1 hour or until the chickpeas are absolutely tender and squashy.

While they're cooking prepare the rest of the soup ingredients. The coriander and cumin seeds should be dry-roasted in a small pre-heated pan for 2–3 minutes, then crushed in a pestle and mortar. After that melt the butter in the pan, add the crushed spices along with the chopped garlic and chillies and cook over a low heat for about 5 minutes. Now add the turmeric, stir and heat that gently before removing the pan from the heat.

As soon as the chickpeas are tender, drain them in a colander placed over a bowl to reserve the cooking water. Transfer the chickpeas to a liquidizer together with a couple of ladles of cooking water and purée them until fine and smooth. Now add the lemon zest, coriander stalks and spices from the pan along with another ladleful of cooking water and blend once more until fine and smooth.

Next the whole lot needs to go back into the saucepan with the rest of the reserved cooking water. Bring it all up to a gentle simmer, give it a good stir, season, then simmer gently for a further 30 minutes. All this can be done in advance, then when you're ready to serve the soup re-heat very gently without letting it come to the boil. Stir in half the crème fraîche and the lemon juice, taste to check the seasoning, then serve in hot soup bowls with the rest of the crème fraîche swirled in and scatter with the shredded chilli and coriander leaves as a garnish.

———————◇———————

Next page: Roasted Pumpkin Soup with Melting Cheese (see page 14)

Roasted Pumpkin Soup with Melting Cheese

SERVES 6

The lovely thing about pumpkin is that it has a really velvety texture in soup, and if it's oven-roasted before you add it to the soup, it gives an unusual nuttiness to the flavour. Just before serving, add little cubes of quick melting cheese like Gruyère or, if you're lucky enough to get it, Fontina. Then finding little bits of half-melted cheese in the soup that stretch up on the spoon is an absolute delight. (See photograph on pages 12–13.)

1 pumpkin weighing 3–3½ lb (1.35–1.6 kg)
1 tablespoon groundnut oil
1 large onion, peeled and finely chopped
1½ pints (850 ml) stock, vegetable or chicken
15 fl oz (425 ml) whole milk
1 oz (25 g) butter
Freshly grated nutmeg
Salt and freshly milled black pepper

TO SERVE:
4 oz (110 g) Gruyère or Fontina, cut into ¼-inch (5-mm) dice
2 oz (50 g) Gruyère or Fontina, coarsely grated
6 teaspoons crème fraîche
Croûtons (see page 10)
Flat-leaf parsley

You will also need a solid baking sheet that won't buckle in the high heat, and a 6-pint (3.5-litre) saucepan.

Pre-heat the oven to gas mark 9, 475°F (240°C).

Begin by cutting the pumpkin in half through the stalk, then cut each half into 4 again and scoop out the seeds using a large spoon. Then brush the surface of each section with the oil and place them on the baking sheet. Season with salt and pepper, then pop them on a high shelf of the oven to roast for 25–30 minutes or until tender when tested with a skewer.

Meanwhile melt the butter in a large saucepan over a high heat, add the onion, stir it round and when it begins to colour around the edges, after about 5 minutes, turn the heat down. Let it cook very gently without a lid, giving it a stir from time to time, for about 20 minutes.

Then remove the pumpkin from the oven and leave it aside to cool. Now add the stock and the milk to the onions, and leave them with the heat turned low to slowly come up to simmering point. Next scoop out the flesh of the pumpkin with a sharp knife and add it to the stock together with a seasoning of salt, pepper and nutmeg. Then let it all simmer very gently for about 15–20 minutes.

Next the soup should be processed to a purée. Because there's a large volume of soup, it's best to do this in two halves. What you need to do is whizz it until it's smoothly blended, but as an extra precaution it's best to pass it through a sieve as well in case there are any unblended fibrous bits. Taste and season well, then when you're ready to serve the soup re-heat it gently just up to simmering point, being careful not to let it boil.

Finally, stir in the diced cheese, then ladle the soup into warm soup bowls. Garnish each bowl with a teaspoonful of crème fraîche and scatter with the grated cheese, a few croûtons as well, if you like them, and a sprinkling of parsley.

Polish Beetroot Soup

SERVES 4

Beetroot is either loved or hated – mostly the latter I suspect, because in this country people have a surfeit of it doused in strong vinegar. But its lovers know of its earthy charm and delicious but distinctive flavour. It makes wonderful soup, and this one is Polish in origin and especially good. Although the soup is a dazzling colour, you won't want your hands to match it, so it's best to wear gloves while you're handling it!

FOR THE STOCK:
6 oz (175 g) belly pork cut in cubes
1 large carrot, cut in chunks
1 medium onion, roughly chopped
1 bay leaf
A handful of parsley stalks
1 dessertspoon of oil
2 pints (1.2 litres) water
Salt and freshly milled black pepper

FOR THE SOUP:
1½ lb (700 g) uncooked beetroot, whole but with stalks removed
1 level tablespoon plain flour, mixed to a paste with 1 oz (25 g) butter
5 fl oz (150 ml) soured cream
2 tablespoons lemon juice
Salt

You will also need a large saucepan of about 6-pint (3.5-litre) capacity.

First of all you need to make a stock: heat the oil in a large saucepan and when it's really hot, brown the pieces of pork, carrot and onion, keeping the heat high so they turn brownish-black at the edges. This is important because it gives the stock a good flavour.

When you're happy with the colour (after about 6 minutes) add the water, bay leaf and parsley stalks, followed by a good seasoning of salt and freshly milled pepper. As soon as it begins to simmer turn the heat down and let it simmer very gently without a lid for 40 minutes. After that strain it through a sieve into a bowl, throw out the stock ingredients and rinse the saucepan to use again.

While the stock is cooking you can deal with the beetroot. Place it in another saucepan, add enough boiling water to just cover, then add salt. Put on a lid and simmer gently for 40 minutes or until tender when pierced with a skewer. After that drain off the water, then cover the beetroot with cold water to cool it down. As soon as it's cool enough to handle, take off the skin. Now reserve one beetroot (about 4 oz, 110 g) for the garnish and cut the rest into cubes. Next transfer it to the saucepan in which you made the stock, add the stock, bring to simmering point, cover and simmer gently for 20 minutes.

Now, using a draining spoon, transfer the beetroot to a liquidizer or food processor, put the lid on, switch on the motor and whilst it's running add the flour and butter paste, the soup stock followed by 3 fl oz (75 ml) of soured cream. When it's all blended pour it back into the saucepan, add the lemon juice, taste to check the seasoning and re-heat very gently, without letting it come to the boil. Grate the reserved beetroot on the fine side of the grater. Then serve the soup in warmed soup bowls, swirl in the remaining soured cream and scatter the grated beetroot on top as a garnish. For entertaining, croûtons (see page 10) made with black rye bread would be a good addition.

Curried Parsnip and Apple Soup with Parsnip Crisps

SERVES 6

This is such a lovely soup. The sweetness of the parsnips is sharpened by the presence of the apple, and the subtle flavour of the spices comes through beautifully. If you're entertaining, the soup can be enhanced by some crunchy parsnip crisps sprinkled over as a garnish (see right).

1½ lb (700 g) young parsnips	1 heaped teaspoon cumin seeds
1½ oz (40 g) butter	6 whole cardamom pods, seeds only
1 tablespoon groundnut oil	1 heaped teaspoon turmeric
2 medium onions, chopped	1 heaped teaspoon ground ginger
2 cloves garlic, chopped	Salt and freshly milled black pepper
2 pints (1.2 litres) good flavoured stock (see page 9)	
1 medium Bramley apple (6 oz, 175 g)	
1 heaped teaspoon coriander seeds	

You will also need a large saucepan of about 6-pint (3.5-litre) capacity.

Begin by heating a small frying pan and dry-roasting the coriander, cumin and cardamom seeds – this is to toast them and draw out their flavour. After 2–3 minutes they will change colour and start to jump in the pan. Remove them from the pan and crush them finely with a pestle and mortar.

Next heat the butter and oil in a saucepan until the butter begins to foam, then add the onions and gently soften for about 5 minutes before adding the garlic. Let that cook along with the onions for another 2 minutes, then add all the crushed spices along with the turmeric and ginger, stir and let it all continue to cook gently for a few more minutes while you peel and chop the parsnips into 1-inch (2.5-cm) dice. Add the parsnips to the saucepan, stirring well, then pour in the stock, add some seasoning and let the soup simmer as gently as possible for 1 hour without putting on a lid.

After that remove it from the heat, then liquidize it if possible; if not, use a food processor and then a sieve – or even just a sieve, squashing the ingredients through using the bowl of a ladle. After the soup.has been puréed return it to the saucepan, taste to check the seasoning, then when you're ready to serve re-heat very gently. While that's happening, peel the apple and as the soup just reaches simmering point grate the apple into it. Be careful to let the soup barely simmer for only 3–4 minutes. Serve in hot soup bowls garnished with parsnip crisps.

⸻ ◊ ⸻

Parsnip Crisps

1 medium to large parsnip (10–12 oz, 275–350 g)	6 tablespoons groundnut oil
	Salt

First peel the parsnip and then slice it into rounds as thinly as you possibly can, using a sharp knife. Now heat the oil in a 10-inch (25.5-cm) frying pan until it is very hot, almost smoking, then fry the parsnip slices in batches until they are golden brown, about 2–3 minutes (they will not stay flat or colour evenly but will twist into lovely shapes). As they're cooked remove them with a slotted spoon and spread them out on kitchen paper to drain. Sprinkle lightly with salt. If you like you can make these in advance as they will stay crisp for a couple of hours.

◇

Black Bean Soup with Black Bean Salsa

SERVES 4–6

This soup is simply stunning, one you'll want to make over and over again. Black beans don't have a strong flavour of their own but they do carry other flavours superbly, while at the same time yielding a unique velvety texture. If you forget to soak the beans overnight, bring them up to the boil for 10 minutes and then pre-soak them for three hours. Serving salsa with soup makes a clever contrast of the cold refreshing textures of the vegetables and the hot lusciousness of the soup.

9 oz (250 g) black beans
1 x 70 g pack (or 3 oz) pancetta, or smoked bacon, finely chopped
1 large onion, chopped small
2 oz (50 g) carrot, chopped small
2 oz (50 g) swede, chopped small
1 fat clove garlic, crushed
1 teaspoon cumin seeds
1 teaspoon Tabasco sauce
1 x 15 g pack (or ½ oz) coriander, stalks finely chopped and leaves reserved for the salsa
2 pints (1.2 litres) chicken stock
2 tablespoons olive oil
Salt and freshly milled black pepper
1 heaped tablespoon crème fraîche

Juice of ½ lime (keep other ½ for the salsa)

FOR THE SALSA:

3 large spoons cooked beans – see method
2 large tomatoes, not too ripe
1 small red onion, finely chopped
1 green chilli, de-seeded and chopped
Coriander leaves reserved from above
1 dessertspoon extra virgin olive oil
Juice of ½ lime
Salt and freshly milled black pepper

You will also need a large saucepan of about 6-pint (3.5-litre) capacity.

It's best to start the soup the night before by throwing the beans into a pan and covering them with approximately twice their volume of cold water. Next day, drain them in a colander and rinse them under a cold running tap. Now take the saucepan and heat the 2 tablespoons of olive oil. As soon as it's really hot, add the chopped pancetta and cook for about 5 minutes. Then turn the heat down to medium, stir in the onion, garlic, carrot, swede and coriander stalks and continue to cook for another 10 minutes with the lid on, stirring everything round once or twice.

While that's happening heat a small frying pan over a medium heat, then add the cumin seeds and dry-roast them for 2–3 minutes until they become very aromatic, begin to change colour and start to dance in the pan. At that point remove them from the pan and crush them to a coarse powder with a pestle and mortar. Add this to the vegetables along with the drained beans, Tabasco sauce and stock (but no salt at this stage), then bring everything up to a gentle simmer for about 1½ hours with the lid on. It's very important to keep the simmer as gentle as possible, so you might need to use a heat diffuser here.

When the time is up, use a slotted spoon to remove 3 rounded spoonfuls of the beans, rinse and drain them in a sieve and reserve them for the salsa. Now you need to purée the soup and the best way to do this is in a liquidizer – if not, a processor and a sieve will do or even just a sieve. When the soup is liquidized, return it to the saucepan, add the lime juice, season with salt and pepper and it's now ready for re-heating later when you want to serve it.

TO MAKE THE SALSA

Pour boiling water over the tomatoes, leave them for 1 minute, then slip the skins off, cut them in half and gently squeeze each half in your hand to remove the seeds. After the seeds are removed, chop the tomato into small dice and place it in a bowl along with the reserved beans, the finely chopped red onion, green chilli, coriander leaves and the extra virgin olive oil. Then add the juice of half a lime, some salt and freshly milled black pepper and leave it aside for about 1 hour for the flavours to mingle and be absorbed.

To serve the soup, re-heat it very gently, being careful not to allow it to come to the boil, as boiling always spoils the flavour of soup. Serve in warm soup bowls, adding a spoonful of crème fraîche and an equal portion of salsa sprinkled over the surface.

If you're entertaining and really want to have some fun, make this soup *and* the White Bean Soup on page 22, and serve them together with one or other of the garnishes. All you do is re-heat both soups, then using two ladles pour both ladlefuls into the warmed bowls simultaneously, one from the left, the other from the right. It works a treat (see photograph on page 20) and makes a lovely contrast. Any leftover soup can be frozen.

———————————◇———————————

Next page: Black Bean Soup and Tuscan White Bean Soup (see page 22)

Smoked Haddock Chowder with Poached Eggs

SERVES 4

*S*moked haddock makes a very fine soup, and this I've adapted from a famous version invented in Scotland where it is called Cullen skink. If you add poached quails' eggs to the soup this makes a delightful surprise as you lift up an egg on your spoon. For a main course meal you could use poached hens' eggs to make it more substantial. Either way it is lovely served with brown bread and butter.

1 lb 4 oz (560 g) undyed smoked haddock, cut into 4 pieces	1 tablespoon lemon juice
18 fl oz (500 ml) milk	8 quails' eggs (or 4 hens' eggs)
18 fl oz (500 ml) water	1 tablespoon chopped flat-leaf parsley
1 bay leaf	Salt and freshly milled black pepper
1½ oz (40 g) butter	
1 medium onion, finely chopped	
1 oz (25 g) flour	

You will also need a large saucepan of about 6-pint (3.5-litre) capacity, and 4 warmed shallow soup bowls.

Start off by placing the haddock pieces in a large saucepan, pour in the milk and water, season with pepper (but no salt yet) and add the bay leaf. Now gently bring it up to simmering point and simmer very gently for 5 minutes before taking it off the heat and pouring it all into a bowl to steep for 15 minutes.

Meanwhile, wipe the saucepan with kitchen paper and melt the butter, add the chopped onion and let it sweat very gently without browning for about 10 minutes. By that time the haddock will be ready, so remove it with a draining spoon (reserving the liquid) to a board, discard the bay leaf and peel off the skin.

Next stir the flour into the pan to soak up the juices, then gradually add the fish-cooking liquid, stirring after each addition. When that's all in, add half the haddock separated into flakes.

Now pour the soup into a liquidizer or food processor and blend thoroughly. After that pass it through a sieve back into the saucepan, pressing any solid bits of haddock that are left to extract all the flavour. Discard what's left in the sieve then separate the remaining haddock into flakes and add these to the soup. Taste it now and season with salt, pepper and lemon juice and leave to one side to keep warm.

Now poach the eggs: pour boiling water straight into a medium-sized frying pan and place over a heat gentle enough for there to be the merest trace of bubbles simmering on the base of the pan. Break the 8 quails' eggs (or 4 hens' eggs) into the water and let them cook for just 1 minute. Then remove the pan from the heat and let the quails' eggs stand in the water for 3 minutes, and the hens' eggs for 10, after which time the whites will be set and the yolks creamy. Use a draining spoon and a wad of kitchen paper underneath to remove the eggs, place 2 quails' eggs (or one hen's egg) in each warmed serving bowl, ladle the soup on top and serve sprinkled with the chopped parsley.

Tuscan White Bean Soup with Frizzled Shallots and Pancetta

SERVES 4

If you look down the list of ingredients here you might be forgiven for thinking this doesn't sound very exciting. Yet Italian cannellini beans transformed into a soup are just wonderful, both in texture and in flavour. The other essential ingredients are fresh herbs and the best Italian extra virgin olive oil you can lay your hands on. (See photograph on page 20.)

8 oz (225 g) cannellini beans	2 pints (1.2 litres) chicken stock
1 large onion, peeled and chopped	4 tablespoons extra virgin olive oil
2 fat cloves garlic, crushed	Juice of ½ lemon
1 stalk celery, chopped	Salt and freshly milled black pepper
1 good sprig each of parsley, thyme and rosemary	
1 bay leaf	

You will also need a 6-pint (3.5-litre) saucepan.

First of all you need to soak the beans in twice their volume of cold water overnight or, failing that, use the same amount of cold water, bring them up to the boil, boil for 10 minutes and leave them to soak for 2 hours.

When you're ready to make the soup, heat 2 tablespoons of the olive oil in the saucepan and gently soften the onion in it for 5 minutes. Then add the garlic and continue to cook gently for about 1 minute. After that add the drained beans, celery, herbs, bay leaf and black pepper, but no salt at this stage. Now pour in the stock and stir well. As soon as it reaches a gentle simmer put a lid on and keep it at the gentlest simmer for 1½ hours, stirring it from time to time. When the time is up, check the beans are tender and if not continue to cook them for a further 15–30 minutes.

When the beans are ready, season with salt, liquidize the soup or process it and pass it through a sieve (or simply sieve the whole lot). When you are ready to serve the soup, re-heat gently without letting it come to the boil and add the lemon juice, check the seasoning and add 2 more tablespoons of olive oil just before serving. While you're re-heating the soup, make the garnish as follows.

————————— ◇ —————————

Frizzled Shallots and Pancetta Garnish

4 shallots, peeled and finely sliced into rings	**3 tablespoons olive oil**
1 x 70 g pack (or 3 oz) thinly sliced pancetta or streaky bacon	

Roll the pancetta or bacon strips into a cigar shape then with a sharp knife cut them into fine shreds, which you then need to separate out. Now heat 2 tablespoons of olive oil in a large frying pan over a high heat, and when the oil is hot and shimmering add the shallots and fry them for 3–4 minutes, stirring occasionally so they don't catch on the base of the pan. When they are crisp and golden brown lift them onto crumpled kitchen paper to drain, using a draining spoon.

Now heat another tablespoon of olive oil in the same pan and fry the pancetta or bacon strips over a high heat for about 2 minutes until they too are golden and crunchy. Drain on kitchen paper then serve a little of the shallots and pancetta on the soup as it goes to the table. If you want to make the garnish in advance you can re-frizzle both in a hot frying pan just before serving.

◇

Libyan Soup with Couscous

SERVES 6

This recipe first appeared in 'The Food Aid Cookery Book', published in 1986. Its contributor Mary El-Rayes has kindly given me permission to reprint it here. It's a truly wonderful soup, meaty with lots of fragrant flavour, and perfect for serving on a really cold winter's day with pitta bread warm from the oven.

6 oz (175 g) finely chopped raw lamb, leg steak or similar	**4 oz (110 g) dried chickpeas (soaked overnight in twice their volume of cold water)**
1 heaped teaspoon coriander seeds	**2 oz (50 g) couscous**
1 heaped teaspoon cumin seeds	**1 tablespoon chopped fresh parsley**
1 large onion, peeled and chopped	**1 tablespoon chopped fresh mint**
2 cloves garlic, peeled and crushed with 1 level teaspoon sea salt in a pestle and mortar	**2 tablespoons oil**
	Salt to taste
1 heaped teaspoon ground allspice	
2 heaped teaspoons mild chilli powder	TO SERVE:
1 x 140 g tin tomato purée	**Pitta bread**
1 green chilli, de-seeded and chopped	**Lemon wedges**
2 teaspoons caster sugar	
1½ pints (850 ml) water	You will also need a large saucepan of about 6-pint (3.5-litre) capacity with a well-fitting lid.
1 pint (570 ml) good lamb stock	

Begin by pre-heating a small frying pan over a medium heat, then add the coriander and cumin seeds and dry-roast them for about 2–3 minutes, moving them around the pan until they change colour and begin to dance. This will draw out their full spicy flavour. Now crush them quite finely with a pestle and mortar.

Next heat 1 tablespoon of the oil in the saucepan and gently cook the onion until soft and lightly browned, about 5 or 6 minutes, then add the crushed garlic and let that cook for another 2 minutes. After that add the crushed spices, the allspice and chilli powder and stir them into the juices in the pan. Now transfer all this to a plate and keep it aside while you heat the other tablespoon of oil in the same pan until it's very hot. Then add the pieces of lamb and brown them, quickly turning them over and keeping them on the move.

Turn the heat down and now return the onion and spice mixture to the pan to join the meat, adding the tomato purée, chopped chilli and caster sugar. Stir everything together, then add the water and stock. Give it all another good stir then drain the soaked chickpeas, discarding their soaking liquid, and add these to the pan. Give a final stir then put a lid on and simmer as gently as possible for 1 hour or until the chickpeas are tender.

When you're ready to serve the soup taste it, add some salt, then add the couscous, parsley and mint and take the pan off the heat. Put the lid back on and let it stand for 3 minutes before serving in hot soup bowls. Serve with lemon wedges to squeeze into the soup and some warm pitta bread.

French Onion Soup (see page 26)

French Onion Soup

SERVES 6

There are few things more comforting than making a real French Onion Soup – slowly cooked caramelized onions that turn mellow and sweet in a broth laced with white wine and Cognac. The whole thing is finished off with crunchy baked croûtons of crusty bread topped with melted, toasted cheese. If ever there was a winter stomach warmer, this is surely it! (See photograph on page 25.)

1½ lb (700 g) onions, thinly sliced	FOR THE CROUTONS:
2 tablespoons olive oil	**French bread or *baguettine*, cut into**
2 oz (50 g) butter	**1-inch (2.5-cm) diagonal slices**
2 cloves garlic, crushed	**1 tablespoon olive oil**
½ teaspoon granulated sugar	**1–2 cloves garlic, crushed**
2 pints (1.2 litres) good beef stock	
10 fl oz (275 ml) dry white wine	TO SERVE:
2 tablespoons Cognac	**6 large or 12 small croûtons**
Salt and freshly milled black pepper	**8 oz (225 g) Gruyère, grated**

Pre-heat the oven to gas mark 4, 350°F (180°C).

You will also need a heavy based saucepan or flameproof casserole of 6-pint (3.5-litre) capacity and a heatproof tureen or soup bowls.

First make the croûtons – begin by drizzling the olive oil on a large, solid baking sheet, add the crushed garlic and, then, using your hands, spread the oil and garlic all over the baking sheet. Now place the bread slices on top of the oil, then turn over each one so that both sides have been lightly coated with the oil. Bake for 20–25 minutes till crisp and crunchy.

Next place the saucepan or casserole on a high heat and melt the oil and butter together. When this is very hot, add the onions, garlic and sugar, and keep turning them from time to time until the edges of the onions have turned dark – this will take about 6 minutes. Then reduce the heat to its lowest setting and leave the onions to carry on cooking very slowly for about 30 minutes, by which time the base of the pan will be covered with a rich, nut brown, caramelized film.

After that pour in the stock and white wine, season, then stir with a wooden spoon, scraping the base of the pan well. As soon as it all comes up to simmering point, turn down the heat to its lowest setting, then go away and leave it to cook very gently, without a lid, for about 1 hour.

All this can be done in advance, but when you're ready to serve the soup, bring it back up to simmering point, taste to check for seasoning – and if it's extra-cold outside, add a couple of tablespoons of Cognac! Warm the tureen or soup bowls in a low oven and pre-heat the grill to its highest setting. Then ladle in the hot soup and top with the croûtons, allowing them to float on the top of the soup.

Now sprinkle the grated Gruyère thickly over the croûtons and place the whole lot under the grill until the cheese is golden brown and bubbling. Serve immediately – and don't forget to warn your guests that everything is very hot!

CHAPTER TWO

———————————◇———————————

WARM SALADS, HOT STARTERS *and* SUPPER DISHES

———————◇———————

Winter salads have become much more popular in recent years, mainly due to the improving quality of imported salad vegetables. There was a time when these were limp and tasteless, but now they're getting better and better all the time. For instance our English Fenland Celery Growers move their whole operation to Spain during the winter to provide us with crisp and crunchy celery all year round. There is also a dazzling array of salad leaves constantly winging their way to us from around the world, not to mention fresh herbs and an enormous choice of vinegars and oils.

What is also helpful in winter is the current fashion for warm salads, where some of the ingredients are warm or even hot but the crisp fresh texture of the salad is retained. Most of the hot starters included in this chapter can double up as supper dishes serving fewer people.

If you are entertaining you may like to consider other starters elsewhere in the book. There are dishes that translate easily from lunch to evening meal in almost every chapter: try Linguini with Mussels and Walnut Parsley Pesto (page 66), Fillets of Sole Véronique (page 49), Oven-Baked Wild Mushroom Risotto (page 101), Red Onion Tarte Tatin (page 94), Roasted and Sun-Dried Tomato Risotto (page 99), Warm Roquefort Cheesecake with Pears in Balsamic Vinaigrette (page 92), Pancake Cannelloni with Spinach and Four Cheeses (page 89), Mashed Black-Eyed Beancakes with Ginger Onion Marmalade (page 104).

————————

Pan-Roasted Italian Onions with San Daniele Ham and Shaved Pecorino

SERVES 4 AS A STARTER

I *first tasted this at one of my favourite London restaurants, Le Caprice, and loved it so much I asked for the recipe, which the chefs Mark Hix and Tim Hughes very kindly gave me. It is really one of the nicest first courses I have ever had. San Daniele is available from specialist food shops but if you can't get hold of it use thinly sliced Parma ham. And the same applies to the sheep's cheese Pecorino, which can be replaced by Parmigiano Reggiano.*

12 oz (350 g) flat Italian onions or shallots, peeled	**1 teaspoon thyme leaves**
6–8 oz (175–225 g) San Daniele ham, thinly sliced	**2 fl oz (55 ml) balsamic vinegar**
4 oz (110 g) mature Pecorino Romano	**Salt and coarsely crushed peppercorns**
2 fl oz (55 ml) extra virgin olive oil	
1 teaspoon brown sugar	

Begin by heating the olive oil in a thick-based saucepan, stir in the onions or shallots, cover and cook over a medium heat for 5 minutes. After that add the brown sugar, thyme leaves, the salt and pepper and 2 tablespoons water. Cover the pan and cook slowly over a low heat – stirring the onions from time to time to prevent them sticking to the base of the pan – for about 30–35 minutes or until the liquid caramelizes slightly and the onions are soft, with a little colour.

After that, add the balsamic vinegar to the pan, stir well then remove it straight away from the heat, and allow the onions to cool (if you want to prepare this part in advance you can store them at this stage in an airtight jar in the fridge).

Just before you are ready to serve, pre-heat the oven to gas mark 4, 350°F (180°C) and place the onions in a shallow, lidded casserole for 15 minutes. After that arrange them on a plate with a little of the balsamic dressing spooned over. Lay the ham over the onions and use a potato peeler to shave the Pecorino over it. Now spoon a little more of the dressing around the plate and sprinkle some crushed black pepper over the cheese. Serve with ciabatta and some good butter.

––––––––––––––– ◇ –––––––––––––––

Baked Eggs in Wild Mushroom Tartlets

SERVES 6 AS A STARTER

It's quite a long time since I made a large quiche or tart for entertaining. I feel that serving them individually is prettier and more practical, and people seem to really enjoy them. This recipe contains a base of a very concentrated mixture of fresh mushrooms and dried porcini, and this is a delight coupled with a softly baked egg and crisp pastry. (See photograph on page 32.)

FOR THE PASTRY:

3 oz (75 g) soft butter

6 oz (175 g) plain flour, sifted

1½ oz (40 g) Parmesan (Parmigiano Reggiano), finely grated

FOR THE FILLING:

1 oz (25 g) dried porcini mushrooms

3 oz (75 g) butter

2 small red onions, finely chopped

2 cloves garlic, chopped

6 oz (175 g) chestnut mushrooms

6 oz (175 g) open cap mushrooms

2 teaspoons lemon juice

1 heaped tablespoon chopped fresh parsley

6 x size 1 eggs

1 oz (25 g) Parmesan (Parmigiano Reggiano), finely grated, for sprinkling over the tarts

Sea salt and freshly milled black pepper

You will also need 6 quiche tins, 4-inch (10-cm) base diameter, ½ inch (1 cm) deep, and a 5½-inch (14-cm) plain cutter.

Begin by placing the porcini in a bowl. Pour 7 fl oz (200 ml) boiling water over them and leave to soak for 30 minutes.

Now make the pastry. This can easily be done in a processor or by rubbing the butter into the flour and stirring in the grated Parmesan and sufficient water (approximately 3 tablespoons) to mix to a soft but firm dough. Place the dough in a plastic bag and leave in the fridge for 30 minutes to rest. This pastry will need a little more water than usual as the cheese absorbs some of it.

For the filling, heat 2 oz (50 g) of the butter in a heavy-based frying pan, add the onions and garlic and fry until they are soft and almost transparent (about 15 minutes). While that's happening, finely chop the chestnut and open cap mushrooms. When the porcini have had their 30 minutes' soaking, place a sieve over a bowl and strain them into it, pressing to release the moisture. You can reserve the soaking liquid and freeze it for stocks or sauces if you don't want to throw it out.

Then chop the porcini finely and transfer them with the other mushrooms to the pan containing the onions. Add the remaining 1 oz (25 g) of butter, season and cook till the juices of the mushrooms run, then add the lemon juice and parsley. Raise the heat slightly and cook the mushrooms without a lid, stirring from time to time to prevent them sticking, until all the liquid has evaporated and the mixture is of a spreadable consistency. This will take about 25 minutes.

While the mushrooms are cooking, pre-heat the oven to gas mark 6, 400°F (200°C). Now roll out the pastry to a thickness of ⅛ inch (3 mm) and cut out 6 rounds, re-rolling the pastry if necessary.

Grease the tins with a little melted butter and line each tin with the pastry, pushing it down from the top so the pastry will not shrink while cooking. Trim any surplus pastry from around the top and prick the base with a fork. Now leave this in the fridge for a few minutes until the oven is up to temperature.

Now place the tins on a solid baking sheet and bake on the middle shelf of the oven for 15–20 minutes until the pastry is golden and crisp. Remove them from the oven and reduce the temperature to gas mark 4, 350°F (180°C).

Divide the filling between the tarts, making a well in the centre with the back of a spoon. Then break an egg into a saucer or a small ramekin, slip it into the tart and scatter a little Parmesan over the top. Repeat this process with the other five tarts and return them to the oven for 12–15 minutes until they are just set and the yolks are still soft and creamy. Serve straight away, because if they wait around the eggs will go on cooking.

Spaghetti alla Carbonara

SERVES 2 AS A SUPPER DISH

his is my favourite, and the very best version I know of the great classic Italian recipe for pasta with bacon and egg sauce. This is one that is made using authentic ingredients: pancetta (Italian cured bacon which has a wonderful flavour) and Pecorino Romano (a sheep's cheese) which is sharper than Parmesan. However, if you can't get either of these ingredients it's still marvellous made with streaky bacon and Parmigiano Reggiano.

8 oz (225 g) spaghetti	**4 tablespoons crème fraîche**
2 x 70 g packs (or 5 oz) pancetta, sliced or ready cubed	**Salt and freshly milled black pepper**
1½ tablespoons extra virgin olive oil	TO SERVE:
4 tablespoons Pecorino Romano, finely grated	**Extra grated Pecorino**
2 x size 1 eggs plus 2 extra yolks	

First of all take your largest saucepan and fill it with at least 4 pints (2.25 litres) of hot water and then put it on the heat to come up to simmering point, adding salt and a few drops of olive oil. As soon as it reaches simmering point add the pasta and stir it once, then put a timer on and time it for 8 minutes exactly. (Some pasta might need 10 minutes so follow the instructions on the packet.)

Meanwhile, heat the olive oil in a frying pan and fry the pancetta until it's crisp and golden, about 5 minutes. Next, whisk the eggs, yolks, cheese and crème fraîche in a bowl and season generously with black pepper. Then when the pasta is cooked, drain it quickly in a colander, leaving a little of the moisture still clinging. Now quickly return it to the saucepan and add the pancetta and any oil in the pan, along with the egg and cream mixture. Stir very thoroughly so that everything gets a good coating – what happens is that the liquid egg cooks briefly as it comes into contact with the hot pasta.

Serve the pasta on really hot deep plates with some extra grated Pecorino.

Warm Lentil Salad with Walnuts and Goats' Cheese

SERVES 4

I think we should all be eating more pulses, so the more recipes that include them the better. In this warm salad, I've chosen the little tiny black-grey Puy lentils, but the green or brown variety will work just as well, given slightly less cooking time.

	FOR THE DRESSING:
8 oz (225 g) Puy lentils	
1½ oz (40 g) walnuts, roughly chopped	**1 fat clove garlic, peeled**
1 small red onion, finely chopped	**1 level teaspoon sea salt**
1 bay leaf	**1 rounded teaspoon powdered mustard**
1 fat clove garlic, crushed	**2 tablespoons balsamic vinegar**
1 heaped teaspoon thyme leaves, chopped	**2 tablespoons walnut oil**
	3 tablespoons extra virgin olive oil
1 tablespoon extra virgin olive oil	**1 x 30 g pack (or 1 oz) of rocket leaves**
Salt and freshly milled black pepper	**Freshly milled black pepper**
	2 crottin goats' cheese or 4 oz (110g) of any other firm goats' cheese

First you need to cook the lentils. To do this, heat the oil in a medium saucepan and when it's hot, lightly fry the chopped walnuts for about 1 minute. Then remove them with a draining spoon to a plate and keep them aside for later.

Now to the oil left in the pan, add the onion and crushed garlic and let these cook and soften for about 5 minutes. After that, stir in the lentils, bay leaf and thyme and make sure they all get a good coating with oil. Next add 10 fl oz (275 ml) of boiling water, but don't add any salt – just put a lid on, turn the heat down to a gentle simmer and let the lentils cook for 30–40 minutes or until they're tender and all the liquid has been absorbed. You really need to bite one to test if they're done.

While the lentils are cooking you can prepare the dressing. Use a pestle and mortar and crush the garlic with the salt until it's creamy, then add the mustard and work that into the garlic paste. After that, whisk in the balsamic vinegar, followed by the oils. Then season well with freshly milled black pepper.

As soon as the lentils are cooked, add salt to taste. Empty them into a warm serving bowl and while they're still hot, pour the dressing over. Give everything a good toss and stir, then crumble the goats' cheese all over and add the rocket leaves, torn in half. Give everything one more toss and stir, and serve straight away with the walnuts scattered over.

———————— ◇ ————————

Baked Eggs in Wild Mushroom Tartlets (see page 30)

Blinis with Smoked Salmon, Crème Fraîche and Dill

SERVES 8 AS A STARTER

*B*linis originated in Russia and are traditionally made with buckwheat flour, but I find them better and lighter if made with a mixture of strong plain flour and buckwheat. Buckwheat is available in healthfood shops and some supermarkets, but if you can't get hold of it you can replace it with wholewheat flour. (See photograph on pages 36–7.)

2 oz (50 g) buckwheat flour	1 teaspoon salt
6 oz (175 g) strong white plain flour	1½ oz (40 g) butter
1 x 6 g sachet easy-blend dried yeast	
1 x 500 ml tub crème fraîche	FOR THE TOPPING:
(reserve 300 ml for the topping)	1 lb (450 g) smoked salmon
8 fl oz (225 ml) whole milk	300 ml crème fraîche
2 x size 1 eggs	A few dill sprigs

Begin by sifting the salt, buckwheat flour and plain flour together into a large roomy bowl and then sprinkle in the yeast. Place 7 fl oz (200 ml) of the crème fraîche into a measuring jug and add enough milk to bring it up to the 15 fl oz (425 ml) level. Place this in a small saucepan and warm it gently – it must only be slightly warm, as too much heat will kill the yeast. Next separate the eggs, reserving the whites until later, then add the yolks to the milk, mix them in with a whisk and after that pour the whole lot into the flour mixture. Whisk everything until you have a thick batter, then cover the bowl with a clean tea-cloth and leave it in a warm place for about 1 hour – this can simply be a matter of placing the bowl in another larger bowl filled with warm water.

After 1 hour the batter will be spongy and bubbly. Now you whisk up the egg whites until they form stiff peaks and gently fold them into the batter. Cover with the cloth again and leave as before for another hour.

When you're ready to make the blinis, begin by melting the butter in a heavy based frying pan, then tip the melted butter out into a cup and use it – with the help of a tightly rolled wodge of kitchen paper – to brush the pan all over as you make each blini. To do this keep the pan on a medium heat and add 1½ tablespoons of batter (1 tablespoon goes in first then another ½ tablespoon on top) – it won't spread out much and the underneath sets as soon as it touches the pan. This amount should give you a blini approximately 4 inches (10 cm) in diameter.

Don't worry at this stage if it looks too thick, it isn't, it's just light and puffy. After 40 seconds, no longer, flip the blini over and give it just 30 seconds on the other side. Transfer it to a wire cooling rack and repeat, brushing the pan with butter each time. This mixture should give you 24 blinis.

When all the blinis are made and have cooled, wrap them in foil parcels, with 6 laid out flat in each one. To serve, pre-heat the oven to gas mark 1, 275°F (140°C) and place the foil parcels on a high shelf for 10 minutes.

Serve the blinis on warm plates, giving each person 2 to start with, and top with slices of smoked salmon, about 2 oz (50 g) per person, add a tablespoon of very cold crème fraîche on the side of the plate and garnish with sprigs of fresh dill.

NOTE: Any unused blinis can be warmed and served for breakfast or tea with honey or jam. They also freeze very well if left in the foil parcels and can be re-heated in the oven, as above, after defrosting. If you want to serve blini canapés, these are made in the same way with teaspoonfuls of the mixture. Cook them for about 15 seconds on each side. Then re-heat, as above, and top with smoked salmon, crème fraîche and dill.

———————————◇———————————

Next page: Blinis with Smoked Salmon,
Crème Fraîche and Dill

Camembert Croquettes with Fresh Date and Apple Chutney

SERVES 6 AS A STARTER

Ripe Camembert is essential for this recipe, so plan ahead and buy a Camembert which will be ready to use roughly on its sell-by date. I keep mine in the garage or in the boot of a car, which is cool enough in the winter, though you have to warn people about the smell!

1 x 250 g (9 oz) round, ripe unpasteurized Normandy Camembert, chilled
1 small carrot
½ small onion
½ stick celery
10 fl oz (275 ml) whole milk
1 pinch or blade of mace
1 bay leaf
6 peppercorns
1½ oz (40 g) butter
2 oz (50 g) plain flour
Groundnut oil for frying

FOR THE COATING:

2 x size 1 eggs
2 tablespoons milk
6 oz (175 g) fine white breadcrumbs
1 tablespoon seasoned flour

TO SERVE:

6 flat-leaf parsley sprigs

You will also need 6 x 4-fl oz (110-ml) straight-sided ramekins 2¾ inches (7 cm) diameter and some clingfilm.

First of all peel and roughly chop the vegetables and place them in a saucepan with the milk, mace, bay leaf and peppercorns. Bring everything up to simmering point, then turn the heat off and leave to infuse for 30 minutes.

After that strain the milk into a jug, using a sieve and pressing the vegetables with the back of a spoon to extract all the juices. Now rinse and dry the saucepan and, over a medium heat, melt the butter in it, then add the flour and, using a wooden spoon, stir briskly until the mixture has turned a pale straw colour.

Now add the milk a little at a time and switch to a balloon whisk, whisking vigorously after each addition until you have a very thick, glossy mixture. Then take the pan off the heat and allow it to cool slightly.

While the mixture is cooling you can deal with the cheese – although it needs to be ripe, it makes life a lot easier if it has been chilled. So all you do is cut the Camembert in half and, using a small sharp knife, peel it carefully, paring the skin away from the cheese. After that, add the cheese to the sauce in smallish pieces and give it all a really good mixing to combine it as thoroughly as possible. Then leave it aside for 10 minutes or so to cool.

Meanwhile, prepare the ramekins. The easiest way to do this is to lightly oil each one, then take pieces of clingfilm about 8 inches (20 cm) long and lay them across the centre of each ramekin. Then, using a clean pastry brush, push the clingfilm into the ramekins all round the edges – it doesn't matter if it creases. Now divide the cheese mixture between each one and press it in evenly. Fold the surplus clingfilm over the top, smooth it out, then place them in the fridge for several hours, but preferably overnight.

The croquettes can be coated with the egg and breadcumbs in advance, provided that you keep them well chilled afterwards. Sprinkle the seasoned flour onto a piece of greaseproof paper, then lightly beat the eggs and milk together and spread the breadcrumbs out on a plate. Also, have another flat plate to hand.

Now all you do is unfold the clingfilm and flip each croquette onto the flour and lightly coat it on all sides. Next dip it in the beaten egg, then in the breadcrumbs, shaking off any surplus. Now return it to the egg and then back again to the breadcrumbs. This double coating gives good protection while the croquettes are cooking.

When the croquettes are coated, if you're not cooking them straight away, put them on the flat plate and return them to the fridge, uncovered. When you're ready to cook them, have some crumpled kitchen paper spread out on a plate and then heat up enough groundnut oil to just cover the base of a solid frying pan. The oil needs to be really hot, so test it by dropping in a little cube of bread and if it turns golden in 30 seconds the oil is ready. Now fry the croquettes for about 2 minutes on each side and transfer them to kitchen paper to drain while you fry the rest. You need to take some care here not to overcook them – it's okay for little bits to ooze out of the sides, but if you leave them in too long they tend to collapse. Serve as soon as possible after they are cooked. Garnish with sprigs of parsley and the chutney alongside.

◇

Fresh Date and Apple Chutney

3 oz (75 g) fresh stoned dates	2 whole cloves
(or dried if not available)	3 tablespoons balsamic vinegar
2 small Granny Smith apples	2 shallots, peeled and roughly chopped
⅓ teaspoon allspice berries	Pinch cayenne pepper

This chutney is best made a couple of hours in advance. First, using a pestle and mortar, crush the spices to a fine powder. Quarter and core the apples, but leave the peel on, then cut each quarter into 8.

Place the apples, dates and all the rest of the ingredients in a food processor, give it all a good whizz to start, then use the pulse action to chop everything evenly. Then transfer the whole lot into a serving bowl, cover with clingfilm and chill before serving.

◇

Apple, Cider Salad with Melted Camembert Dressing

SERVES 6 AS A STARTER OR 2 AS A LIGHT LUNCH

When I wrote the 'Summer Collection' I felt I'd got Caesar salad as perfect as it could be, but then I ate so many Caesar salads that I began to get bored. If this has happened to you too, then let me tell you that this makes an absolutely brilliant alternative, especially in the winter months. It does need ripe Camembert, but if you don't live near a supplier, a supermarket Camembert will have a date stamp to show when it will have fully ripened, so you can gauge the best time to make the salad (see previous recipe). The piquancy of the apple combined with cheese is absolutely superb.

FOR THE SALAD:

1 Cos lettuce

4 oz (110 g) Cox's apple (1 medium)

1 x 30 g pack (or 1 oz) rocket leaves

FOR THE DRESSING:

1 x 250 g (9 oz) round, ripe unpasteurized Normandy Camembert, chilled

2 rounded tablespoons crème fraîche

1 or 2 tablespoons dry cider (if Camembert isn't quite ripe)

TO SERVE:

1 quantity of garlic croûtons (see page 10)

First make the garlic croûtons (see page 10). Then prepare the dressing – cut the cheese in half and use a small, sharp knife to peel it carefully like a potato, paring away the skin from the soft cheese. Place the cheese in a small saucepan. Next measure in the crème fraîche but don't heat it until just before you are going to serve the salad.

When you're ready, mix the salad leaves together, breaking up the larger ones into manageable pieces, and arrange the salad on the serving plates. Slice the apple, leaving the skin on, and put the slices in a small bowl, then sprinkle on a little cider – just enough to give the slices a covering. After that, pat them dry and arrange over the salad leaves.

Now place the saucepan over a gentle heat and blend the cheese and crème fraîche together for about 3–4 minutes – using a small balloon whisk – until the mixture is smooth. If the cheese is very ripe and runny, you may not need the dry cider, but if the centre is less ripe, you will need to add a little cider to keep the mixture smooth. The main thing is to melt the cheese just sufficiently for it to run off the whisk in ribbons, while still retaining its texture. Don't allow the cheese to overheat or it may go stringy – it needs to be melted rather than cooked.

Next, using a small ladle, pour the dressing equally over the salad and finish with a scattering of croûtons. Alternatively, you can hand the dressing round the table and let everyone help themselves.

NOTE: You can, if you want to, prepare the dressing ahead, then just gently melt it again before serving.

Apple, Cider Salad with Melted Camembert Dressing

Rillettes of Duck with Confit of Cranberries

SERVES 6 AS A STARTER

This is one of my favourite starters: a terrine of tiny shreds of tender, succulent duck melded together like a pâté, then served with the dazzling depth of colour and sharpness of a confit of cranberries to counteract the richness. It's very simple to make and instead of serving it as a starter you could, as I did recently, offer it as a lunch for three people with a green salad and some slightly chilled Beaujolais. Magnificent!

1 duck, cut into quarters, approximately 4–5 lb (1.8–2.25 kg), or buy it ready quartered with the bones in
1 level tablespoon chopped fresh thyme leaves
½ teaspoon powdered mace
2 cloves garlic, chopped
15 black peppercorns
15 juniper berries
8 fl oz (225 ml) dry white wine
1 level teaspoon salt

TO GARNISH:

A few thyme sprigs
2 or 3 bay leaves
A few whole cranberries
Whole peppercorns and juniper berries
1 bunch watercress

You will also need a 1½-pint (850-ml) terrine or loaf tin.

Pre-heat the oven to gas mark 6, 400°F (200°C).

Begin by placing the duck joints on a rack in a shallow roasting tin, pierce them with a skewer, sprinkle salt on the skins then place them on a high shelf of the oven and leave them for 1 hour. Then remove them from the oven and drain off all the fat from the roasting tin into a bowl. The fat is excellent for cooking, so hang on to it.

Now place the duck joints in a solid flameproof casserole or saucepan, and sprinkle in the thyme, mace and garlic. Then use a pestle and mortar to crush the peppercorns and juniper berries coarsely, and add these as well. Next pour in the wine, bring everything up to simmering point, then turn the heat right down to the gentlest simmer possible and leave it like that for 2 hours.

After that pour off all the liquid into a bowl and reserve it, then have ready the terrine or loaf tin. Take a quarter of duck, place it on a board and simply strip away the skin and bones, which will part very easily from the flesh. Then, using either two forks or just your hands, shred the pieces of duck flesh as finely as possible, and pack them into the terrine. When you have repeated this with the other duck quarters, press all the shreds of meat down very firmly into the terrine, then pour in all the cooking juices (there's no need to strain them).

Lastly decorate the surface with the thyme, bay leaves, peppercorns, juniper berries and a few whole cranberries. Then as soon as it's cool put a lid on the terrine or cover with foil and place in the fridge until needed. You can make it well in advance as it will keep for about three days.

Serve the terrine with thickish slices of toasted bread, garnish with sprigs of watercress and spoon some cranberry confit onto the plate, saving some to hand round separately.

Confit of Cranberries

1 lb (450 g) cranberries	**2 tablespoons best quality**
4 oz (110 g) granulated sugar	**red wine vinegar**
15 fl oz (425 ml) red wine	**Grated zest and juice of 1 orange**

To make the confit, place the cranberries in a saucepan with the rest of the ingredients. Bring the mixture up to a very gentle simmer, give it all a good stir and let it barely simmer without a lid for about an hour, stirring from time to time. What you end up with is a concentrated mass of glazed cranberries which tastes absolutely wonderful. Remove it from the heat, leave to cool then spoon it into a serving bowl and cover until needed.

NOTE: Cranberry confit provides the perfect balance of sharpness for rich game dishes as well as this terrine. If you were serving it with a hot game dish, you might even like to gently re-heat it, but it's excellent cold.

———————◇———————

Home-made Mayonnaise

*H*ome-made mayonnaise made by the traditional method is unbeatable. First a couple of tips: (a) use a small basin with a narrow base – a 1-pint (570-ml) pudding basin is ideal, and (b) place the basin on a damp tea towel so it will remain steady and leave you two hands free, one to drip the oil, the other to hold the beater.

10 fl oz (275 ml) groundnut oil	**1 level teaspoon salt**
2 x size 1 egg yolks	**Freshly milled black pepper**
1 clove garlic, crushed	**1 teaspoon white wine vinegar**
1 heaped teaspoon powdered mustard	

First of all put the egg yolks into the basin, add the crushed garlic, mustard powder, salt and a little freshly milled black pepper. Mix all of these together well. Then, holding the groundnut oil in a jug in one hand and an electric hand whisk in the other, add 1 drop of oil to the egg mixture and whisk this in.

However stupid it may sound, the key to a successful mayonnaise is making sure each drop of oil is thoroughly whisked in before adding the next drop. It won't take all day, because after a few minutes – once you've added several drops of oil – the mixture will begin to thicken and go very stiff and lumpy. When it gets to this stage you need to add a teaspoon of vinegar, which will thin the mixture down.

Now the critical point has passed so you can then begin pouring the oil in a very, very thin but steady stream, keeping the beaters going all the time. When all the oil has been added, taste and add more salt and pepper if it needs it. If you'd like the mayonnaise to be a bit lighter, at this stage add 2 tablespoons of boiling water and whisk it in.

Mayonnaise only curdles when you add the oil too quickly at the beginning. If that happens, don't despair. All you need to do is put a fresh egg yolk into a clean basin, add the curdled mixture to it (drop by drop), then continue adding the rest of the oil as though nothing had happened.

The mayonnaise should be stored in a screw-top jar in the bottom of the fridge, but for no longer than a week.

———————— ◇ ————————

Home-made Mayonnaise

Prawn Cocktail 2000

SERVES 6

This recipe is part of my sixties revival menu. In those days it used to be something simple but really luscious, yet over the years it has suffered from some very poor adaptations, not least watery prawns and inferior sauces. So here, in all its former glory, is a starter quite definitely fit for the new millennium!

2 lb (900 g) large prawns in their shells (see recipe)	FOR THE SAUCE:
	1 quantity of mayonnaise (see page 45)
1 crisp-hearted lettuce, such as Cos	**1 dessertspoon Worcestershire sauce**
1 x 30 g pack (or 1 oz) rocket leaves	**A few drops Tabasco sauce**
1 ripe but firm avocado pear	**1 dessertspoon lime juice**
1 whole lime, divided into 6 wedge-shaped sections	**2 tablespoons tomato ketchup (preferably organic)**
Cayenne pepper	**Salt and freshly milled black pepper**

The very best version of this is made with prawns (either fresh or frozen in their shells) that you have cooked yourself. Failing that, buy the large cooked prawns in their shells, or if you can only get shelled prawns cut the amount to 1 lb (450 g). To prepare them: if frozen put them in a colander and allow to defrost thoroughly at room temperature for about 1 hour. After that heat a large solid frying pan or wok and dry-fry the prawns for 4–5 minutes until the grey turns a vibrant pink. As soon as they're cool, reserve 6 in their shells for a garnish and peel the remainder. Then take a small sharp knife, make a cut along the back of each peeled prawn and remove any black thread. Place them in a bowl, cover with clingfilm and keep in the fridge until needed.

To make the cocktail sauce, prepare the mayonnaise (see page 45) and add it to the rest of the sauce ingredients. Stir and taste to check the seasoning, then keep the sauce covered with clingfilm in the fridge until needed.

When you are ready to serve, shred the lettuce and rocket fairly finely and divide them between 6 stemmed glasses, then peel and chop the avocado into small dice and scatter this in each glass amongst the lettuce. Top with the prawns and the sauce, sprinkle a dusting of cayenne pepper on top and garnish with 1 section of lime and 1 unpeeled prawn per glass. Serve with brown bread and butter.

———————— ◇ ————————

Warm Poached Egg Salad with Frizzled Chorizo

SERVES 4

This makes a fun starter for four people, or a zappy light lunch or supper dish for two. For poaching you need very fresh eggs, so watch the date stamp on the box when you buy them and, to be absolutely sure, pop them into a glass measuring jug filled with cold water: if the eggs sit horizontally on the base they're very fresh. A slight tilt is acceptable, but if they sit vertically your supplier's date stamps are in doubt.

Chorizo is a spicy Spanish pork sausage made with paprika. At specialist food shops you can also buy 'chorizo piccante', a more spicy version, which gives the whole thing a wonderful kick.

4 x very fresh size 1 eggs	**1½ tablespoons sherry vinegar**
6 oz (175 g) chorizo sausage, skinned and cut into ¼-inch (5-mm) cubes	**Salt and freshly milled black pepper**
3 tablespoons extra virgin olive oil	**3 oz (75 g) assorted green salad leaves**
1 medium onion, finely chopped	
2 cloves garlic, finely chopped	TO SERVE:
1 red pepper, de-seeded and chopped small	**1 quantity of croûtons (see page 10) with the addition of 1 level tablespoon hot paprika**
3 tablespoons dry sherry	

First make the croûtons by following the basic recipe on page 10 but sprinkle the paprika over the bread cubes before the olive oil.

When you're ready to make the salad, start with the eggs. A useful way to poach 4 eggs without any last-minute hassle is to pour boiling water straight from the kettle into a medium-sized frying pan. Place it over a heat gentle enough for there to be the merest trace of bubbles simmering on the base of the pan. Now carefully break the 4 eggs into the water and let them cook for just 1 minute. Then remove the pan from the heat and leave the eggs in the hot water for 10 minutes, after which time the whites will be set and the yolks creamy.

Now arrange the salad leaves on 4 plates. Then, in another frying pan, heat 1 tablespoon of the olive oil until it's very hot, then add the chorizo, cook for 2–3 minutes then add the onion, garlic and pepper. Keeping them on the move and turning down the heat if it gets too hot, cook for about 6 minutes until the ingredients are toasted round the edge. Now add the sherry, sherry vinegar and the remaining 2 tablespoons of olive oil to the pan. Let it all bubble a bit and season with salt and pepper.

To remove the eggs from the first pan, use a draining spoon with a wad of kitchen paper underneath to absorb the moisture. Place them centrally on the salad leaves on the serving plates, pour the warm chorizo dressing over everything, and finally sprinkle on the croûtons. We eat this with olive bread to mop up the juices – a wonderful accompaniment.

NOTE: If you like you can make this with red wine and red wine vinegar or white wine and white wine vinegar just to ring the changes.

CHAPTER THREE

SEAFOOD *in* WINTER

◇

I wouldn't be at all surprised if fish became *the* food for the 21st century. Fish has just about everything going for it: what other food can you think of that provides first-class protein, is low in fat and calories yet at the same time cooks faster than almost anything else? While I was researching and preparing this chapter, I actually made a personal vow to include much more fish in my daily cooking routine, not least because it's so quick. You can provide such a great variety of interesting and up-to-the-minute supper dishes in as little as 10 minutes – and very few fish dishes take longer than half an hour.

One of the reasons it all got so much easier is that although, sadly, the high street fishmonger is an endangered species, fish in supermarkets has taken on a whole new dimension in that it has become far more accessible and a great deal of the tedious work once involved in its preparation has been removed. Fish nowadays comes cleaned and gutted, boned and filleted and sometimes even skinned. Also with supplies now coming in from all corners of the world and at all times of the year, there is a far wider choice than ever. So for a more varied and interesting diet without too much work, let's all of us vow to eat more fish!

Fillets of Sole Véronique

SERVES 2 AS MAIN COURSE OR 4 AS A STARTER

This famous French classic has always been a favourite of mine and, as it has somehow been neglected on restaurant menus, I think it's time for a revival! Personally I love to serve it with the grapes well chilled, which beautifully complements the warm rich sauce. However, if you prefer you could add the grapes to the fish before it goes under the grill, so they would be warmed through.

2 good-sized Dover or lemon sole about 12–16 oz (350–450 g). Ask your fishmonger to fillet and skin them for you	½ oz (10 g) butter
	½ oz (10 g) plain flour
3 oz (75 g) Muscat-type grapes	5 fl oz (150 ml) whipping cream
1 heaped teaspoon chopped fresh tarragon	Salt and freshly milled black pepper
6 fl oz (175 ml) Chambéry vermouth or dry white wine	

You will also need an ovenproof serving dish.

First peel the grapes well in advance by placing them in a bowl and pouring boiling water over them. Leave them for 45 seconds, then drain off the water and you will find the skins will slip off easily. Cut the grapes in half, remove the seeds, then return them to the bowl and cover and chill in the refrigerator until needed.

When you are ready to start cooking the fish, begin by warming the serving dish and have a sheet of foil ready. Then wipe each sole fillet and divide each one in half lengthways by cutting along the natural line, so you now have 8 fillets. Season them and roll each one up as tightly as possible, keeping the skin side on the inside and starting the roll at the narrow end. Next put a faint smear of butter on the base of a medium frying pan and arrange the sole fillets in it. Then sprinkle in the tarragon followed by the vermouth.

Now place the pan on a medium heat and bring it up to simmering point. Cover, then put a timer on and poach the fillets for 3–4 minutes, depending on their thickness. While the fish is poaching pre-heat the grill to its highest setting.

Meanwhile take a small saucepan, melt the butter in it, stir in the flour to make a smooth paste and let it cook gently, stirring all the time, until it has become a pale straw colour. When the fish is cooked transfer the fillets with a fish slice to the warmed dish, cover with foil and keep warm.

Next boil the fish-poaching liquid in its pan until it has reduced to about a third of its original volume. Stir in the cream and let that come up to a gentle simmer, then gradually add this cream and liquid mixture to the flour and butter mixture in the small saucepan, whisking it in well until you have a thin, creamy sauce. Taste and season with salt and freshly milled black pepper.

Pour the sauce over the fish and pop it under the pre-heated grill (about 4 inches from the source of the heat) and leave it there for approximately 3 minutes, until it is glazed golden brown on top. Serve each portion on to warmed serving plates, garnished with grapes.

Luxury Fish Pie with Rösti Caper Topping

SERVES 4–6

This is a perfect recipe for entertaining and wouldn't need anything to go with it other than a simple green salad. The fish can be varied according to what's available as long as you have 2¼ lb (1 kg) in total.

FOR THE FISH MIXTURE:

1½ lb (700 g) halibut

8 oz (225 g) king scallops, including the coral, cut in half

4 oz (110 g) uncooked tiger prawns, throughly defrosted if frozen, and peeled

5 fl oz (150 ml) dry white wine

10 fl oz (275 ml) carton of fish stock

1 bay leaf

2 oz (50 g) butter

2 oz (50 g) plain flour

2 tablespoons crème fraîche

6 cornichons (continental gherkins), drained, rinsed and chopped

1 heaped tablespoon chopped fresh parsley

1 dessertspoon chopped fresh dill

Salt and freshly milled black pepper

FOR THE ROSTI CAPER TOPPING:

2 lb (900 g) Désirée or Romano potatoes, even-sized if possible

1 tablespoon salted capers or capers in brine, drained, rinsed and dried

2 oz (50 g) butter, melted

2 oz (50 g) strong Cheddar cheese, finely grated

You will also need a baking dish about 2 inches (5 cm) deep of 2½-pint (1.5-litre) capacity, well-buttered.

Pre-heat the oven to gas mark 7, 425°F (220°C).

First of all, prepare the potatoes by scrubbing them, but leaving the skins on. As they all have to cook at the same time, if there are any larger ones cut them in half. Then place them in a saucepan with enough boiling, salted water to barely cover them and cook them for 12 minutes after they have come back to the boil, covered with the lid. Strain off the water and cover them with a clean tea-cloth to absorb the steam.

Meanwhile, heat the wine and stock in a medium saucepan, add the bay leaf and some seasoning, then cut the fish in half if it's a large piece, add it to the saucepan and poach the fish gently for 5 minutes. It should be slightly undercooked.

Then remove the fish to a plate, using a draining spoon, and strain the liquid through a sieve into a bowl.

Now rinse the pan you cooked the fish in, melt the butter in it, whisk in the flour and gently cook for 2 minutes. Then gradually add the strained fish stock little by little, whisking all the time. When you have a smooth sauce turn the heat to its lowest setting and let the sauce gently cook for 5 minutes. Then whisk in the crème fraîche, followed by the cornichons, parsley and dill. Give it all a good seasoning and remove it from the heat.

To make the rösti, peel the potatoes and, using the coarse side of a grater, grate them into long shreds into a bowl. Then add the capers and the melted butter and, using two forks, lightly toss everything together so that the potatoes get a good coating of butter.

Now remove the skin from the white fish and divide it into chunks, quite large if possible, and combine the fish with the sauce. Next, if you're going to cook the fish pie more or less immediately, all you do is add the raw scallops and prawns to the fish mixture then spoon it into a well-buttered baking dish. Sprinkle the rösti on top, spreading it out as evenly as possible and not pressing it down too firmly. Then finally scatter the cheese over the surface and bake on a high shelf of the oven for 35–40 minutes.

If you want to make the fish pie in advance, this is possible as long as you remember to let the sauce get completely cold before adding the cooled white fish and raw scallops and prawns. When the topping is on, cover the dish loosely with clingfilm and refrigerate it until you're ready to cook it. Then give it an extra 5–10 minutes' cooking time.

———————————◇———————————

Fried Herring Fillets with a Lime Pepper Crust

SERVES 2

For me the humble herring, once the food of the poor, is a great delicacy with all the gutsy flavours of fresh sardines but lots more juicy flesh. Now they can be bought boned and filleted and are cooked in moments. This recipe is probably the fastest in this chapter. The lime and pepper crust is fragrant and slightly crunchy. Squeeze lots of lime juice over before you start eating – it cuts through the richness perfectly.

2 herring fillets weighing 6–7 oz (175–200 g) each	**Grated zest and juice of 2 limes**
	1 rounded dessertspoon plain flour
1 rounded teaspoon whole mixed peppercorns	**2 tablespoons olive oil**
	Crushed salt flakes

First of all crush the peppercorns with a pestle and mortar – not too fine, so they still have some texture. Then grate the zest of the limes and add half of it to the peppercorns, then add the flour. Mix them all together and spread the mixture out on a flat plate. Wipe the herrings dry with kitchen paper and coat the flesh side with the flour-pepper mixture. Press the fish well in to give it a good coating – anything left on the plate can be used to dust the skin side lightly.

Now in your largest frying pan, heat the oil until it is very hot and fry the herrings flesh-side down for about 2–3 minutes. Have a peek by lifting up the edge with a fish slice – it should be golden. Then turn the fish over on to the other side and give it another 2 minutes, and drain on crumpled greaseproof or kitchen paper before serving. Serve sprinkled with crushed salt, the rest of the lime zest and the limes cut into quarters to squeeze over.

———————————◇———————————

Roasted Fish Topped with Sun-Dried Tomato Tapenade

SERVES 6

This is quite simply a fantastic recipe – it takes no time at all but has the kind of taste that makes people think you have spent hours in the kitchen. And another of its great virtues is that, apart from the fish itself and fresh basil leaves, the whole thing is made from store-cupboard ingredients. (See photograph on pages 52–3.)

6 tail-end pieces of cod or haddock weighing 6–7 oz (175–200 g) each, skin removed

FOR THE TAPENADE:
1 x 10 oz (275 g) jar sun-dried tomatoes, drained, but reserve the oil

1 x 185 g tin pitted black olives in brine, drained and rinsed, or 6 oz (175 g) bought loose

2 x 15 g packs (or 1 oz) basil leaves

1 heaped teaspoon (about 36) green peppercorns in brine, rinsed and drained

2 fat cloves garlic, peeled

1 x 50 g tin anchovies including the oil

3 heaped tablespoons capers, drained and pressed between double layers of absorbent kitchen paper

3 tablespoons oil from the tomatoes

Freshly milled black pepper

Pre-heat the oven to gas mark 6, 400°F (200°C).

Begin by reserving 6 whole olives and 6 medium basil leaves from the above, then all you do to make the tapenade – which can be made 2 or 3 days in advance – is place all the ingredients in a food processor and blend them together to a coarse paste. It's important not to over-process; the ingredients should retain some of their identity, as shown in the photograph (see pages 52–3).

When you're ready to cook the fish, wipe the fillets with kitchen paper, season then fold them by tucking the thin end into the centre then the thick end on top of that so you have a neat, slightly rounded shape. Place the fish on an oiled baking sheet, then divide the tapenade mixture equally between them, using it as a topping. Press it on quite firmly with your hands, then lightly roughen the surface with a fork. Dip the reserved basil leaves in olive oil and place one on the top of each piece of fish, following that with an olive. Now place the baking tray on a high shelf in the oven, bake the fish for 20–25 minutes, and serve straight away.

———————◇———————

Previous page: Roasted Fish Topped with Sun-Dried Tomato Tapenade

Pepper-Crusted Monkfish with Red Pepper Relish

SERVES 4

Filleted monkfish can be quite pricey, but there is no waste with head or bones. It has a lovely firm, meaty texture, and I think this particular recipe would be a superb choice for someone who wants to cook something quite special but has very little time. The pieces of fish are coated with crushed mixed peppercorns and this simplest of sauces not only tastes divine but looks amazingly colourful in contrast to the fish.

2 lb (900 g) monkfish (off-the-bone weight)	**2 medium tomatoes, skinned (tinned Italian tomatoes would be fine)**
1½ rounded tablespoons mixed whole peppercorns	**1 fat clove garlic, peeled**
	3 anchovy fillets, chopped
4 tablespoons olive oil	**1 tablespoon balsamic vinegar**
2 rounded tablespoons plain flour, seasoned with 1 teaspoon salt	**1 tablespoon olive oil**
	Salt and freshly milled black pepper
FOR THE RED PEPPER RELISH:	**Sprigs of watercress or fresh coriander leaves to garnish**
2 medium red peppers, de-seeded and cut into strips	

Begin the relish by heating the oil in a medium-sized saucepan. When it's really hot add the strips of pepper and toss them around, keeping them on the move so they get nicely toasted and browned at the edges. Then add the tomatoes, the whole garlic clove and the chopped anchovies. Give it all a good stir, put a lid on and, keeping the heat at its lowest possible setting, let the whole thing stew gently, stirring once or twice, for 25 minutes or until the peppers are soft. Then whizz the whole lot to a coarse purée in a liquidizer or food processor. Taste and season with salt and freshly milled pepper, then empty into a serving bowl and stir in the balsamic vinegar. It is now ready for serving and can be made in advance.

To cook the fish first cut it into small rounds about ¾ inch (2 cm) thick. Crush the peppercorns with a pestle and mortar – or using the end of a rolling pin in a small bowl – to a fairly coarse texture, then combine them with the flour.

Next heat the oil until very hot in a good solid frying pan. Dip each piece of fish in the flour and peppercorn mixture, pressing them gently on all sides to get an even coating. Now fry the fish in two batches, for about 2–3 minutes on each side, until they're tinged nicely brown. Keep the first batch warm while you cook the second.

Serve garnished with watercress or fresh coriander sprigs, and the sauce handed round separately.

◇

Smoked Haddock with Spinach and Chive Butter Sauce

SERVES 4

My thanks to top chef and dear friend Simon Hopkinson for this superb recipe which he cooked for me at his restaurant Bibendum one day for lunch – and had invented that day! Now, thanks to his generosity, all of us can make and savour what has become one of my very favourite fish recipes.

4 pieces smoked haddock, approximately 6 oz (175 g) each, skinned and boned	**3 x size 1 egg yolks**
	2 tablespoons chopped chives
10 fl oz (275 ml) milk	**Salt and freshly milled black pepper**
Freshly milled black pepper	
	FOR THE SPINACH:
	2 lb (900 g) raw spinach, picked over, trimmed and thoroughly washed
FOR THE HOLLANDAISE SAUCE:	
6 oz (175 g) butter, melted	**1 oz (25 g) butter**
1 tablespoon lemon juice	**Salt and freshly milled black pepper**

First you need to make the Hollandaise sauce: place the butter in a small saucepan and let it melt slowly. Meanwhile blend the egg yolks and seasoning in a liquidizer or food processor.

Then turn the heat up and when the butter reaches the boil, pour it into a jug and start to pour this very slowly into the liquidizer, in a thin trickle, with the motor running, until all the butter is added and the sauce is thickened. Then, with the motor still switched on, slowly add the lemon juice. Then keep the sauce warm by placing it in a basin over some hot water.

To cook the fish, place it in a frying pan, pour in the milk, add some freshly milled pepper then bring it all up to a gentle simmer. Cover and poach for 6–7 minutes. While that is happening, cook the spinach – melt the butter in a large saucepan and pile the spinach in with a teaspoon of salt and some freshly milled black pepper. Put the lid on and cook it over a medium heat for 2–3 minutes, turning it all over halfway through. Quite a bit of water will come out so what you need to do then is drain it in a colander and press down a small plate on top to squeeze out every last bit of juice. Cover with a cloth and keep warm.

When the haddock is ready divide the spinach between 4 warm serving plates, and place the haddock pieces on top. Now just add a little of the poaching liquid (about 2 tablespoons) to the sauce and whisk it in along with the chives then pour the sauce over the haddock and spinach, and serve straight away.

───────◇───────

Smoked Haddock with Spinach and Chive Butter Sauce

Parmesan-Coated Fish with Walnut Romesco Sauce

SERVES 4

This method of cooking fish with a light dusting of flour and grated Parmesan is excellent, but to make it even more special serve it with a Romesco sauce made with walnuts. The advantage of Romesco is that you can make it well ahead; it's always served at room temperature, so keep it in the fridge and remove it about 1 hour before serving.

4 x 6 oz (175 g) thick fillets of fish (skinned cod, haddock, monkfish or halibut)	FOR THE SAUCE:
	3 large cloves garlic
2 tablespoons plain flour	**2 green chillies, halved and de-seeded**
1 dessertspoon finely grated Parmesan (Parmigiano Reggiano)	**1½ oz (40 g) walnuts**
	3 ripe plum tomatoes, skins removed
2 fl oz (55 ml) milk	**6 fl oz (175 ml) extra virgin olive oil**
1 oz (25 g) butter	**2 tablespoons balsamic vinegar**
1 tablespoon oil for frying	**Salt and freshly milled black pepper**
Salt and freshly milled black pepper	
	FOR THE GARNISH:
	A few fresh flat-leaf parsley sprigs

To make the sauce, take a good solid frying pan and heat 1 tablespoon of the oil over a medium heat, then lightly sauté the whole garlic cloves for about 3 minutes or until they feel softened and have turned golden. Then add the chillies and walnuts and continue to cook for another 2 minutes.

Now tip them into a processor, then return the pan to a high heat and when the oil begins to smoke cut the tomatoes in half lengthways and place them in the hot pan cut side down. Keep the heat high and cook the tomatoes until they are charred and blackened all over – this will take about 1½–2 minutes on each side.

Next add the tomatoes to the processor, turn it onto a low speed and with the motor running add the rest of the oil in a slow, steady stream. The sauce will then begin to thicken and assume the consistency of mayonnaise. After that add some seasoning, then transfer the sauce to a jug or a bowl and stir in the balsamic vinegar. Cool, cover with clingfilm, and chill until needed. But let it come back to room temperature before serving.

When you're ready to cook the fish, mix the flour, seasoning and cheese together on a plate and pour the milk into a shallow dish. Now wipe and dry the fish with kitchen paper. Then dip each piece first into the milk and then into the flour mixture, making sure it's well coated and that you shake off any surplus.

Next heat the butter and oil in a large frying pan and as soon as it's really hot cook the fish for 2–3 minutes on each side, depending on its thickness. The coating should be golden brown and as soon as it's cooked remove the fillets carefully with a fish slice to warm serving plates.

Serve with a little of the sauce spooned over, and garnish with the parsley. A nice accompaniment to this would be Puy lentils (see page 82).

Oven-Baked Mackerel Stuffed with Pesto Mash

SERVES 4

*I*t takes only one word to describe this recipe – wow! It's simply one of the best fish recipes ever. Easy to make and such a divine combination of flavours, it can also be prepared in advance, so all you have to do is just pop it in the oven, make a salad and a nice lemony dressing. One important point, though: buy fresh pesto, available in tubs from most supermarkets (it's not quite the same with bottled pesto sauce).

4 x 10 oz (275 g) very fresh mackerel, heads removed	**Salt and freshly milled black pepper**
12 oz (350 g) red potatoes, peeled and cut into evenly sized pieces	TO SERVE:
1 x 120 g tub fresh pesto sauce	**Lemon quarters**
6 spring onions, finely chopped including green part	**Flat-leaf parsley sprigs**
1 oz (25 g) brown bread (about 1½ slices)	You will also need a solid baking tray, approximately 16 x 12 inches (40 x 30 cm), lined with foil and brushed with a little olive oil.
1 tablespoon porridge oats	
A little olive oil	Pre-heat the oven to gas mark 6, 400°F (200°C).

First cook the potatoes in boiling salted water for 20 minutes. Test them with a skewer and when they're absolutely tender drain them well. Leave them in the saucepan and cover with a tea-cloth to absorb some of the steam. Next add all but 1 tablespoon of the pesto to the potatoes, then use an electric hand whisk to mash them – start with a slow speed to break them up, then going on to high until you have a smooth, lump-free purée. Now fold in the spring onions and taste to check the seasoning.

Next make the topping for the fish by dropping cubes of bread into a processor or liquidizer with the motor switched on, then follow with the porridge oats until everything is uniformly crumbled.

To prepare the fish, wipe them inside and out with kitchen paper, lay them on the foil-lined baking tray and make three diagonal cuts about 1 inch (2.5 cm) in depth all along the top side of the mackerel. Spoon the pesto mash into the body cavities, pack it in neatly, then fork the edges to give some texture. Now brush the surface of the fish with olive oil, scatter it with the crumbs and finally add a dessertspoon of olive oil to the remaining pesto and drizzle it over the crumbs using a teaspoon.

Now it's ready for the oven: bake for 25 minutes on a high shelf, then serve with lemon quarters and sprigs of flat-leaf parsley.

Next page: Seared Spiced Salmon Steaks with Black Bean Salsa (see page 61)

Seared Spiced Salmon Steaks with Black Bean Salsa

SERVES 6

*E*veryone *I know who has eaten this has loved it. The black bean salsa looks very pretty along-side the salmon and provides a marvellous contrast of flavours and textures, and what's more the whole thing is so little trouble to prepare.*

6 salmon steaks, 5–6 oz (150–175 g) each	FOR THE SALSA:
3 fat cloves garlic	**4 oz (110 g) black beans soaked overnight in twice their volume of cold water**
2 level teaspoons rock salt	
1½-inch (4-cm) piece of root ginger	
Grated zest of 2 limes, reserve the juice for the salsa	**12 oz (350 g) ripe but firm tomatoes, skinned, de-seeded and finely chopped**
A good pinch of ground cinnamon	**1 red chilli, de-seeded and finely chopped**
A good pinch of ground cumin	
1 x 15 g pack (or ½ oz) fresh coriander leaves (reserve 6 sprigs and finely chop the remainder)	**1 x 15 g pack (or ½ oz) coriander leaves, finely chopped**
	1 medium red onion, finely chopped
2 tablespoons light olive oil	**1 tablespoon extra virgin olive oil**
Freshly milled black pepper	**Juice of the limes reserved from the salmon recipe**
You will also need a solid baking sheet that won't buckle under the heat.	**½ level teaspoon salt**

A few hours before you want to cook the salmon, wipe each of the steaks with damp kitchen paper and remove any visible bones using tweezers. Place the salmon on a plate, then, with a pestle and mortar, crush the garlic cloves and rock salt together until you have a creamy purée. Now add the grated ginger, lime zest, cinnamon and cumin, 1 tablespoon of olive oil and the chopped coriander, and a good grind of black pepper. Mix everything together and spread a little of this mixture on each salmon steak. Cover with clingfilm and set aside for the flavours to develop and permeate the salmon.

To make the salsa, rinse the beans in plenty of cold water, put them in a saucepan with enough water to cover, bring to the boil and boil rapidly for 10 minutes. Then reduce the heat and simmer the beans for 30 minutes until tender. Drain and allow them to cool completely before adding all the other ingredients. Then leave them covered for several hours to allow the flavours to develop.

When you're ready to cook the salmon, pre-heat the grill to its highest setting. Brush the baking sheet with the olive oil and put it under the grill to heat up. When the grill is really hot, remove the baking sheet using an oven glove, and place the salmon pieces on it. They will sear and sizzle as they touch the hot metal. Position the tray 3 inches (7.5 cm) from the heat and grill them for 7 minutes exactly. Use a kitchen timer as the timing is vital.

Remove them when the time is up and use a sharp knife to ease the skins off. Transfer to warm plates and garnish with sprigs of coriander. Serve immediately with the black bean salsa.

Salmon Coulibiac

SERVES 6

*T*his is one of the best fish pies ever invented. It's perfect for entertaining as it can all be made well in advance and popped into the oven just before you serve the first course. Serve it cut in slices, with a large bowl of mixed leaf salad tossed in a sharp lemony dressing and hand round some foaming Hollandaise sauce. Or you can simply melt some butter with an equal quantity of lemon juice and serve it with that.

1 x 375g pack of ready-rolled fresh puff pastry
1¼ lb (560 g) salmon tail fillet, skinned
3 oz (75 g) butter
3 oz (75 g) white basmati rice
8 fl oz (225 ml) fish stock
1 medium onion, finely chopped
4 oz (110 g) small button mushrooms, finely sliced
1 tablespoon freshly chopped dill
1 teaspoon lemon zest
2 tablespoons fresh lemon juice
2 x size 1 eggs, hard boiled (7 minutes from simmering), roughly chopped

1½ tablespoons chopped fresh parsley
Salt and freshly milled black pepper

TO FINISH:

1 egg, lightly beaten
1 oz (25 g) butter, melted

You will also need a good solid baking tray 16 x 12 inches (40 x 30 cm) and a lattice cutter.

Pre-heat the oven to gas mark 4, 350°F (180°C).

First melt 1 oz (25 g) of the butter in a medium saucepan and stir in the rice. When the rice is coated with butter, add the stock and a little salt and bring it up to simmering point, then stir well and cover with a lid. Cook the rice for 15 minutes exactly, then take the pan off the heat, remove the lid and allow it to cool.

As soon as the rice is cooking, take a sheet of buttered foil, lay the salmon on it and add some seasoning. Then wrap it up loosely, pleating the foil at the top and folding the edges in. Place it on a baking sheet and pop it in the oven for just 10 minutes – the salmon needs to be only half cooked. After that remove it from the oven, open the foil and allow it to cool.

While the salmon and the rice are cooling, melt the other 2 oz (50 g) of butter in a small saucepan and gently sweat the onion in it for about 10 minutes until it softens. After that add the sliced mushrooms and half the dill, then carry on cooking gently for a further 5 minutes. After that stir in the lemon zest and juice, some salt and freshly milled black pepper, and allow this mixture to cool.

Next take a large bowl and combine the salmon, broken up into large flakes, the hard-boiled eggs, the remaining dill and half the parsley. Give all this a good seasoning of salt and freshly milled black pepper. Next, in another bowl, combine the rice mixture with onion, mushroom and the rest of the parsley, giving this some seasoning too.

Now for the pastry. What you need to do here is take it out of its packet, unfold it and place it lengthways on a lightly floured surface, then using a tape measure, roll the pastry into a 14-inch (35-cm) square. Now cut it into 2 lengths, one 6½ inches (16 cm) and one 7½ inches (19 cm). Lightly brush the baking sheet and surface of the pastry with melted butter and lay the narrower strip of pastry onto it. Then first spoon half the rice mixture along the centre leaving a gap of at least 1 inch (2.5 cm) all the way round. Next spoon the salmon mixture on top of the rice, building it up as high as possible and pressing and moulding it with your hands – what you're aiming for is a loaf shape of mixture. Then lightly mould the rest of the rice mixture on top of the salmon and brush the 1-inch (2.5-cm) border all round with beaten egg.

Next take the lattice cutter and run it along the centre of the other piece of pastry leaving an even margin of about 1 inch (2.5 cm) all round. Brush the surface of the pastry with the remaining melted butter, then very carefully lift this and cover the salmon mixture with it. The idea here is not to let the lattice open too much as you lift it, because it will open naturally as it goes over the filling. Press the edges together all round to seal, then trim the pastry so that you're left with a ¾-inch (2-cm) border. Now using the back edge of a knife, knock up the edges of the pastry, then crimp it all along using your thumb and the back of the knife, pulling the knife towards the filling each time as you go round. Alternatively just fork it all around.

When you're ready to cook the coulibiac raise the oven temperature to gas mark 7, 425°F (220°C) and brush the surface of the pastry all over with beaten egg and any remaining butter. And, if you feel like it, you can re-roll some of the trimmings and cut out little fish shapes to decorate the top. Now place the coulibiac onto the high shelf of the oven and bake it for 20–25 minutes until it's golden brown. Remove it from the oven and leave it to rest for about 10 minutes before cutting into slices and serving with the sauce.

NOTE: Provided everything is cooled thoroughly first you can make the coulibiac in advance. Cover it with clingfilm and leave in the fridge until you want to cook it.

◇

Foaming Hollandaise

2 x size 1 eggs, separated	4 oz (110 g) salted butter
1 dessertspoon white wine vinegar	Salt and freshly milled black pepper
1 dessertspoon lemon juice	

To make the foaming Hollandaise sauce, begin by placing the egg yolks in a food processor or blender together with some salt, switch on and blend them thoroughly. In a small saucepan heat the vinegar and lemon juice till the mixture simmers, then switch the processor on again and pour the hot liquid onto the egg yolks in a steady stream. Switch off.

Now in the same saucepan melt the butter – not too fiercely: it mustn't brown. When it is liquid and foaming, switch on the processor once more and pour in the butter, again in a steady thin stream, until it is all incorporated and the sauce has thickened. Next, in a small bowl, whisk the egg whites until they form soft peaks and then fold the sauce, a tablespoon at a time, into the egg whites and taste to check the seasoning. When you've done that it's ready to serve or it can be left till later and placed in a bowl over barely simmering water to gently warm through.

Foil-Baked Salmon served with English Parsley Sauce

SERVES 4

*N*ow *that farmed salmon is plentiful and available all the year round, we can all enjoy luxury fish at affordable prices. However, this recipe works equally well using cod cutlets, halibut or other firm white fish. Another luxury – perhaps because of its sheer rarity nowadays – is a classic parsley sauce, so simple but so delightfully good.*

4 salmon steaks weighing approximately 6 oz (175 g) each	**1 blade mace**
A few parsley stalks	**A few chopped parsley stalks**
4 small bay leaves	**10 whole black peppercorns**
4 slices lemon	**¾ oz (20 g) plain flour**
4 dessertspoons dry white wine	**1½ oz (40 g) butter**
Salt and freshly milled black pepper	**4 heaped tablespoons finely chopped parsley**
FOR THE PARSLEY SAUCE:	**1 tablespoon single cream**
15 fl oz (425 ml) milk	**1 teaspoon lemon juice**
1 bay leaf	**Salt and freshly milled black pepper**
1 slice of onion, ¼ inch (5 mm) thick	

You will also need a solid baking sheet.

To make the sauce, place the milk, bay leaf, onion slice, mace, peppercorns and a few chopped parsley stalks in a saucepan. Bring slowly up to simmering point, pour the mixture into a bowl and leave it aside to get completely cold. Meanwhile, to prepare the salmon, take a sheet of foil large enough to wrap all the fish steaks in, and lay it over a shallow baking tray. Wipe the pieces of salmon with kitchen paper and place on the foil. Then place the parsley stalks, a bay leaf and a slice of lemon over each steak, and season with salt and pepper. Finally, sprinkle the wine over, bring the foil up either side, then pleat it, fold it over and seal it at the ends.

When you need to cook the salmon, pre-heat the oven to gas mark 4, 350°F (180°C) and bake the salmon on a highish oven shelf for 20 minutes exactly. Then, before serving, slip off the skin, using a sharp knife to make a cut and just pulling it off all round.

When you're ready to make the sauce, strain the milk back into the saucepan, discarding the flavourings, then add the flour and butter and bring everything gradually up to simmering point, whisking continuously with a balloon whisk until the sauce has thickened. Now turn the heat down to its lowest possible setting and let the sauce cook for 5 minutes, stirring from time to time. When you're ready to serve the sauce, add the parsley, cream and lemon juice. Taste and add seasoning, then transfer to a warm jug to pour over the fish at the table.

◇

Gratin of Mussels with Melted Camembert

SERVES 6 AS A STARTER

I first sampled this concept in Normandy where the Camembert was used as a topping for oysters. Then back home, I discovered it goes superbly well with mussels too.

2 lb (900 g) mussels, cleaned and prepared	**2 oz (50 g) fresh breadcrumbs**
1 tablespoon olive oil	**2 tablespoons finely chopped fresh parsley**
1 shallot, chopped	**2 cloves garlic, finely chopped**
1 clove garlic	**Salt and freshly milled black pepper**
6 fl oz (175 ml) dry white wine	
Salt and freshly milled black pepper	TO SERVE:
	Crusty bread

FOR THE TOPPING:

1 x 250 g (9 oz) slightly under-ripe Normandy Camembert, de-rinded and cut into small cubes

You will also need a baking tray measuring 12 x 16 inches (30 x 40 cm).

First you need to deal with the mussels: heat the olive oil in a large pan, add the shallot and garlic and cook these over a medium heat for about 5 minutes or until they're just soft. Now turn the heat up high, tip in the prepared mussels and add the wine and some salt and pepper. Put on a close-fitting lid, turn the heat down to medium and cook the mussels for about 5 minutes, shaking the pan once or twice, or until they have all opened. Discard any that remain closed. When the mussels are cooked pull away the top shells and discard them. Arrange the mussels sitting on their half shells on a baking tray. Then put ½ teaspoon of strained mussel juice into each shell.

Now place a cube of Camembert on top of each mussel. Then, in a bowl, combine the breadcrumbs, parsley, garlic and a seasoning of salt and pepper and sprinkle this mixture on top.

When you are ready to finish the mussels, pre-heat the grill to its highest setting for at least 10 minutes, then place the tray of mussels fairly close to the heat source and don't go away. You need to watch them like a hawk. It will only take about 3–4 minutes for the cheese to melt and turn golden brown and bubbling. Serve straight away with lots of crusty bread.

———————◇———————

Linguine with Mussels and Walnut Parsley Pesto

SERVES 2

*F*or me, mussels are still a luxury food that cost very little money. I don't think anything can match their exquisite, fresh-from-the-sea flavour. In this recipe every precious drop of mussel juice is used which gives a lovely, concentrated flavour. Now that mussels come ready cleaned and prepared, it makes the whole thing very simple and easy: all you have to do is put them in cold water, then pull off any beardy strands with a sharp knife, use them as soon as possible and discard any that don't close tightly when given a sharp tap.

2 lb (900 g) mussels, cleaned and prepared	FOR THE PESTO:
	½ oz (10 g) walnuts, chopped
6 oz (175 g) linguine or other pasta	**1 oz (25 g) fresh parsley leaves**
1 tablespoon olive oil	**1 clove garlic**
1 shallot, chopped	**2 tablespoons olive oil**
1 clove garlic, chopped	**Salt and freshly milled black pepper**
6 fl oz (175 ml) dry white wine	
Salt and freshly milled black pepper	TO SERVE:
	2 tablespoons chopped fresh parsley

First prepare the pesto: select a large pan that will hold the mussels comfortably, then in it heat a tablespoon of olive oil and sauté the walnuts in the hot oil to get them nicely toasted on all sides – this will take 1–2 minutes. Place the walnuts and any oil left in the pan into a liquidizer or food processor, add the parsley and garlic, the remaining tablespoon of oil and seasoning, then blend everything to make a purée.

Next you need to deal with the mussels: heat the olive oil in the same pan that you sautéed the walnuts in, add the shallot and chopped garlic and cook these over a medium heat for about 5 minutes or until they're just soft. Now turn the heat up high, tip in the prepared mussels and add the wine and some salt and pepper. Put on a close-fitting lid, turn the heat down to medium and cook the mussels for about 5 minutes, shaking the pan once or twice or until they have all opened. Discard any that remain closed.

During those 5 minutes bring another large pan of salted water up to the boil. Then, when the mussels are cooked, remove them from the heat and transfer them to a warm bowl using a slotted spoon and shaking each one well so that no juice is left inside. Keep 8 mussels aside still in their shells, for a garnish. Then remove the rest from their shells and keep them warm, covered with foil in a low oven.

Then place a sieve lined with muslin or gauze over a bowl and strain the mussel liquor through it. This is very important as it removes any bits of sand or grit that get lodged in the shells.

Now it's time to pop the pasta into the boiling water and put a timer on for 8 minutes (some pasta might need 10 minutes so follow the instructions on the packet). Then pour the strained mussel liquor back into the original saucepan and fast-boil to reduce it by about one-third. After that turn the heat to low and stir in the pesto.

Now add the shelled mussels to the pesto sauce and remove from the heat. As soon as the pasta is cooked, quickly strain it into a colander and divide it between two hot pasta bowls. Spoon the mussels and pesto over each portion, add the mussels in their shells and scatter over the parsley. Serve absolutely immediately with some well-chilled white wine. Yummy!

CHAPTER FOUR

———————————— ◇ ————————————

POULTRY *and*
THE GAME SEASON

—————◇—————

Something that I've discovered since I last wrote about game in the *Christmas* book is the changing face of venison. Naturally lean with a low fat content, it has quite rightly come to be regarded as fashionably healthy meat, and in this country it is reared in natural herds that roam free in parklands.

Thus the emotive question of inhumane animal rearing does not apply. Because the farmed herds are controlled – which means they are culled at the right season and at the right age – we no longer have to introduce to the cooking-pot some tough and veteran trophy of the hunter that needs weeks of marinating to tenderize the flesh and has an overpowering gamey flavour. Instead, and in increasing quantities, we have tender, lean meat with a very good flavour. And it is for these reasons that I've included some new venison recipes in this chapter.

The same thing more or less could be said of pheasants which in my part of Suffolk range well and truly free (often in our garden). There's nothing to beat a well-roasted pheasant, but it *does* have to be young and tender and I must admit to having had one occasionally which turned out tough and dry. That problem shouldn't occur here because the recipes in this chapter are for alternative ways of cooking them – poaching and pot roasting.

Roast Duck with Sour Cherry Sauce

SERVES 4

This is a very old favourite of mine, quite nostalgic really because it was one of the first things I learned to cook when I started washing up in a restaurant. Now all these years afterwards it suddenly has taken on a whole new dimension with the arrival of dried sour cherries and some very high quality Morello cherry jams that are now available.

1 large duck, 6 lb (2.7 kg) in weight
1 x 12 oz (345 g) jar Morello cherry jam (with a high fruit content)
1½ oz (40 g) dried sour cherries
15 fl oz (425 ml) red wine
Salt and freshly milled black pepper
Watercress to garnish

You will also need a good solid roasting tin and either a roasting rack or a large piece of crumpled roasting foil.

Pre-heat the oven to gas mark 7, 425°F (220°C).

The most important thing to remember when you're roasting a duck is that if you like the skin really crisp it must be perfectly dry before it goes in the oven. This means if you buy it with any kind of plastic wrapping on, remove it as soon as you get it home, dry the duck thoroughly with kitchen paper and leave it in the fridge without covering, preferably for a day or so before you want to cook it.

When you're ready to cook the duck place it on a rack or on some crumpled foil in a roasting tin. Prick all the fleshy parts with a skewer, as this allows some of the fat to escape, and season it well with salt and freshly milled black pepper. Now pop it onto the highest shelf of the pre-heated oven and give it 30 minutes' initial cooking time, then reduce the heat to gas mark 4, 350°F (180°C) and continue to roast the duck for a further 2 hours. From time to time during the cooking remove the tin from the oven and drain off the fat into a bowl – don't be alarmed at the amount of fat, it is quite normal and if you keep it to use later it makes wonderful roast potatoes.

Fifteen minutes before the end of the cooking time measure the wine into a jug and add the cherries to pre-soak. Then take 1 tablespoon of the jam and pass it through a sieve. Remove the duck from the oven, brush it all over with the sieved jam to make a glaze then return it to the oven for another 15 minutes.

After that, remove the duck to a carving board and let it rest for 10 minutes. Meanwhile spoon off any excess fat from the roasting tin then place it over direct heat, and stir in the wine and soaked cherries, scraping all the base and sides of the tin to incorporate all the crusty bits. Turn the heat up and let it bubble and reduce to about two-thirds of its original volume, then add 4 tablespoons of Morello cherry jam. Whisk the jam in, let it bubble and reduce for a couple of minutes more. Then carve the duck simply by using a very sharp knife to cut it into 4 sections, then pull each section away from the backbone. Spoon some of the sauce over each portion, garnish with watercress and hand the rest around the table.

NOTE: This might seem a long time to cook duck, but it's essential if you like it really crispy.

Chicken Breasts with Wild Mushroom and Bacon Stuffing and Marsala Sauce

SERVES 4

This is a very simple way to deal with four boneless chicken breasts. The use of wild porcini mushrooms combined with the beautifully rich flavour of Marsala wine in the sauce turns them into something quite unusual and special.

4 boneless, skinless chicken breasts, each weighing about 5 oz (150 g)
1 x ½ oz (10 g) pack porcini mushrooms
6 oz (175 g) open cap mushrooms, finely chopped
1 x 70 g pack (or 3 oz) pancetta (or streaky bacon)
1 oz (25 g) butter
1 medium onion, finely chopped
1 fat garlic clove, crushed
1 heaped teaspoon chopped fresh sage leaves
A grating of nutmeg

Salt and freshly milled black pepper
FOR THE SAUCE:
5 fl oz (150 ml) dry Marsala
1 teaspoon oil
Reserved pancetta
1 shallot, peeled and chopped
3 small mushrooms, finely sliced
1 teaspoon chopped fresh sage leaves
¾ level dessertspoon plain flour
Soaking liquid from porcini
Salt and freshly milled black pepper

You will also need 4 squares of foil measuring approximately 10 inches (25.5 cm).

First you need to soak the porcini mushrooms, so pop them into a jug, pour 5 fl oz (150 ml) of boiling water over them and leave them to soak for 20 minutes. After that strain them in a sieve placed over a bowl and squeeze every last bit of liquid out of them because you are going to need it for the sauce.

Now melt the butter in a good solid frying pan, finely chop the pancetta and cook half of it in the hot butter until golden and crisp, and remove it to a plate. Then add the chopped onion to the pan and fry that gently for about 5 minutes to soften.

While that is happening, chop the strained porcini finely and add these to the pan along with the garlic, sage and finely chopped open cap mushrooms, a little nutmeg and the cooked pancetta. Stir well to get everything coated with the oil, then, as soon as the juices start to run out of the mushrooms, reduce the heat to very low and let the whole lot cook gently without covering until all the juices have evaporated and all you have left is a thick mushroom paste. This will take about 30 minutes in all. After that remove it from the heat, taste and season well with salt and freshly milled black pepper, then allow it to get completely cold.

Now take each of the chicken breasts and remove the silvery sinew from the back. Fold back the fillet, making a deeper cut if necessary, so that it opens out almost like a book. Season the chicken and spread a quarter of the mushroom mixture over it, fold back the flap and then roll it up lengthways like a Swiss roll. When they are all filled, lay each chicken breast on a lightly buttered piece of foil.

Wrap each in its foil, folding over the ends to seal. At this stage the parcels should be chilled for at least an hour to firm up.

When you're ready to cook them, pre-heat the oven to gas mark 8, 450°F (230°C). Place the chicken parcels on a baking sheet and cook for 20 minutes. Then remove them from the oven and allow them to rest, still in the foil, for 10 minutes before serving.

While the chicken is cooking you can make the sauce. First add the oil to the pan in which you cooked the mushroom filling, then gently fry the remaining pancetta and shallot for about 5 minutes, then add the sliced mushrooms and chopped sage, stir and continue to cook for about 1 minute, by which time the juices of the mushrooms will begin to run. Next stir in the flour to soak up the juices, then gradually add the porcini soaking liquid, followed by the Marsala and give a good seasoning of salt and freshly milled black pepper. Keep stirring until it bubbles and thickens, then turn the heat down and add a spoonful more of Marsala if you think it's too thick. Now let the sauce cook very gently for about 20 minutes.

To serve, unwrap each parcel onto a plate and cut each one into 4 pieces – at an angle to show the stuffing. Then pour the sauce over each one and serve straight away.

―――――――――◇―――――――――

tablespoon of the olive oil in the flameproof casserole and when it's really hot, brown the chicken pieces on all sides – don't overcrowd the pan, it's best to do it in 2 batches, 4 pieces at a time.

After that remove the chicken pieces to a plate, then add the second tablespoon of oil and turn the heat to its highest setting. When the oil is really hot add the peppers and onions and cook them in the hot oil, moving them around until their edges are slightly blackened – this should take about 5 minutes – then turn the heat down. Strip the coriander leaves from the stalks, wrap them in a piece of cling-film and keep them in the fridge. Then chop the coriander stalks finely and add these to the peppers and onions along with the garlic, chillies, crushed spices, the chickpeas and rice, giving everything a good stir to distribute all the ingredients.

Season well with salt and pepper, then combine the lemon and saffron mixture with the stock and wine, pour it all into the casserole and stir well. Cut the remaining lemon into thin slices and push these well into the liquid. Now scatter the olives in and finally place the pieces of chicken on top of everything. Cover with a tight-fitting lid and place in the pre-heated oven for 1 hour or until the rice and the chickpeas are tender. Then just before serving scatter the coriander leaves on top, and serve straight away on warmed serving plates.

——————————◇——————————

Traditional Roast Stuffed Chicken with Cranberry, Sage and Balsamic Sauce

SERVES 8

*W*hen *roasting a chicken the skill is to ensure that the cooked bird is not dry, but juicy and succulent. Placing a pork-based stuffing inside the chicken ensures that the juices from the pork provide a kind of internal basting. Most of it is placed around the breast end, which is potentially the driest, then a small amount is tucked inside so the flavours can permeate all through. At the same time the buttery bacon juices do much the same from the outside. The cook can help the process by basting the chicken at least three times during the cooking. For eight people you will need two chickens, or for four just halve the recipe.*

2 x 4 lb (1.8 kg) free-range chickens with giblets	FOR THE APPLE, SAGE AND ONION STUFFING:
12 rashers smoked streaky bacon	**4 oz (110 g) fresh white bread, crusts removed**
3 oz (75 g) butter, softened to room temperature	**1 tablespoon parsley**
Salt and freshly milled black pepper	**1 heaped tablespoon fresh sage leaves**
	1 dessert apple, cored and quartered
FOR THE SAUCE:	**1 small onion, peeled and quartered**
3 tablespoons cranberry jelly	**Chicken livers from the giblets**
1½ tablespoons balsamic vinegar	**8 oz (225 g) minced pork or pork sausage meat**
1 dessertspoon fresh sage, chopped	**¼ teaspoon powdered mace**
Salt and freshly milled black pepper	**Salt and freshly milled black pepper**

Pre-heat the oven to gas mark 5, 375°F (190°C).

First of all the chickens need to be stuffed. If you have a food processor, then making stuffing is a doddle; all you do is switch the motor on, add the pieces of bread and process to crumbs, then add the parsley, sage leaves, apple and onion quarters and process till everything is finely chopped. Next trim the chicken livers (use the rest of the giblets for stock (see page 9), rinse under cold water, pat them dry. Then add them together with the sausage meat, mace and seasoning. Give a few pulses in the processor or until it is all thoroughly blended. Remove the stuffing with a spatula, then place in a polythene bag and store in the fridge until it is needed.

To stuff the chickens, you begin at the neck end where you'll find a flap of loose skin: gently loosen this away from the breast and you'll be able to make a triangular pocket.

Pack about one-third of the stuffing inside as far as you can go and make a neat round shape on the outside. Then tuck the neck flap under the bird's back and secure it with a small skewer. Repeat with the other chicken, then divide the stuffing you have left and place a small amount in each body cavity.

Now place the chickens side by side in a large solid roasting tin. Divide the butter in half and simply smear it over each chicken, using your hands and making sure you don't leave any part of the surface unbuttered.

Season the chickens all over with salt and freshly milled pepper, then arrange 6 slices of the smoked bacon, slightly overlapping in a row along each breast (I like to leave the rind on the bacon for extra flavour but you can remove it if you prefer).

Place the chickens in the oven on the centre shelf and cook them for 1¾ hours (i.e. 20 minutes to the pound plus 10–20 minutes extra). The chickens are cooked when the thickest part of the leg is pierced with a skewer and the juices run clear. It is important to baste the chickens at least three times during the cooking – the juices mingling with the bacon fat and butter spooned over help to keep the flesh succulent.

During the last basting (about half an hour before the chickens are cooked) remove the crisped bacon slices and keep warm. If they are not crisp, leave them around the chicken to finish off. For the final 15 minutes of the cooking, turn up the heat to gas mark 7, 425°F (220°C) which will give the skin that golden crispness.

When the chickens are cooked it is important to leave them in the warm kitchen (near the oven) covered in foil for 30 minutes, which will allow them to relax. This is because when a chicken is cooking all the juices bubble up to the surface (if you look inside the oven you can actually see this happening just under the skin) and what relaxing does is allow time for all those precious juices to seep back into the flesh. It also makes it much easier to carve.

You can make the sauce and the gravy while the chicken is relaxing – all you do to make the sauce is combine everything in a small saucepan by whisking over a gentle heat until the cranberry jelly has melted. Then pour the sauce into a serving jug and leave till needed (it doesn't need re-heating – it's served at room temperature).

Next make the giblet gravy using the giblet stock as on page 9. When you have spooned off the excess fat from the roasting tin and only the dark juices are left, work about 2 level tablespoons of flour into these juices over a low heat. Now, using a balloon whisk, whisk in the giblet stock bit by bit, until you have a smooth gravy. Let it bubble and reduce a little to concentrate the flavour, and taste and season with salt and pepper. Pour it into a warm serving jug and hand round separately.

―――――――――◇―――――――――

Poached Pheasant with Celery

SERVES 2

*C*elery has a wonderful affinity with poultry and game and the two have often appeared together in English recipes over the centuries. This recipe is what I would call old-fashioned comfort food. It has the purest of flavours, as the juices from the pheasant and celery combine to make a wonderful, light creamy sauce. (See photograph on page 80.)

1 pheasant (or guinea fowl, or small chicken), dressed weight about 1 lb 6 oz (625 g)

1 head of celery

10 smallish shallots, about 1 inch (2.5 cm) in diameter

FOR THE SAUCE:

¾ oz (20 g) butter

¾ oz (20 g) plain flour

2 fl oz (55 ml) double cream

Salt and freshly milled black pepper

FOR THE STOCK:

2 pints (1.2 litres) water

The trimmings from the bird

Celery trimmings

1 large onion, halved

2 thyme sprigs

2 stalks parsley

A few peppercorns

1 large carrot, chopped into chunks

1 bay leaf

2 rosemary sprigs

1 level teaspoon salt

FOR THE GARNISH:

About 10 celery leaves, reserved (see below)

1 egg white

1 dessertspoon seasoned flour

Groundnut oil

You will also need a large saucepan with a close-fitting lid, of approximately 4-pint (2.25-litre) capacity.

Begin by making the stock for the sauce. First of all remove any tough outer stems of the celery, and trim the root minimally but leave most of the base on. Then cut the tops off the celery about 3 inches (7.5 cm) up from the base and set aside the base half, reserving about 10 of the prettiest leaves for later. Next wash the other stems from the top half, chop them roughly and place them in a saucepan.

Now add all the other stock ingredients along with the wings of the pheasant. Pheasant wings can be removed very easily – all you do is insert a small knife at the point where the wing is attached to the bone, push your thumb into the incision and feel the little ball-and-socket joint, then use the knife again to cut the ball away from the socket. Repeat with the other wing then bring everything up to simmering point, and simmer for 30 minutes.

Meanwhile, cut the lower part of the celery in half vertically (including the base), then into quarters and finally into eighths. Wash the sections carefully, keeping them attached to the base. Now peel the shallots.

When the stock has had its 30 minutes, place a large sieve over a bowl, line it with a single sheet of kitchen paper and strain the stock through it, then return the strained stock to the saucepan. Season the pheasant and lower it into the liquid. Bring it very gently up to simmering point, then put a lid on and let it simmer for 20 minutes.

After that add the shallots and time it for a further 15 minutes, then add the celery and give the whole thing another 15 minutes. After that remove the pheasant to a dish and use a draining spoon to transfer the vegetables to join it. Cover everything with foil and keep warm.

Now boil the liquid left in the pan without a lid until it has reduced to approximately 10 fl oz (275 ml), or a third of the original. Then, once again, line the sieve with a single sheet of kitchen paper, place it over a bowl and give the stock a final straining. Next make the sauce by melting the butter in a small saucepan, adding the flour and cooking it (stirring all the time) until the mixture turns a pale straw colour – this takes 3–4 minutes. Then, starting off with a wooden spoon and finishing with a whisk, add the stock gradually and whisk until you have a smooth, glossy sauce. Simmer the sauce very gently for 5 minutes. Add the cream and check the seasoning. Then make the garnish.

Heat up ½ inch (1 cm) of groundnut oil in a shallow pan. Whisk the egg white till just frothy, then dip about 10 of the celery leaves first in flour, shaking off the surplus, then in the egg white and briefly fry them in the hot oil for about 10 seconds till pale gold. Then drain them on kitchen paper.

To serve the pheasant: put the bird on its back, take a sharp knife and run the blade down the breastbone and along the wishbone, keeping as close to the bone as you can. Using the knife as a lever, gently pull the breast away from the frame. Now insert your fingers along the rib cage and you'll find you can ease the leg and thigh away from the bone. Trim the bits of skin off, and repeat with the other side. Now cut each half in half again and serve them on warmed plates with the vegetables, the sauce poured over and garnished with the celery leaf fritters.

———————————◇———————————

Venison Steaks with Cranberry Cumberland Sauce

SERVES 2

This is a perfect meal for two for a special occasion, and has the added bonus of being super-fast. For Cumberland sauce redcurrant jelly is traditionally used, but when it's made with cranberry jelly, as it is here, it has a new, deliciously different dimension.

FOR THE STEAKS:	FOR THE SAUCE:
2 venison steaks, each about 7–8 oz (200–225 g)	2 rounded tablespoons cranberry jelly
1 tablespoon groundnut oil	Zest and juice of ½ large orange
1 dessertspoon crushed peppercorns	Zest and juice of ½ small lemon
2 medium shallots, finely chopped	1 teaspoon freshly grated root ginger
Salt	1 slightly rounded teaspoon mustard powder
	3 tablespoons port

Make the sauce way ahead of time – preferably a couple of hours or even several days ahead – so there is time for the flavours to develop. Take off the outer zest of half the orange and the lemon using a potato peeler, then with a sharp knife shred these into really fine hairlike strips, about ½ inch (1 cm) long.

Then place the cranberry jelly, ginger and mustard in a saucepan, add the zest and the squeezed orange and lemon juice, and place it over a medium heat. Now bring it up to simmering point, whisking well to combine everything together, then as soon as it begins to simmer turn the heat off, stir in the port and pour it into a jug to keep till needed.

When you're ready to cook the steaks, heat the oil in a medium-sized, thick-based frying pan. Dry the venison thoroughly with kitchen paper, then sprinkle and press the crushed peppercorns firmly over both sides of each steak. When the oil is smoking hot, drop the steaks into the pan and let them cook for 5 minutes on each side for medium (4 minutes for rare and 6 minutes for well done).

Halfway through add the shallots and move them around the pan to cook and brown at the edges. Then 30 seconds before the end of the cooking time pour in the sauce – not over but around the steaks. Let it bubble for a minute or two, season with salt, and then serve the steaks with the sauce poured over. A garnish of watercress would be nice, and a good accompaniment would be mini jacket potatoes and a mixed-leaf salad.

◇

Poached Pheasant with Celery
(see page 78)

Grilled Chicken with Lemon, Garlic and Rosemary, served with Puy Lentils

SERVES 2

This recipe is for the stressed, overworked man or woman who still wants to eat real food when they finally get home. All you do is shove the chicken in the marinade, go off to have a nice relaxing shower, followed by something that includes the sound of ice tinkling on glass, and then when you're finally ready for supper it will only take about 40 minutes. On the other hand, if you have time, marinate it for longer or even the night before.

2 boneless chicken breasts, 6 oz (175 g) each, skin on

1 medium-sized red onion, peeled and halved

2 bay leaves, snipped in half

1 level tablespoon fresh rosemary leaves, bruised and finely chopped

1 clove garlic, crushed

Grated zest of 1 lemon

3 tablespoons fresh lemon juice

3 tablespoons extra virgin olive oil

Salt and freshly milled black pepper

FOR THE LENTILS:

5 oz (150 g) Puy lentils

½ red onion (see left)

1 dessertspoon extra virgin olive oil

8 fl oz (225 ml) water or red or white wine

A rosemary sprig

Salt and freshly milled black pepper

TO GARNISH:

Flat-leaf parsley

You will also need 2 bamboo skewers which should be soaked in water while the chicken is marinating.

Begin by cutting each chicken breast into 5 evenly sized pieces and place these in a bowl. Then cut 1 half of the onion into quarters and separate into layers, adding them to the chicken, along with the rest of the ingredients. Now give everything a good mixing, cover with a cloth and go away and leave it for at least half an hour.

When you're ready to cook the chicken, pre-heat the grill to its highest setting and set the grill tray 5 inches (13 cm) from the element. Next see to the lentils. Just chop the other half of the onion finely, heat the oil in a medium saucepan, fry the onion for about 5 minutes, then stir in the lentils, making sure they get a good coating of oil. Then add the liquid and sprig of rosemary, but no salt. Put on a lid and let the lentils simmer gently for about 30–40 minutes until the liquid has been absorbed.

To cook the chicken thread the pieces on the skewers, putting half a bay leaf first, then a piece of chicken, then a piece of onion, finishing with the other half of the bay leaf. Then, keeping the skin side of the chicken pieces upwards, lay the skewers on the grill rack with a dish underneath to catch the juices. Season them well, then grill for 20 minutes, turning once and basting with the marinade juices once or twice. When the chicken is ready, taste and season the lentils with salt and a little freshly milled black pepper, and arrange them on warm serving plates. Slide the chicken, onion and bay leaf off the skewers between the prongs of a fork, then spoon the warm basting juices over everything. Garnish with flat-leaf parsley and serve with the lentils and a green salad.

Pot-Roasted Venison with Shrewsbury Sauce

SERVES 4

As the title suggests this is a warming, fragrant and very inviting supper dish that will do wonders to cheer up the long winter nights. Serve it with clouds of fluffy mashed potato which will absorb the sublimely good sauce. You can if you wish use beef instead of venison, in which case I would choose brisket or silverside and cook it for $2\frac{1}{2}$ hours.

2 lb (900 g) boneless, tied venison joint
1 tablespoon groundnut oil
½ oz (10 g) butter
1 small carrot, chopped
1 small onion, chopped
A few thyme sprigs
1 bay leaf
½ bottle (37.5 cl) red wine, something light like Beaujolais
A grating of nutmeg
Salt and freshly milled black pepper

FOR THE SAUCE:

4 level tablespoons good quality redcurrant jelly
2 tablespoons Worcestershire sauce
1–2 tablespoons lemon juice
½ oz (10 g) soft butter
½ oz (10 g) plain flour
1 rounded teaspoon mustard powder
Salt and freshly milled black pepper

You will also need a flameproof casserole with a tight-fitting lid, which will hold the meat comfortably.

First of all wipe the venison joint with kitchen paper and season the surface with salt and freshly milled pepper. Now heat up the oil and butter together in the casserole and when it is foaming hot add the meat to brown on all sides with the carrot and onion alongside it to brown as well. When everything is browned add the thyme and bay leaf, wine, nutmeg and seasoning. Bring this up to a very gentle simmer, cover with a lid (if the lid is not really tight place a sheet of foil under it and press down firmly to seal it).

Give the meat an initial cooking time of 30 minutes. Then turn it over in the liquid, so it will cook to an even colour, and give it a further 30 minutes. After that remove the meat to a warm plate, cover it with foil and keep warm.

Now to make the sauce. Place a sieve over a bowl and strain the liquid through it, pressing the vegetables to extract their juices, then discard them. Next pour the liquid back into the casserole, boil it up and let it reduce slightly. Then add the redcurrant jelly and Worcestershire sauce and whisk it very thoroughly to dissolve the jelly. Now mix the softened butter, flour and mustard powder together to a paste then whisk this, in small pieces, into the sauce so that it thickens slightly and takes on a glossy appearance.

Now add 1 tablespoon of the lemon juice, adding more if needed, taste and check the seasoning. Simmer the sauce gently for 3–4 minutes, then carve the venison and serve with the sauce spooned over.

Pot-Roast of Pheasant with Shallots and Caramelized Apples

SERVES 4–6

This is a superb way to cook pheasants and would make an excellent alternative Christmas lunch for four people. The pheasants are first browned and flamed in calvados (apple brandy) and then are slowly braised in cider. If you don't have any calvados you could use brandy or omit altogether. When the pheasant season comes to an end in mid-February, this works just as well with guinea fowl.

2 pheasants	**Salt and freshly milled black pepper**
1 tablespoon butter	
1 tablespoon oil	FOR THE CARAMELIZED APPLES:
12 shallots, peeled	**3 medium Cox's apples, unpeeled,**
2 fresh thyme sprigs	**quartered and each quarter sliced in 2**
1 bay leaf	**1½ oz (40 g) butter, melted**
3 tablespoons calvados	**4 oz (110 g) granulated sugar**
1½ pints (850 ml) medium cider	
1 heaped teaspoon flour and 1 heaped teaspoon butter mixed to a paste	

You will also need a flameproof casserole in which 2 pheasants can sit comfortably.

Start off by heating the butter and oil together in a heavy frying pan, then brown the pheasants in the hot fat until they're a good golden colour all over. Then place them, breasts uppermost, in the casserole and season them well. Then brown the shallots in the fat remaining in the frying pan and add these to the pheasants along with the thyme and bay leaf.

Next pour the calvados into a small saucepan and warm it gently, then ignite with a match. When it is alight, pour the flaming calvados all over the pheasants. The alcohol will burn off, leaving just the beautiful essence to flavour the birds. Now pour in the cider and bring everything up to a very gentle simmer, put a tight lid on and let the pheasants braise slowly on top of the stove for 1–1¼ hours or until they're tender.

Towards the end of the cooking time, pre-heat the grill to its highest setting. Line the grill pan with foil and brush it with melted butter. Then brush each piece of apple with melted butter and dip it in sugar to coat it well all over. Place these on the foil and grill them about 2 inches (5 cm) away from the element for 6 minutes or until the sugar caramelizes, then turn them over and caramelize on the other side. When they're done they will keep warm without coming to any harm.

When the pheasants are cooked, remove them and the shallots to a warmed serving plate and keep warm. Discard the herbs, then boil the liquid in the casserole briskly without a lid until it has reduced slightly. Then whisk in the flour and butter paste with a balloon whisk, which will slightly thicken it when it comes back to the boil. Carve the pheasant and serve with the shallots and sauce poured over and garnished with the caramelized apples.

Venison Sausages Braised in Red Wine (see page 87)

Terrine of Venison with Juniper and Pistachio Nuts

SERVES 10–12

This is just about the easiest terrine in the world to make because you can buy the venison and the pork ready minced. The result is a lovely, rough country pâté. Serve it with thick slices of toasted country bread, and an excellent accompaniment would be the Confit of Cranberries on page 43.

1 lb (450 g) minced venison, available in large supermarkets	**1 heaped teaspoon chopped fresh thyme**
1 lb (450 g) ready-minced pork	**2 rounded teaspoons salt**
8 oz (225 g) rindless smoked streaky bacon	**6 fl oz (175 ml) dry white wine**
30 juniper berries, crushed	**1 fl oz (25 ml) brandy**
1 rounded dessertspoon mixed peppercorns	You will also need a 2-lb (900-g) loaf tin 7½ x 4¾ x 3½ inches (19 x 12 x 9 cm) deep, preferably non stick, or a terrine of 3-pint (1.75-litre) capacity.
4 oz (110 g) ready-shelled pistachio nuts	
¼ teaspoon powdered mace	Pre-heat the oven to gas mark 2, 300°F (150°C).

First of all, place the venison and the pork in a large bowl then place the bacon slices on a board stacked on top of one another and cut them into thin strips about ⅛ inch (3 mm), then add these to the bowl. After that crush the juniper berries quite coarsely with a pestle and mortar, add these to the bowl then crush the peppercorns, also quite coarsely, and add these. To deal with the pistachio nuts all you need to do is chop them in half, then they can go in along with the thyme, mace, salt and then finally the wine and brandy.

Now you've got quite a lot of mixing to do, so either use your hands or take a large fork and thoroughly combine everything. Cover the bowl with a cloth and leave it all to marinate for about 2 hours, then pack it into the loaf tin or terrine and cover the surface with a double thickness of foil, pleat the corners and fold it under the rim. Now place the terrine in a roasting tin and put it on the middle shelf of the oven, then pour in about 1 inch (2.5 cm) of boiling water from the kettle and let the terrine cook for 1¾ hours. After that, remove it from the oven, leaving the foil on, then after 30 minutes place two 1 lb (450 g) weights on top or the equivalent in tins of tomatoes or something similar. When the terrine is completely cold, place it in the fridge with the weights still on top and leave it overnight to really firm up. Don't forget to take it out of the fridge about an hour before serving, and serve cut in slices.

◇

Venison Sausages Braised in Red Wine

SERVES 2–3

Bangers are bangers, but there are some bangers that are extremely special – and venison sausages are positively five-star, especially when you serve them braised slowly with herbs, shallots, mushrooms and red wine. Then all you need is a dreamy pile of light, creamy mashed potato to go with them. (See photograph on page 84.)

1 lb (450 g) venison sausages	2 bay leaves
1 dessertspoon olive oil	6 oz (175 g) medium-sized, open cap
8 oz (225 g) diced bacon or pancetta	mushrooms
1 large clove garlic, peeled	1 heaped teaspoon plain flour
8 oz (225g) shallots, peeled	1 rounded teaspoon mustard powder
1 dessertspoon juniper berries	1 oz (25 g) soft butter
10 fl oz (275 ml) red wine	1 rounded tablespoon redcurrant jelly
1 teaspoon chopped fresh thyme	Salt and freshly milled black pepper

First take a large flameproof casserole and heat the oil in it. Then, with the heat at medium, brown the sausages evenly all over, taking care not to split the skins by turning them over too soon. Next, using a slotted spoon, transfer them to a plate while you brown the diced bacon along with the garlic and shallots. Now crush the juniper berries very slightly without breaking them – just enough to release their flavour. Return the sausages to the casserole, pour in the wine and add the berries, then thyme and bay leaves. Now season lightly, bring it all up to a gentle simmer, put a lid on the casserole, turn the heat as low as possible and let it all simmer gently for 30 minutes.

After that, add the mushrooms, stirring them in well, then leave everything to cook gently for a further 20 minutes – this time without the lid so the liquid reduces slightly. To finish off remove the sausages and vegetables to a warm serving dish, mix the flour and the mustard powder with the softened butter until you have a smooth paste and whisk this, a little at a time, into the casserole. Let everything bubble for a few more minutes, then take the casserole off the heat, return the sausages to the casserole, whisk in the redcurrant jelly – and it's ready to serve.

CHAPTER FIVE

◇

THE WINTER VEGETARIAN

◇

I find vegetarian cooking a challenge, and I love a challenge – in particular finding ways to make meals without meat or fish more varied and interesting when it comes to entertaining. Vegetarian food has certainly become much more integrated into mainstream cooking in recent years, and, because it has become far more inventive, most people barely notice the absence of fish or meat. In fact I often see committed carnivores actually choosing something vegetarian from a menu.

For something really special, why not go for a soufflé? It is such a treat and if you follow a few very simple rules (like getting the right sized dish) there's never any need to worry. For a family vegetarian meal I would personally go for the Moussaka (page 102), or Pancake Cannelloni with Spinach and Four Cheeses (see opposite). For a supper party the Strudel with Spiced Pickled Pears (page 106) has won high praise among my vegetarian friends.

The vegetarian recipes included in this chapter are by no means the only ones in the book as a whole. For instance have a look at the chapter on soups – Roasted Pumpkin Soup with Melting Cheese (page 14), Chickpea, Chilli and Coriander Soup (page 11), or Curried Parsnip and Apple Soup (page 16) are all ideal. For other inspiration look up Camembert Croquettes (page 38), Apple, Cider Salad with Melted Camembert Dressing (page 40), or Warm Lentil Salad with Walnuts and Goats' Cheese (page 33), to mention just a few.

Pancake Cannelloni with Spinach and Four Cheeses

SERVES 4–6

P*ancakes make brilliant cannelloni – better and lighter, I think, than pasta. Four star Italian cheeses and spinach make this a simply wonderful vegetarian version. It can be made, as described here, in one large family-sized dish, or if you're entertaining it's rather nice to serve it as a starter in individual heatproof baking dishes, with two pancakes per person.*

1 quantity of basic pancakes (see page 179)

FOR THE SAUCE:

1 pint (570 ml) milk

2 oz (50 g) butter

1¼ oz (30 g) plain flour

1 bay leaf

Good grating of fresh nutmeg

2½ fl oz (60 ml) double cream

Salt and freshly milled black pepper

FOR THE FILLING:

1 lb (450 g) raw spinach

½ oz (10 g) butter

5 oz (150 g) Ricotta cheese

5 oz (150 g) Gorgonzola cheese, crumbled

2½ oz (60 g) Parmesan (Parmigiano Reggiano) cheese, grated

1 bunch spring onions, finely sliced including the green parts

Fresh nutmeg

FOR THE TOPPING:

4 oz (110 g) Mozzarella cheese, grated

1½ oz (40 g) Parmesan (Parmigiano Reggiano) cheese, grated

You will also need a well-buttered dish measuring 9 x 9 x 2 inches (23 x 23 x 5 cm).

Pre-heat the oven to gas mark 6, 400°F (200°C).

Begin by making the sauce, and to do this place the milk, butter, flour and bay leaf in a saucepan and bring everything up to simmering point, whisking all the time until the sauce has thickened. Season it with salt, pepper and a good grating of fresh nutmeg. Then turn the heat down to its lowest and let it simmer very gently for 2 minutes, and remove it from the heat before stirring in the cream.

Meanwhile cook the spinach by placing it in a large saucepan with a knob of butter and cooking it briefly for 1–2 minutes, tossing it around until it wilts and collapses down, then drain it in a colander and squeeze it hard to get rid of all the excess juice. Now place the spinach in a bowl, chop it roughly with a knife and then add the Ricotta, Gorgonzola, Parmesan and a grating of the nutmeg. Mix everything together, seasoning with pepper, but no salt as the cheeses can be quite salty. Next add the chopped spring onions and 4 or 5 tablespoons of the sauce.

Then lay a pancake out and place a tablespoonful of the filling onto it, then roll it up, tucking in the edges and repeat this with the remaining pancakes. Lay the filled pancakes side by side in individual gratin dishes or a baking dish and scatter the Mozzarella all over them. Next pour over the sauce. Finally sprinkle the rest of the Parmesan all over the surface. Then bake the cannelloni on the highest shelf of the oven for 25–30 minutes until the top is brown and sauce is bubbling. If you make individual cannelloni in separate dishes, the cooking time will be about 20 minutes.

Broccoli Soufflé with Three Cheeses

SERVES 4 AS A LIGHT LUNCH TOGETHER WITH A GREEN SALAD, OR 6–8 AS A STARTER

The secret of a well-risen soufflé lies precisely in the size of dish you use. If you want it to look amazing use a small dish with a collar tied around – this way you can pile the mixture up high, then when it's cooked remove the collar to reveal a spectacular height! Of course it all tastes the same, but it's good to have some fun when you're cooking, and this is great fun! One thing to remember when making soufflés is that you must have the bowls and whisks spanking clean, then wipe them with a little lemon juice and kitchen paper to ensure they're absolutely grease-free.

1 lb (450 g) broccoli, with the very thick stalks trimmed off
3 x size 1 eggs
2 x extra size 1 egg whites
1 oz (25 g) butter
1¼ oz (30 g) plain flour
5 fl oz (150 ml) milk
¼ teaspoon cayenne pepper
¼ whole nutmeg, grated
1 oz (25 g) strong Cheddar cheese, grated
1 oz (25 g) Gruyère, grated
2 tablespoons Parmesan (Parmigiano Reggiano), grated

Salt and freshly milled black pepper
Melted butter for the dish and collar

You will also need silicone paper, string and a 1¼-pint (725-ml) soufflé dish measuring 5 inches (13 cm) diameter and 3 inches (7.5 cm) high, such as Pillivuyt (available from specialist kitchen shops).

Pre-heat the oven to gas mark 6, 400°F (200°C). Place the oven shelf in the lower third of the oven with no shelf above.

First of all prepare the soufflé dish and its collar. To do this, cut a piece of silicone paper from the roll, 20 x 12 inches (51 x 30 cm) in length. Fold in half along its length so that it now measures 20 x 6 inches (51 x 15 cm) doubled. Now turn up a 1-inch (2.5-cm) fold all along the length to stabilize the base of the collar.

Next butter the dish really well and sprinkle the inside with some of the Parmesan, tipping the dish from side to side to give the base and sides a light coating. Empty out the excess then tie the paper collar around the dish with the 1-inch (2.5-cm) folded bit at the bottom. The paper will overlap around the circumference by 3 inches (7.5 cm) and stand 2 inches (5 cm) above the rim of the dish. Fix the collar in place with string and tie with a bow so that when it comes out of the oven you can remove it quickly and easily. Now butter the inside of the paper and that's it – the dish is now ready to receive the soufflé.

To make the soufflé, place the broccoli in a steamer, sprinkle with salt and steam over simmering water until tender – approximately 8–10 minutes. While the broccoli is cooking, prepare the eggs. Have ready a large bowl containing the extra egg whites and two small ones, separate the eggs into the small bowls one at a time, transferring the whites from the small bowl into the larger bowl as you go. When the broccoli is tender, remove it and leave to cool until barely warm. Then pop it into the processor and whizz it almost to a purée.

Next make the sauce. Place the butter, flour and milk in a small saucepan and whisk with a balloon whisk over a medium heat until you have a smooth, glossy paste. Season to taste with salt and pepper, then season with about the same amount again – this extra is really to season the large volume of eggs. Transfer to a mixing bowl and add the cayenne, nutmeg, Cheddar, Gruyère and 1 tablespoon of the grated Parmesan. Add the 3 egg yolks plus the broccoli and mix everything together thoroughly.

Now the vital part – the beating of the egg whites. If you're using an electric whisk, switch it on to low and beat the whites for approximately 30 seconds or until they begin to start foaming. Then increase the speed of the whisk to medium and then to high, moving the whisk round and round the bowl while it's beating, until you get a smooth glossy mixture that stands in stiff peaks when the whisk is removed from the bowl. It's better to underbeat than overbeat, so watch carefully.

Next, using a large metal spoon, stir 1 tablespoon of the egg whites into the broccoli to lighten the mixture, then empty the broccoli mixture into the egg whites and fold, using cutting and turning movements, until everything is well amalgamated. Don't be tempted to do any mixing – it must be careful folding done as quickly as possible. Now pour the mixture into the prepared dish, sprinkle the top with the remaining Parmesan and place on a shelf in the lower third of the oven (with no shelf above) for 40–45 minutes. When it's done it should be nicely browned on top, well risen and beginning to crack. It should feel springy in the centre but it's important not to overcook it, as it should be nice and moist, almost runny inside because as you are taking it from the oven to the table, and even as you're serving it, it will go on cooking. Divide between warm serving plates and serve it absolutely immediately.

NOTE: This soufflé can be made with other vegetable purées: parsnips, Jerusalem artichokes or courgettes would make lovely alternatives.

———————————◇———————————

Warm Roquefort Cheesecake with Pears in Balsamic Vinaigrette

SERVES 8

*T*his *savoury cheesecake includes a clever blend of three cheese flavours, as the smooth fromage frais and curd cheese gently complement the sharpness of the Roquefort. And, while cheese and pears are always good partners, this particular combination is a marriage made in heaven.*

FOR THE BASE:

4 oz (110 g) white breadcrumbs

2 oz (50 g) Pecorino Romano, finely grated (or Parmesan)

1 oz (25 g) melted butter

Freshly milled black pepper

FOR THE FILLING:

3 x size 1 eggs

8 oz (225 g) medium-fat curd cheese

4 oz (110 g) fromage frais (8% fat)

6 oz (175 g) Roquefort

1 tablespoon snipped chives

4 spring onions, finely sliced

Salt and freshly milled black pepper

FOR THE PEARS IN BALSAMIC VINAIGRETTE:

4 firm but ripe pears

1 fat clove garlic, peeled

1 level teaspoon Maldon sea salt

1 rounded teaspoon mustard powder

1 tablespoon balsamic vinegar

4 tablespoons extra virgin olive oil

Freshly milled black pepper

You will also need a springform cake tin 9 inches (23 cm) in diameter.

Pre-heat the oven to gas mark 5, 375°F (190°C).

First of all make the base of the cheesecake by mixing the breadcrumbs and cheese together, then pour in the butter, adding a good grinding of pepper. Press the crumb mixture firmly down over the base of the tin, then bake in the pre-heated oven for 10–15 minutes. (This time will vary slightly, so it does need careful watching – the aim is for the base to be crisp and toasted. If it is undercooked it does not have the lovely crunchy texture so necessary to the finished cheesecake.) Then remove it from the oven and turn the heat down to gas mark 4, 350°F (180°C).

Now make the filling. First beat together the eggs and curd cheese in a bowl, then stir in the fromage frais and seasoning. After that crumble the Roquefort fairly coarsely and stir it in, together with the chives. Pour the mixture into the tin and scatter the sliced spring onion over the top, then place it on the high shelf of the oven and bake for 30–40 minutes or until the centre feels springy to the touch. Allow the cheesecake to cool and settle for about 20 minutes before serving cut into slices.

The pears in balsamic vinaigrette can be prepared up to 2 hours before serving. Thinly pare off the skins of the pears using a potato peeler and being careful to leave the stalks intact. Now lay each pear on its side with the stalk flat on a board, then take a very sharp knife and make an incision through the tip of the stalk. Turn the pear the right way up and gently cut it in half, first sliding the knife through the stalk and then through the pear.

Now remove the central core of each half, then, with the pear core-side down-wards, slice it thinly but leave the slices joined at the top. Press gently and the slices will fan out.

Make up the vinaigrette by crushing the clove of garlic and sea salt together with a pestle and mortar until it becomes a creamy paste. Now add the mustard and several grinds of black pepper. Work these into the garlic, then, using a small whisk, add the balsamic vinegar and then the oil – whisking all the time to amalgamate. Serve one pear half with each portion of the cheesecake, with a little of the vinai-grette spooned over.

————————◊————————

Red Onion Tarte Tatin

SERVES 6 AS A STARTER OR 4 AS A MAIN COURSE

This is simply the old favourite apple tarte tatin turned into a savoury version. The red onions are mellowed and caramelized with balsamic vinegar, and look spectacularly good. And the cheese and thyme pastry provides the perfect background. Everyone in my family says this is ace.

2½ lb (1.15 kg) red onions
1 oz (25 g) butter
1 level teaspoon caster sugar
6 small thyme sprigs
1 tablespoon chopped fresh thyme
1 tablespoon balsamic vinegar
Salt and freshly milled black pepper

FOR THE PASTRY:

3 oz (75 g) plain flour
2 oz (50 g) plain wholemeal flour
2 oz (50 g) soft butter
1 oz (25 g) Cheddar cheese, grated

1 teaspoon chopped fresh thyme leaves
2–3 tablespoons cold water

TO SERVE:

A few shavings Parmesan (Parmigiano Reggiano)

You will also need either a cast-iron ovenproof pan with a base diameter of 9 inches (23 cm) or a good solid baking tin of the same size (see page 248).

Pre-heat the oven to gas mark 4, 350°F (180°C) and pre-heat a solid baking sheet as well.

Begin by preparing the onions, which should have their outer papery skins removed and then be cut in half lengthways from stem to root. After that, place the pan over a medium heat and as soon as it's hot, add the butter and the sugar, then as soon as the butter begins to sizzle, quickly scatter the sprigs of thyme in, then arrange the onions on the base of the pan, cut side down. As you do this you need to think 'jigsaw puzzle', so that after the onion halves have been placed in the pan to cover the surface, all of those left over need to be cut into wedges and fitted in between to fill the gaps. Bear in mind that what you see when you turn the tart out is the cut side of the onions.

When the onions have all been fitted in, give them a good seasoning of salt and freshly milled black pepper, then scatter over the chopped thyme and sprinkle in the vinegar.

Now turn the heat down under the pan and let the onions cook very gently for about 10 minutes. After that cover the pan with foil and place it on the baking sheet on the shelf just above the centre of the oven and leave it there for the onions to cook for 50–60 minutes.

While the onions are cooking, make the pastry and this, if you like, can be done by mixing all the ingredients, except the water, in a processor. When the mixture resembles fine crumbs, gradually add enough cold water to make a soft dough. Then pop the dough into the fridge in a polythene bag for 30 minutes to rest.

As soon as the onions have had their cooking time, test them with a skewer: they should be cooked through but still retain some texture. Then, protecting your hands well, remove the pan from the oven back onto the hob and increase the oven temperature to gas mark 6, 400°F (200°C). Then turn on the heat under the pan containing the onions to medium, as what you now need to do is reduce all the lovely buttery oniony juices – this will probably take about 10 minutes, but do watch them carefully so that they do not burn. By this time you'll be left with very little syrupy liquid at the base of the pan.

While that's all happening, roll out the pastry to a circle about 10 inches (25.5 cm) in diameter, then – again being careful to protect your hands – turn the heat out under the pan, fit the pastry over the onions, pushing down and tucking in the edges all round the inside of the pan. Then return the tart to the oven on the same baking sheet but this time on the higher shelf and give it another 25–30 minutes until the pastry is crisp and golden.

When the tart is cooked, remove it from the oven and allow it to cool for 20 minutes before turning it out. When turning it out it's important to have a completely flat plate or board. Then protecting your hands with a tea-cloth, place the plate on top of the pan, then turn it upside down, give it a good shake and hey presto – Red Onion Tarte Tatin! If for any reason some of the onions are still in the pan, fear not: all you need to do is lift them off with a palette knife and replace them into their own space in the tart. I think it's nice to serve this tart just warm with a few shavings of Parmesan sprinkled over.

———————————◇———————————

Next page: Italian Stuffed Aubergines
(see page 98)

Italian Stuffed Aubergines

SERVES 2 AS A LIGHT SUPPER DISH OR 4 AS A STARTER

*A*part from tasting superb this is particularly pretty to look at. I like to serve it as a first course, but with a salad and some good bread it would make a lovely supper dish for two people. Strict vegetarians can replace the anchovies with an extra teaspoon of capers. (See photograph on pages 96–7.)

1 medium to large aubergine, approximately 12–14 oz (350–400 g)	**1½ level tablespoons fine fresh breadcrumbs**
3 large ripe tomatoes	**2 level tablespoons Parmesan (Parmigiano Reggiano), freshly grated**
1 medium onion, finely chopped	
1 large clove garlic, crushed	**2 tablespoons olive oil**
1 tablespoon torn fresh basil leaves	**8 basil leaves, lightly oiled**
2 teaspoons sun-dried tomato paste	**Salt and freshly milled black pepper**
6 drained anchovy fillets, chopped	
1 rounded tablespoon drained small capers	
5 oz (150 g) Mozzarella, drained	

You will also need a large solid baking sheet 16 x 12 inches (40 x 30 cm), lightly oiled, and a baking dish 16 x 12 inches (40 x 30 cm), also oiled.

Pre-heat the oven to gas mark 4, 350°F (180°C).

First of all wipe the aubergine and trim off the stalk end, then use the very sharpest knife you have to cut it lengthways into 8 thin slices about ¼ inch (5 mm) thick. When you get to the bulbous sides these slices should be chopped into small pieces and kept aside for the filling. Now arrange the slices of aubergine in rows on the baking sheet, then brush each slice lightly with olive oil and season with salt and pepper. Pop them into the oven on a high shelf and let them pre-cook for 15 minutes, by which time they will have softened enough for you to roll them up easily.

Next pour boiling water on the tomatoes and after 1 minute drain and slip the skins off. Then cut the tomatoes in half and, holding them in the palm of your hand, gently squeeze them until the seeds come out – it's best to do this over a plate or a bowl! Next using a sharp knife, chop the tomatoes into approximately ¼-inch (5-mm) dice. Now heat 1 tablespoon of oil in a large solid frying pan and fry the onion, chopped aubergine and garlic for about 5 minutes. Then add the chopped tomatoes, torn basil leaves and sun-dried tomato paste and continue to cook for about another 5 minutes. Give everything a good seasoning and add the chopped anchovies and capers. Then remove the pan from the heat and let the mixture cool slightly.

Now chop the Mozzarella into very small dice. As soon as the aubergines are cool enough to handle, sprinkle each one with chopped Mozzarella, placing it all along the centre of each slice. On top of that put an equal amount of stuffing ingredients, leaving a border all round to allow for expansion. Roll up the slices and put them in the baking dish, making sure the overlapping ends are tucked underneath. Finally brush each one with oil, combine the fresh breadcrumbs and Parmesan, sprinkle the mixture over them, pop a basil leaf on top, then bake in the oven (same temperature) for about 20 minutes and serve immediately.

Roasted and Sun-Dried Tomato Risotto

SERVES 2 AS A SUPPER DISH OR 3–4 AS A LIGHT LUNCH

Oven-roasted tomatoes, which have been slightly blackened and become really concentrated in flavour, are the mainstay of this superb dish. Add to them some sun-dried tomatoes, Parmesan, a hint of saffron and some creamy, nutty rice and you have one of the nicest risottos imaginable.

FOR THE ROASTED TOMATOES:

1½ lb (700 g) tomatoes

1 dessertspoon extra virgin olive oil

1 fat clove garlic, chopped

1 x 15 g pack (or ½ oz) basil leaves

Salt and freshly milled black pepper

FOR THE RISOTTO:

1 red onion, finely chopped

1 oz (25 g) butter

8 oz (225 g) Italian carnaroli rice (risotto rice)

10 fl oz (275 ml) dry white wine

12 fl oz (330 ml) boiling water

2 teaspoons sun-dried tomato paste

4 oz (110 g) sun-dried tomatoes, roughly chopped

2 oz (50 g) Parmesan (Parmigiano Reggiano), freshly grated, plus 1 oz (25 g) extra shaved into flakes with a potato peeler

¼ teaspoon saffron stamens

1 tablespoon double cream

Salt and freshly milled black pepper

You will also need a solid roasting tray 14 x 10 inches (35 x 25.5 cm), and a 9-inch (23-cm) shallow ovenproof dish of about 3-pint (1.75-litre) capacity.

Pre-heat the oven to gas mark 6, 400°F (200°C).

First of all skin the tomatoes by pouring boiling water over them, then leave them for 1 minute exactly before draining them and slipping the skins off (if they're too hot protect your hands with a cloth). Now slice each tomato in half and arrange the halves on the roasting tray, cut side uppermost, then season with salt and pepper, sprinkle a few droplets of olive oil on each one, followed by the chopped garlic, then finally top each one with half a basil leaf dipped in oil first to get a good coating.

Now pop the whole lot into the oven and roast the tomatoes for 50–60 minutes or until the edges of the tomatoes are slightly blackened. After that, remove them from the oven and then put the dish in the oven to pre-heat it, reducing the temperature to gas mark 4, 350°F (180°C) first. Now put the tomatoes and all their juices into a processor and blend. Next melt the butter in a large heavy saucepan and fry the onion for about 7 minutes until it is just tinged brown at the edges. After that add the rice and stir to coat all the grains with the buttery juices. Now crush the saffron stamens to a powder with a pestle and mortar, then add this to the rice, together with the wine. Bring it up to boiling point, let it bubble for a minute then add the tomato paste and boiling water. Give it all a good stir, season with salt and pepper and then add all the processed tomato mixture plus the dried tomatoes. Stir again and bring it just up to simmering point, then transfer the whole lot to the warm dish, return the dish to the oven and, using a timer, give it 35 minutes.

After that stir in the grated Parmesan and give it another 5–10 minutes – what you'll have to do here is to bite a grain of rice to check when it's ready. It should be tender but still retain some bite. Just before serving stir in the cream and top each portion with shavings of Parmesan and any leftover basil leaves.

Oven-Baked Wild Mushroom Risotto

SERVES 6 AS A STARTER

I've always loved real Italian risotto, a creamy mass with the rice grains 'al dente' – but oh, the bother of all that stirring to make it. Then one day I was making a good old-fashioned rice pudding and I thought, why not try a risotto in the oven?

Why not indeed – it works like a dream and leaves you in peace to enjoy the company of your friends while it's cooking. I have since discovered, in fact, that in Liguria they do make a special kind of baked risotto called 'arrosto', so my version turns out to be quite authentic after all.

½ oz (10 g) dried porcini mushrooms (see page 233)	**2 tablespoons freshly grated Parmesan (Parmigiano Reggiano), plus 2 oz (50 g) extra, shaved into flakes with a potato peeler**
8 oz (225 g) fresh dark-gilled mushrooms	**Salt and freshly milled black pepper**
2½ oz (60 g) butter	
1 medium onion, finely chopped	
6 oz (175 g) Italian carnaroli rice (risotto rice)	
5 fl oz (150 ml) dry Madeira	

You will also need a 9-inch (23-cm) shallow ovenproof dish of 2½-pint (1.5-litre) capacity, approximately 2 inches (5 cm) deep.
Pre-heat the oven to gas mark 2, 300°F (150°C).

First of all you need to soak the dried mushrooms, and to do this you place them in a bowl and pour 1 pint (570 ml) of boiling water over them. Then just leave them to soak and soften for half an hour. Meanwhile chop the fresh mushrooms into about ½-inch (1-cm) chunks – not too small, as they shrink down quite a bit in the cooking.

Now melt the butter in a medium saucepan, add the onion and let it cook over a gentle heat for about 5 minutes, then add the fresh mushrooms, stir well and leave on one side while you deal with the porcini.

When they have had their half-hour soak, place a sieve over a bowl, line the sieve with a double sheet of absorbent kitchen paper and strain the mushrooms, reserving the liquid. Squeeze any excess liquid out of them, then chop them finely and transfer to the pan to join the other mushrooms and the onion. Keep the heat low and let the onions and mushrooms sweat gently and release their juices – which will take about 20 minutes. Meanwhile put the dish in the oven to warm.

Now add the rice and stir it around to get a good coating of butter, then add the Madeira, followed by the strained mushroom-soaking liquid. Add a level teaspoon of salt and some freshly milled black pepper, bring it up to simmering point, then transfer the whole lot from the pan to the warmed dish. Stir once then place it on the centre shelf of the oven without covering. Set a timer and give it 20 minutes exactly.

After that, gently stir in the grated Parmesan, turning the rice grains over. Now put the timer on again, and give it a further 15 minutes, then remove from the oven and put a clean tea-cloth over it while you invite everyone to be seated. Like soufflés, risottos won't wait, so serve *presto pronto* on warmed plates and sprinkle with shavings of Parmesan.

Vegetarian Moussaka with Ricotta Topping

SERVES 4–6

Yes, it is possible to make an extremely good Greek-style moussaka without meat, and even non-vegetarians will admit it tastes every bit as good. Serve it with a large bowl of crunchy salad along with some warm pitta bread.

2 aubergines, 8 oz (225 g) each
10 fl oz (275 ml) vegetable stock
2 oz (50 g) Puy lentils
2 oz (50 g) green lentils
4 tablespoons olive oil
2 medium onions, finely chopped
1 large red pepper, de-seeded and chopped into ¼-inch (5-mm) dice
2 cloves garlic, peeled and crushed
1 x 14 oz (400 g) tin chopped tomatoes
7 fl oz (200 ml) red wine
2 tablespoons tomato purée or sun-dried tomato paste
1 level teaspoon ground cinnamon
2 tablespoons chopped fresh parsley
Salt and freshly milled black pepper

FOR THE TOPPING:
10 fl oz (275 ml) whole milk
1 oz (25 g) plain flour
1 oz (25 g) butter
¼ whole nutmeg, grated
9 oz or 1 x 250 g tub Ricotta cheese
1 x size 1 egg
1 oz (25 g) Parmesan (Parmigiano Reggiano), freshly grated
Salt and freshly milled black pepper

You will also need a shallow dish approximately 9 x 9 x 2½ inches (23 x 23 x 6 cm) deep.

Pre-heat the oven to gas mark 4, 350°F (180°C).

Begin by preparing the aubergines: to do this cut them into ½-inch (1-cm) dice leaving the skins on. Place them in a colander, sprinkling with a little salt between each layer, then put a small plate with a heavy weight on top – this will draw out any excess juices.

Meanwhile pour the stock into a saucepan together with the Puy lentils (but no salt), cover and simmer for 15 minutes before adding the green lentils. Cover again and cook for a further 15 minutes, by which time most of the liquid will have been absorbed and the lentils will be soft. While they're cooking heat 2 tablespoons of oil in a large solid frying pan and fry the onions until they're soft and tinged brown at the edges (about 5 minutes), then add the chopped pepper and soften and brown that too for about another 4 minutes. Next add the garlic, cook for 1 minute more, then transfer the whole lot to a plate.

Now transfer the aubergines to a clean tea-cloth to squeeze them dry, then add a further 2 tablespoons of oil to the frying pan, turn the heat up to high and toss the aubergines in it so they get evenly cooked. When they're starting to brown a little, add the drained tomatoes and the onion and pepper mixture to the pan. In a bowl mix the wine, tomato purée and cinnamon together, then pour it over the vegetables. Add the lentils and the chopped parsley, season well and let everything simmer gently while you make the topping.

All you do is place the milk, flour, butter and nutmeg in a saucepan and, using a balloon whisk, whisk until it comes to simmering point and becomes a smooth glossy sauce. Season with salt and pepper, remove it from the heat and let it cool a little before whisking in the Ricotta cheese followed by the beaten egg.

Finally transfer the vegetable and lentil mixture to the dish and spoon the cheese sauce over the top, using the back of a spoon to take it right up to the edges. Sprinkle with the Parmesan and transfer the dish to the pre-heated oven and bake on the middle shelf for 1 hour. Then allow the moussaka to rest for 15 minutes before serving.

———————————◇———————————

Mashed Black-Eyed Beancakes with Ginger Onion Marmalade

SERVES 4

Black-eyed beans are the lovely nutty beans that are popular in recipes from the deep south of America, and with the addition of other vegetables they make very good beancakes. Fried crisp and crunchy on the outside and served with this delectable Ginger Onion Marmalade, this makes a splendid vegetarian main course.

4 oz (110 g) black-eyed beans	1 clove garlic, chopped
4 oz (110 g) green lentils	¼ teaspoon ground mace
1 pint (570 ml) water	1 teaspoon chopped fresh thyme
1 bay leaf	1 tablespoon sun-dried tomato paste
2 fresh thyme sprigs	2 tablespoons wholewheat flour
1 tablespoon olive oil	4-5 tablespoons olive oil for frying
1 red onion, finely chopped	Salt and freshly milled black pepper
1 medium carrot, finely chopped	
1 small red pepper, de-seeded and finely chopped	TO GARNISH:
1 green chilli, de-seeded and finely chopped	Watercress sprigs

First of all the black-eyed beans need soaking, this can be done by covering them with twice their volume of cold water and leaving them overnight or alternatively bringing them up to the boil, boiling for 10 minutes and then leaving to soak for 2 hours. The green lentils won't need soaking.

Once this is done, take a medium-sized saucepan, add the drained beans and the lentils, then pour in the pint of water, add the bay leaf and sprigs of thyme, then bring everything up to a gentle simmer and let them cook for about 40–45 minutes, by which time all the water should have been absorbed and the beans and lentils will be completely soft. If there's any liquid still left, drain them in a colander. Remove the bay leaf and thyme sprigs. Now you need to mash them to a pulp and you can do this using either a fork, potato masher or an electric hand whisk. After that give them a really good seasoning with salt and freshly milled black pepper and put a clean tea-cloth over them to stop them becoming dry.

Now take a really large frying pan, add the olive oil, then heat it over a medium heat and add the onion, carrot, pepper, chilli and garlic. Sauté them all together for about 6 minutes, moving them around the pan to soften and turn golden brown at the edges.

After that mix all the vegetables into the mashed bean and lentil mixture, add the mace, chopped thyme and tomato paste, then dampen your hands and form the mixture into 12 round cakes measuring approximately 2½–3 inches (6–7.5 cm) in diameter. Then place them on a plate or a lightly oiled tray, cover with cling-film and keep them in the refrigerator until needed, but for 1 hour minimum.

When you're ready to serve the beancakes, coat them lightly with wholewheat flour seasoned with salt and freshly milled black pepper, then heat 2 tablespoons of olive oil. When it is really hot reduce the heat to medium and fry the beancakes in two batches for 3 minutes on each side until they're crisp and golden, adding more oil if needed.

Drain them on kitchen paper and serve garnished with sprigs of watercress and the Ginger Onion Marmalade.

———————◇———————

Ginger Onion Marmalade

This is not only a wonderful accompaniment to the beancakes but is great as a relish for all kinds of other dishes – meat, fish or vegetarian.

12 oz (350 g) onions	2 tablespoons soft dark brown sugar
2 tablespoons olive oil	
3 rosemary sprigs	1 rounded dessertspoon freshly grated ginger
8 fl oz (225 ml) dry white wine	
3 tablespoons white wine vinegar	Salt and freshly milled black pepper

First of all, peel and slice the onions into ¼-inch (5-mm) rings (slice any really large outside rings in half). Then take a solid medium-sized saucepan and heat 2 tablespoons of olive oil. When the oil is hot, add the onions and the rosemary, stir well, and toss the onions around till they're golden and tinged brown at the edges (about 10 minutes).

After that pour in the white wine and white wine vinegar, followed by the brown sugar and the ginger, stir and bring everything up to simmering point. Add salt and pepper, then turn the heat down to low again and let everything simmer very gently for 1¼ hours or until all the liquid has almost disappeared. Then remove the rosemary, pour everything into a serving bowl and you can serve it warm – or I think it's quite nice cold with the hot beancakes.

———————◇———————

Gorgonzola Cheese and Apple Strudel with Spiced Pickled Pears

SERVES 6

*H*ere is a recipe that provides something really stylish for vegetarian entertaining. Serve the strudel with the pickled pears. It's a brilliant combination of crisp pastry, melting cheese and the sharpness of the pears.

12 oz (350 g) young leeks weighed after trimming (this will be about 1½ lb/ 700 g bought weight)

8 oz (225 g) prepared weight of celery (reserve the leaves)

1 small Bramley apple

1 small Cox's apple

8 oz (225 g) Mozzarella, cut in ½-inch (1-cm) cubes

12 spring onions, white parts only, chopped

1 x 3½ oz (100 g) pack ready-chopped walnuts

3 tablespoons chopped parsley, flat-leaf or curly

1 oz (25 g) white bread, crust removed

2 medium cloves garlic, peeled

10 sheets of frozen filo pastry, 18 x 10 inches (45 x 25.5 cm), thawed

6 oz (175 g) Gorgonzola piccante, cut in ½-inch (1-cm) cubes

4 oz (110 g) butter

Salt and freshly milled black pepper

You will also need a large flat baking sheet approximately 16 x 12 inches (40 x 30 cm). Pre-heat oven to gas mark 5, 375°F (190°C).

First of all prepare the leeks by trimming and discarding the outer layers, then slice each one vertically almost in half and wash them under a cold running tap, fanning them out to get rid of any grit and dust. Then dry them in a cloth and cut them into ½-inch (1-cm) pieces. Now wash and chop the celery into slightly smaller pieces.

Then melt 1½ oz (40 g) of the butter in a frying pan 9 inches (23 cm) in diameter. Keeping the heat at medium, sauté the leeks and celery for about 7–8 minutes until just tinged brown, stir them and keep them on the move to stop them catching at the edges. Then tip them into a large bowl and while they are cooling you can deal with the other ingredients.

The apples need to be cored and chopped into ½-inch (1-cm) pieces, leaving the skins on, then as soon as the leeks and celery have cooled, add the apples, diced Mozzarella, spring onions, walnuts and 1 tablespoon of chopped parsley. Season everything well and stir to mix it all together.

Now you need to make a breadcrumb mixture and to do this, place the bread, garlic, the rest of the parsley and reserved celery leaves in a food processor. Switch it on and blend until everything is smooth. If you don't have a food processor, grate the bread, and chop everything else finely and mix together.

Next take a large clean tea-cloth and dampen it under cold water, lay it out on a work surface, then carefully unwrap the filo pastry sheets and lay them on the damp cloth, folding it over. It is important to keep the pastry sheets in the cloth to prevent them drying out.

It is quite complicated to explain how to assemble a strudel, but to actually *do* it is very easy and only takes a few minutes.

Place a buttered baking sheet on a work surface. Because the filo sheets are too small to make a strudel for 6 people, we're going to have to 'weld' them together. To do this, first of all melt the remaining butter in a small saucepan, then take 1 sheet of filo pastry (remembering to keep the rest covered), lay it on one end of the baking sheet and brush it with melted butter. Then place another sheet beside it overlapping it by about 2 inches (5 cm), then brush that with melted butter. Place a third sheet next to the second overlapping it again by 2 inches (5 cm).

Now sprinkle a quarter of the breadcrumb mixture all over the sheets and then place 2 more sheets of filo, this time in the opposite direction, buttering the first one with melted butter and welding the other one with a 2-inch (5-cm) join. Brush that layer as before with melted butter and repeat the sprinkling of breadcrumbs. Then place the next 3 sheets as you did the first 3, again brushing with butter and sprinkling with crumbs. Then place the final 2 sheets as the second ones and brush with butter.

After that place half the cheese and vegetable mixture all the way along the filo, sprinkle the cubes of Gorgonzola on top of that, then finish off with the rest of the mixture on top. Now just pat it together firmly with your hands. Take the edge of the pastry that is nearest to you, bring it up over the filling, then flip the whole lot over as if you were making a giant sausage roll. Neatly push in the vegetables, before tucking the pastry ends underneath. Now brush the entire surface with the remaining butter, scatter the rest of the crumb mixture over the top and bake in the oven for 25–30 minutes or until it has turned a nice golden brown colour.

To serve the strudel, cut off the ends (they are great for the bird table but not for your guests) and cut the strudel into slices, giving each person one pickled pear.

Spiced Pickled Pears

6 hard pears	**4 whole cloves**
(Conference or similar variety)	**6 juniper berries, crushed**
4 oz (110 g) soft brown sugar	You will also need a flameproof casserole approximately 10 inches (25.5 cm) in diameter, large enough to hold the pears.
12 fl oz (330 ml) cider vinegar	
1 tablespoon balsamic vinegar	
1 tablespoon whole mixed peppercorns	Pre-heat the oven to gas mark 5, 375°F (190°C).

To pickle the pears, first peel the pears using a potato peeler, but be very careful to leave the stalks intact as they look much prettier. Place all the rest of the ingredients in a flameproof casserole, bring everything up to simmering point, stirring all the time to dissolve all the sugar. Now carefully lower the pears into the hot liquid, laying them on their sides, then cover with a lid and transfer the pears to the oven for 30 minutes.

After that, remove the lid and carefully turn the pears over. Test with a skewer to see how they are cooking – they'll probably need about another 30 minutes altogether, so cover with the lid and leave them in the oven till they feel tender when pierced with a skewer. Then remove them and allow them to cool in their liquid until needed. When serving, there's no need to re-heat the pears as they taste much better cold.

THE TOP TEN CASSEROLES *and* BRAISED DISHES

◇

I remember going to a very smart, intensely stylish restaurant in the eighties and the chef telling me, rather dismissively, that if he'd known I was coming he'd have made me a casserole. Oh, if only he had! Yet such are the swings of fashion that now my old seventies favourites are back in favour with young chefs. So let us not lament the lean years of nouvelle cuisine, but rather rejoice in this decade of diversity. Back in the charts are oxtails, Irish stews, mashed potatoes, beef, lamb and pork slowly braised in lashings of sauce, real comfort foods for cold days, evoking an aura of homeliness and contentment in the kitchen to dispel the trials of the day.

If casseroles are going to make a comeback in your life, you need to convince yourself that they're really *not* a lot of work. The preparation time is never that long, and while the meal is in the oven you are left completely free – a great deal easier than standing by a grill or frying pan. The other positive side is that all casseroles improve if they're made a day ahead, cooled, refrigerated and gently re-heated when you need them. Just pre-heat the oven to gas mark 4, 350°F (180°C) and place the casserole covered in the oven for 40 minutes. So they're absolutely ideal for serving to friends: you can entertain in a much more relaxed way with no last-minute hurdles to overcome.

Still more good news is that they freeze well. If a casserole has been frozen, defrost it thoroughly then remove the cardboard lid from the foil container and replace it with double foil, and re-heat as above. In all cases make sure it has come to a gentle simmer before serving.

Pork Braised in Cider Vinegar Sauce

SERVES 4

This recipe has an autumnal ring to it and is for me the first casserole of the winter months. Pork shoulder is an excellent cut for braising and this recipe is superb for serving to friends and family, because it just cooks away all by itself until you're ready to serve it. I also think it tastes even better the next day, so if you make it that far ahead, don't add the crème fraîche until it's re-heated. The re-heating will take about 25 minutes in a casserole over gentle direct heat. Note here, though, that it's important to use a good quality cider vinegar.

2 lb (900 g) pork shoulder, trimmed and cut into 1-inch (2.5-cm) cubes
12 shallots, peeled
2 tablespoons groundnut oil
½ oz (10 g) butter
1 pint (570 ml) medium sweet cider
5 fl oz (150 ml) cider vinegar
4 fresh thyme sprigs

2 bay leaves
1½ tablespoons crème fraîche
Salt and freshly milled black pepper

You will also need a wide, shallow flameproof casserole, 4-pint (2.25-litre) capacity.

Pre-heat the oven to gas mark 3, 325°F (170°C).

First place the casserole over a fairly high heat and add half the butter and 1 tablespoon of oil. Meanwhile, dry the pieces of meat with kitchen paper then brown them a few at a time in the hot fat, transferring them to a plate as they brown.

After that add the rest of the butter and oil and when that's very hot add the shallots to the pan and carefully brown these on all sides, to a nice glossy caramel colour. Now pour the cider and cider vinegar into the pan, stir well, scraping the base and sides of the pan then return the meat, add the thyme and the bay leaves and season well.

As soon as it's all come to simmering point, transfer the casserole without a lid to the oven for approximately 1 hour and 15 minutes or until all the liquid is reduced and the meat is tender. Now remove the meat and shallots to a warm serving dish, discarding the herbs, then place the casserole back over direct heat. Bring it up to the boil and reduce the liquid to about half of its original volume. Finally whisk in the crème fraîche, taste to check the seasoning, then pour the sauce over the meat and serve. This is great served with Potato and Apple Rösti (page 154) and Spiced Sautéed Red Cabbage with Cranberries (page 155).

NOTE: If you don't have a wide *shallow* casserole, use an ovenproof dish (same size) but pre-heat it first in the oven. Make sure everything reaches simmering point in the frying pan before you pour it into the dish, then finish the sauce in a saucepan.

—◇—

Braised Lamb with Flageolet Beans

SERVES 4

Though neck fillet of lamb is quite an economical cut, it provides very sweet meat that responds perfectly to long slow cooking and if you add pre-soaked dried green flageolets to cook alongside it, these too absorb all the sweet flavours of the lamb, garlic and herbs, making this an extremely flavoursome and comforting winter warmer.

2 lb (900 g) lamb neck fillets
8 oz (225 g) flageolet beans
2 large onions, peeled, halved and cut into ½-inch (1-cm) rounds
2 cloves garlic, finely chopped
1 oz (25g) plain flour
1 dessertspoon chopped fresh thyme leaves
1 pint (570 ml) supermarket lamb stock or water

3 small bay leaves
8 oz (225 g) cherry tomatoes
4 small fresh thyme sprigs
2 tablespoons oil
Salt and freshly milled black pepper

You will also need a flameproof casserole dish of approximately 4-pint (2.25-litre) capacity.

Pre-heat the oven to gas mark 1, 275°F (140°C).

You need to start this recipe off by soaking the beans. You can do this by covering the beans with twice their volume of cold water, then soaking them overnight. Alternatively, on the same day, boil them for 10 minutes then leave them to soak for a minimum of 2 hours.

When you're ready to cook the lamb, pre-heat the oven, trim off any really excess fat and then cut it into rounds about ¾ inch (2 cm) thick. Now place the casserole over direct heat, add 1 tablespoon of oil then as soon as it's smoking hot, brown the pieces of meat, a few at a time, wiping them first with kitchen paper so that they're absolutely dry when they hit the fat (don't add more than 6 pieces at a time). Then as soon as each piece is nicely browned on both sides, remove the fillets to a plate and carry on until all the meat is browned. Next add the other tablespoon of oil and, keeping the heat high, brown the onions round the edges, moving them around until they take on a nice dark caramel colour – this will take about 5 minutes – then add the garlic, stir that into the onions and let it cook for another minute or so. Now sprinkle in the flour and give it all a good stir, allowing the flour to soak into the juices. Add thyme leaves, then gradually add the stock, stirring all the while as you pour it in. Next return the meat to the casserole and season it well with freshly milled black pepper, but no salt at this stage. After that drain the beans, discarding their soaking water, and add them to the casserole as well. Finally add the thyme sprigs and bay leaves, and as soon as everything has come up to simmering point, place a tight-fitting lid on and transfer the casserole to the centre shelf of the oven. Give it 1½ hours and towards the end of that time pour boiling water over the tomatoes and then after 30 seconds drain off the water and slip the skins off. Add these to the casserole along with a good seasoning of salt, then replace the lid and carry on cooking for a further hour.

Before serving remove the bay leaves and sprigs of thyme and taste to check the seasoning.

A Bit of the Irish Stew
with Crusted Dumplings

SERVES 4–6

*T*his *is an updated version of my 'Cookery Course' recipe, included here simply because Irish Stew is one of the best casserole dishes in the entire world. If you top it with dumplings then bake it in the oven so that they turn crusty and crunchy, you will have a heavenly banquet on your plate. Serve it as the Irish do, with simple boiled cabbage. (See photograph on pages 112–13.)*

3 lb (1.35 kg) neck fillets of lamb and best end of neck cutlets mixed	
2 tablespoons seasoned plain flour	
12 oz (350 g) onions, thickly sliced	
8 oz (225 g) carrots, cut in chunks	
2 medium leeks, washed and sliced	
1 large potato (about 10 oz/275 g), peeled and cut in chunks	
1 rounded tablespoon pearl barley	
Salt and freshly milled black pepper	

FOR THE DUMPLINGS:

6 oz (175 g) self-raising flour

3 tablespoons chopped fresh parsley

3 oz (75 g) shredded suet

Salt and freshly milled black pepper

TO GARNISH:

1 tablespoon chopped fresh parsley

You will also need a 6-pint (3.5-litre) flameproof casserole.

Start off by drying the pieces of meat on kitchen paper, trim away any excess fat, cut the fillets into 1½-inch (4 cm) rounds, then dip them along with the cutlets into the seasoned flour. Now arrange a layer of meat in the base of the casserole, followed by a layer of onion, carrot, leek and potato and a good seasoning of salt and pepper. Then add some more meat and continue layering the ingredients until everything is in.

Next sprinkle in the pearl barley and pour in approximately 2 pints (1.2 litres) of hot water and bring it all up to simmering point. Spoon off any scum that comes to the surface, cover with a well-fitting lid and leave it to simmer over the lowest possible heat for 2 hours.

About 15 minutes before the end of the cooking time pre-heat the oven to gas mark 6, 400°F (200°C), then make up the dumplings. Mix the flour and parsley with a seasoning of salt and pepper in a bowl, then mix in – but do not rub in – the suet. Now add just sufficient cold water to make a fairly stiff but elastic dough that leaves the bowl cleanly. Knead it lightly then shape it into 12 dumplings.

When the stew is ready, remove the lid, place the dumplings all over the surface, then transfer the casserole to the highest shelf of the oven (without a lid) and leave it there for 30 minutes or until the dumplings are golden brown and crusty. Serve the meat surrounding the vegetables and dumplings, with some of the liquid poured over and some in a gravy boat, and sprinkle with chopped fresh parsley.

Next page: A Bit of the Irish Stew with Crusted Dumplings

Pot-Roasted Beef in Red Wine with Red Onion Marmalade

SERVES 4–6

It has to be said that roasting meat does require a little attention, with basting and so on. But the great thing about a pot-roast is that it feeds the same number of people, but leaves you in peace until you're ready to serve. Its other great virtue is that it enables you to use some of those very lean, delicious cuts of meat that are not suitable for roasting, such as brisket or silverside.

2½ lb (1.15 kg) rolled brisket or silverside
15 fl oz (425 ml) red wine
2 bay leaves
A small bunch of thyme
1½ level tablespoons flour
1 oz (25 g) butter
Salt and freshly milled black pepper

You will also need a medium-sized flameproof casserole with a tight-fitting lid.

FOR THE RED ONION MARMALADE:
12 oz (350 g) red onions, very finely chopped
1 oz (25 g) butter
8 fl oz (225 ml) red wine
2 fl oz (55 ml) red wine vinegar
1 teaspoon chopped fresh thyme
Salt and freshly milled black pepper

Pre-heat the oven to gas mark 1, 275°F (140°C).

Take the casserole, melt ½ oz (10 g) of the butter and when it begins to foam turn the heat up high. Dry the meat thoroughly with kitchen paper and then brown it on all sides in the hot butter, browning one flat side first, then turning it over on the other side, and moving it around to get the round edges browned as well.

Then remove the meat, wipe the casserole with some kitchen paper and return the meat to it, adding the herbs, the wine and some salt and pepper. Bring it all up to simmering point, put on a tight-fitting lid, using foil if necessary, then transfer it to the oven and leave it to cook without looking at it for 3 hours.

When the cooking time is up, remove the meat from the casserole, cover it with foil and leave it to relax for 10 minutes. Meanwhile remove the herbs, place the casserole over direct heat and boil briskly to reduce the liquid slightly. Mix the flour and remaining butter to a smooth paste, then add this mixture in small pieces to the hot liquid and whisk with a balloon whisk until it comes back to the boil and you have a smooth, slightly thickened sauce.

While the beef is cooking, make the Red Onion Marmalade. Melt the butter in a medium-sized saucepan, stir in the chopped onion and the thyme and let them soften for about 10 minutes. Then add the wine and wine vinegar, bring it all up to a gentle simmer and add a seasoning of salt and freshly milled black pepper. Turn the heat to its lowest setting and let the whole thing cook really slowly with the lid off for about 50 minutes to 1 hour or until all the liquid has evaporated. Remove it from the heat, but re-heat gently before serving.

◇

Meatballs in Goulash Sauce

SERVES 4–6

This recipe never fails to please – minced beef and pork together with pepper and onion is a wonderful combination of flavours. The meatballs are very light and the sauce rich and creamy. A classic Hungarian accompaniment would be buttered noodles tossed with poppy seeds (see below).

12 oz (350 g) lean minced beef	**1 medium onion, chopped**
12 oz (350 g) minced pork	**½ medium red pepper, de-seeded and finely chopped**
½ medium red pepper, de-seeded and finely chopped	**1 clove garlic, crushed**
1 small onion, very finely chopped	**1 lb (450 g) ripe tomatoes, peeled and chopped, or 1 x 14 oz (400 g) tin Italian chopped tomatoes**
1 fat clove garlic, crushed	
2 tablespoons fresh chopped parsley	
2 oz (50 g) breadcrumbs	**Approximately half 200 ml tub crème fraîche**
1 x size 1 egg, beaten	
1 rounded tablespoon seasoned flour	**A little extra paprika**
2 tablespoons olive oil	**1 tablespoon olive oil**
Salt and freshly milled black pepper	**Salt and freshly milled black pepper**

FOR THE SAUCE:
1 rounded tablespoon hot Hungarian paprika

You will also need a large flameproof casserole, 4 pint (2.25 litre), with a well-fitting lid.

Pre-heat the oven to gas mark 1, 275°F (140°C).

First make the meatballs. In a large bowl place the minced meats, chopped pepper, onion, garlic, parsley and breadcrumbs. Mix well then add the egg and a good seasoning of salt and freshly milled black pepper. Now combine everything as thoroughly as possible, using either your hands or a large fork. Then take pieces of the mixture, about a tablespoon at a time, squeeze and roll each one into a small round – you should get 24 altogether – then coat each one lightly with seasoned flour. Heat up 2 tablespoons of oil in the casserole, and when it's smoking hot, brown the meatballs a few at a time. Then transfer them to a plate.

Next make the sauce in the same pan. Heat the oil, add the onion and the red pepper together and cook for about 5 minutes, then add the garlic, cook for another minute, and stir in the paprika and any remaining bits of seasoned flour. Stir to soak up the juices, then add the tomatoes, season with salt and pepper then bring it all up to simmering point, stirring all the time. Now add the meatballs to the sauce, bring back to simmering point, cover with a tight-fitting lid and transfer it to the middle shelf of the oven for 1½ hours. Just before serving, lightly stir in the crème fraîche to give a marbled effect. Spoon the meatballs onto freshly cooked noodles and sprinkle a little extra paprika on as a garnish as they go to the table.

NOTE: For the noodles use 3 oz (75 g) green tagliatelle per person, drained then tossed in ½ oz (10 g) butter and 1 level teaspoon poppy seeds.

Braised Steak in Madeira with Five Kinds of Mushrooms

SERVES 4–6

This recipe, which uses thick braising steak, is really a very moveable feast. As written it is perfect for entertaining, but for an everyday family version you could replace the Madeira with cider or beer and quite easily use just one variety of mushroom.

2 lb (900 g) braising steak (1 thick slice)
½ oz (10 g) dried porcini mushrooms
6 oz (175 g) oyster mushrooms
6 oz (175 g) shiitake mushrooms
4 oz (110 g) chestnut mushrooms
4 oz (110 g) dark gilled mushrooms
2 medium onions, peeled
10 fl oz (275 ml) dry Madeira
1 rounded tablespoon plain flour

1 fat garlic clove, crushed
1½ oz (40 g) butter
2 tablespoons olive oil
1 bay leaf
A few fresh thyme sprigs
Salt and freshly milled black pepper

You will also need a large shallow flameproof casserole with a tight-fitting lid.

Pre-heat the oven to gas mark ½, 250°F (130°C).

First of all soak the dried porcini by placing them in a jug with 15 fl oz (425 ml) warm water for at least half an hour. Meanwhile, trim the beef of any hard gristle and membrane and if it's a whole slice divide it into 4 pieces. Cut the onions into half lengthways and then into ½-inch (1-cm) wedges. Now in the casserole heat 1 tablespoon of olive oil and sauté the onions until nicely tinged brown at the edges, then remove them to a plate. Heat another tablespoon of oil in the casserole, turning the heat up really high then brown the pieces of meat, 2 at a time on both sides, and remove them as they're done to join the onions.

Next drain the porcini through a sieve lined with kitchen paper, reserving the liquid, and chop them roughly. Now stir the flour into the fat left in the casserole along with ½ oz (10 g) butter, then slowly add the mushroom soaking water, stirring well after each addition and follow that with the Madeira, whisking well to blend everything. As soon as the liquid comes up to simmering point, add the onions and the browned beef to the casserole, along with the chopped porcini. Add the bay leaf and the thyme, season with salt and pepper then put a lid on and place the casserole in the oven for 1½ hours. After that chop the chestnut and dark gilled mushrooms roughly (not too small). Add these to the casserole, sprinkling them on the steak and spooning the juices over, then replace the lid, return the casserole to the oven and let it cook slowly for another 1½ hours.

When you're ready to serve, slice the oyster and shiitake mushrooms into ½-inch (1-cm) strips, reserving a few small whole ones for garnishing, then melt 1 oz (25 g) butter in a frying pan, add the garlic, the mushrooms and season with salt and pepper. Toss everything around in the pan for 2–3 minutes. Now remove the casserole from the oven, taste to check the seasoning, then serve the steaks with the sauce spooned over and garnish with the shiitake and oyster mushrooms.

Braised Steak in Madeira with Five Kinds of Mushrooms

Braised Steak au Poivre in Red Wine

SERVES 4

While the French classic steak au poivre, or peppered steak, is a wonderful idea, steak is expensive and in the winter the original recipe can be adapted to braising – which is far easier for entertaining and tastes every bit as good. I like to serve it with some crispy-skinned buttered jacket potatoes.

2 lb (900 g) good-quality braising steak, cut into 2-inch (5-cm) pieces
1 level dessertspoon whole black peppercorns
2 large onions, finely chopped
2 fat cloves garlic, crushed in a pestle and mortar with 1 teaspoon sea salt
3 tablespoons beef dripping or olive oil
1 rounded tablespoon plain flour

15 fl oz (425 ml) red wine
2 bay leaves
A large thyme sprig
2 rounded tablespoons crème fraîche
Salt and freshly milled black pepper

You will also need a flameproof casserole with a close-fitting lid.

Pre-heat the oven to gas mark 2, 300°F (150°C).

Begin by crushing the peppercorns coarsely with a pestle and mortar, then mix them together with the flour on a plate. Now dip the pieces of meat into this mixture, pressing it well in on all sides. Next heat 2 tablespoons of the dripping or oil in the casserole, and when it is really hot and beginning to shimmer quickly brown the pieces of meat, about 4 at a time, on both sides then transfer them to a plate.

After that add the remaining dripping or oil to the pan and brown the onions for 3–4 minutes, still keeping the heat high. Then add the crushed garlic and cook for another minute. Now add any remaining flour and pepper left on the plate to the pan, stirring well to soak up the juices, then add the wine a little at a time, continuing to stir to prevent any lumps forming, and scraping in any crusty residue from the bottom and edge of the pan. When it's at simmering point, add the meat to the sauce, season it with salt, then pop the bay and thyme leaves in. Bring it back to a simmer then put a lid on the casserole and transfer it to the middle shelf of the oven to cook for 2 hours or until the meat is tender.

When you're ready to serve, remove the herbs, add the crème fraîche, stir it well in, then taste to check for seasoning before serving.

Oxtail Braised in Guinness with Cannellini Beans

SERVES 6

I am not surprised that oxtail has become rather fashionable in restaurants now because any meat that is cooked near the bone has a special sweetness and succulence. But it's still a very economical dish to prepare at home, and the addition of cannellini beans in this recipe means that they too absorb all that lovely flavour. This version is a winner.

8 oz (225 g) cannellini beans	1 pint (570 ml) beef stock
3–3½ lb (1.35–1.6 kg) oxtail	4 whole garlic cloves, peeled
2 large onions, halved and thickly sliced	2 good thyme sprigs
4 tablespoons olive oil	2 bay leaves
1 rounded tablespoon plain flour, seasoned	Salt and freshly milled black pepper
12 oz (350 g) open cap mushrooms	
12 oz (350 g) chestnut mushrooms	
1 x 440 ml can Guinness	

You will also need a flameproof casserole of 8-pint (4.5-litre) capacity.

Pre-heat the oven to gas mark 2, 300°F (150°C).

First the beans need to soak and to do this either put them in a large saucepan with 4 pints (2.25 litres) of cold water and bring them up to the boil for 10 minutes then turn the heat off and leave them to soak for a minimum of 2 hours, or else soak them in cold water overnight.

To make the casserole, heat 2 tablespoons of the oil in a large frying pan then wipe the pieces of oxtail with kitchen paper and coat them lightly in seasoned flour and fry in hot fat on all sides until they are a nutty brown colour, then using a slotted spoon, transfer the pieces of oxtail to a casserole. Now add the rest of the oil and as soon as that's hot, add the onions and fry these for about 5 minutes until brown at the edges before transferring them to join the oxtail in the casserole. Remove the pan from the heat, then drain the beans in a colander. Add them to the casserole along with the garlic cloves, sprigs of thyme and bay leaves and add a good seasoning of black pepper.

Next wipe the open cap mushrooms with some damp kitchen paper, halve them (or quarter them if they are very large), then add these to the casserole as well, tucking them in among the beans and oxtail. Now return the pan to the heat, add any remaining seasoned flour, stir it in to soak up the juices and gradually add the stock and the Guinness, whisking all the time until it reaches simmering point. Pour it over the oxtail and the rest of the ingredients, cover with a tight-fitting lid and place in the pre-heated oven for 2½ hours. Then add the chestnut mushrooms halved and wiped as above, put the lid back on and give the casserole a further hour in the oven. When you next remove it, you will see that some of the fat from the oxtail has bubbled up to the top – spoon this off by skimming a tablespoon across the surface. Then season everything well with salt before serving with a lightly cooked green vegetable.

Black Bean Chilli with Avocado Salsa

SERVES 4–6

*T*he now-familiar chilli con carne has suffered from its fair share of convenience shortcut versions but when it's made properly with the right ingredients, it is still a wonderful concept. I think this version is even better than the original, using black beans and introducing the subtle flavouring of lime and coriander – and adding a contrasting cold garnish at the end. (See photograph on pages 120–1.)

1 lb (450 g) braising steak, cut into very small pieces

8 oz (225 g) black beans

2 x 15 g packs (or 1 oz) fresh coriander (reserving leaves for the salsa)

2 tablespoons olive oil

2 medium onions, chopped

1 garlic clove, crushed

2 green chillies, de-seeded and chopped small

1 rounded tablespoon plain flour

2 x 14 oz (400 g) tins chopped tomatoes

1 large red pepper

Juice of ½ lime

Salt

FOR THE SALSA:

2 large, firm tomatoes

1 ripe, firm avocado

½ small red onion, finely chopped

Reserved chopped coriander leaves

Juice of ½ lime

A few drops Tabasco sauce

Salt and freshly milled black pepper

TO SERVE:

4 tablespoons crème fraîche

You will also need a 4-pint (2.25-litre) flameproof casserole with a well-fitting lid.

Either pre-soak the beans overnight or start this recipe 3 hours ahead of time and begin by placing the beans in a large saucepan, covering them with cold water and bringing them up to boiling point and boiling for 10 minutes. Then turn the heat off and let them soak for 3 hours. Towards the end of the soaking time pre-heat the oven to gas mark 2, 300°F (150°C).

Strip the leaves off the coriander stalks into a bowl, cover with clingfilm and place them in the fridge. Then chop the coriander stalks very finely indeed. After that take the casserole, heat half the oil in it and cook the onions, garlic, coriander stalks and chillies gently for about 5 minutes. Then transfer them to a plate, spoon in the rest of the oil, turn the heat up high, add about a third of the beef and brown it well, keeping it on the move. Then remove it and brown the rest in 2 batches. Now return everything to the casserole and sprinkle in the flour, stir it in to soak up the juices, then add the drained beans, followed by the tomatoes. Stir well and bring it up to simmering point. Don't add any salt at this stage – just

Previous page: Black Bean Chilli with Avocado Salsa

put the lid on and transfer the casserole to the oven to cook for an initial 1½ hours.

Towards the end of that time, de-seed and chop the pepper into smallish pieces. Then when the time is up, stir the pepper in to join the meat and beans. Put the lid back on and give it a further 30 minutes' cooking.

While the meat finishes cooking, make up the salsa. Skin the tomatoes by pouring boiling water over them, then leaving for exactly 1 minute before draining and slipping the skins off when they're cool enough to handle. Then cut each tomato in half and, holding each half over a saucer, squeeze gently to extract the seeds. Now chop the tomato flesh as finely as possible.

Next halve the avocado, remove the stone, cut each half into 4 and peel off the skin. Chop the avocado into minutely small dice, and do the same with the onion. Finally combine everything together in a bowl, adding seasoning, the juice of half the lime, half the chopped coriander and a few drops of Tabasco.

Before serving the chilli, add salt, tasting as you add. Then stir in the rest of the coriander leaves and the juice of half the lime. I like to serve this chilli with some plain brown basmati rice.

———————————◇———————————

Beef in Designer Beer

SERVES 4–6

*I*n *the sixties every other restaurant was a bistro and every other bistro served Carbonnade de Boeuf à la Flamande, a traditional Flemish recipe which translates as Beef in Beer. But like other once-hackneyed sixties recipes, I think it's been neglected and there's a whole new generation now who probably haven't yet tasted it. For them, here is the nineties version, the only difference being that we now have a vast range of beers with smart labels to choose from. Not sure which one to use? Do what I do and go for the prettiest label!*

2 lb (900 g) braising steak cut into 2-inch (5-cm) squares	FOR THE CROUTONS:
15 fl oz (425 ml) designer beer (see above)	**6 x 1-inch (2.5-cm) thick slices French bread cut slightly diagonally**
1 tablespoon olive oil	**1 tablespoon olive oil**
12 oz (350 g) onions, peeled and cut in quarters	**1 garlic clove, crushed**
2 garlic cloves, crushed	**6 level teaspoons wholegrain mustard**
1 heaped tablespoon plain flour	**4 oz (110 g) grated Gruyère cheese**
A few fresh thyme sprigs	
2 bay leaves	
Salt and freshly milled black pepper	You will also need a large, wide, flameproof casserole.

You can make the croûtons well ahead of time and to do this pre-heat the oven to gas mark 4, 350°F (180°C). Then drizzle the olive oil onto a large solid baking sheet, add the crushed garlic, then using either your hands or a piece of kitchen paper, spread the oil and garlic all over the baking sheet. Now place the bread slices on top of the oil, then turn them over so that both sides have been lightly coated with the oil. Bake for 20–25 minutes till crisp and crunchy.

When you're ready to cook the beef, lower the oven temperature to gas mark 2, 300°F (150°C). Take the flameproof casserole, place it over direct heat then heat the oil until sizzling hot and fry the meat 3 or 4 pieces at a time until they turn a dark mahogany colour on all sides. Make sure you don't overcrowd the pan or they will create steam and never become brown. As you brown the meat remove it to a plate, then when all the meat is ready add the onions to the pan keeping the heat still high, and toss them around until they become darkly tinged at the edges – this will take about 5 minutes. After that add the crushed garlic, let that cook for about 30 seconds or so, then turn the heat down, return the meat to the casserole and sprinkle in the flour. Then, using a wooden spoon, stir until all the flour has been absorbed into the juices. It will look rather stodgy and unpromising at this stage but not to worry. The long slow cooking will transform its appearance.

Now gradually stir in the beer and when it's all in, let the whole thing gently come up to simmering point, and while that's happening add salt, freshly milled black pepper and the thyme and bay leaves. Then just as it begins to bubble put the lid on, transfer it to the centre shelf of the oven and leave it there for 2½ hours. Don't be tempted to taste it now or halfway through the cooking as it does take 2½ hours for the beer to mellow and become a luscious sauce.

Just before you want to serve the beef, pre-heat the grill, spread the croûtons with the mustard and sprinkle them with the grated Gruyère, then arrange them on top of the meat and pop the casserole under the grill until the cheese is bubbling. Then serve straight away.

———————————◇———————————

AUTUMN AND WINTER ENTERTAINING

Here are a few menu suggestions for warm occasions during the cold seasons.

AN AUTUMN DINNER FOR SIX PEOPLE

First course

Apple, Cider Salad with Melted Camembert Dressing

Main course

Pork Braised in Cider Vinegar Sauce (recipe x 1½)
Spiced Sautéed Red Cabbage with Cranberries (recipe x 1½)
Potato and Apple Rösti (recipe x 1½)

Dessert

Fallen Chocolate Soufflé with Armagnac Prunes and Crème Fraîche Sauce

———————◇———————

THREE VEGETARIAN SUPPER PARTIES FOR FOUR

Italian Stuffed Aubergines
Warm Roquefort Cheesecake with Pears in Balsamic Vinaigrette
Green Salad
Pears Baked in Marsala Wine

Curried Parsnip and Apple Soup with Parsnip Crisps
Mashed Black-Eyed Beancakes with Ginger Onion Marmalade
Oven-Roasted Cauliflower and Broccoli with Garlic and Coriander
Banoffee Cheesecake with Toffee Pecan Sauce

Oven-Baked Wild Mushroom Risotto
Red Onion Tarte Tatin
Green Salad
Lemon Ricotta Cheesecake with a Confit of Lemons

———————◇———————

HALLOWEEN SUPPER PARTY FOR EIGHT

First course

Roasted Pumpkin Soup with Melting Cheese (recipe x 1½)

Main course

Braised Lamb with Flageolet Beans (recipe x 2)
Mashed Potato with Garlic-Infused Olive Oil (recipe x 2)

Dessert

Four Nut Chocolate Brownies

———————◇———————

Moroccan Baked Chicken with Chickpeas and Rice

SERVES 4

*C*hicken pieces simmered with chickpeas, peppers and olives in a saffron-flavoured rice with coriander and lemons – hope you like it. Chicken Basque was such a huge hit in the 'Summer Collection' because, I imagine, everything needed for a meal for four people was cooked in one large cooking pot with no extra vegetables needed. This has meant I have been under a lot of pressure to produce a recipe that could match it. So to a flourish of trumpets here it is. (See photograph on pages 72–3.)

1 x 3½–4 lb (1.5–2 kg) chicken, jointed in 8 pieces (or you could use a pack of 8 drumsticks and thighs)	3 cloves garlic, chopped
4 oz (110 g) dried chickpeas	10 fl oz (275 ml) carton good chicken stock
6 oz (175 g) brown basmati rice	5 fl oz (150 ml) dry white wine
2 fresh chillies, halved, de-seeded and finely chopped	2 oz (50 g) pitted black olives
1 rounded teaspoon cumin seeds	2 oz (50 g) pitted green olives
1 level tablespoon coriander seeds	2 tablespoons olive oil
½ teaspoon saffron stamens	Salt and freshly milled black pepper
2 x 15 g packs (or 1 oz) fresh coriander	
2 small thin-skinned lemons	
2 large yellow peppers	
2 large onions	

You will also need a wide, shallow flameproof casserole with a domed lid, about 9 inches (23 cm) across the base. Failing that, use any flameproof casserole of 5-pint (3-litre) capacity.

Pre-heat the oven to gas mark 4, 350°F (180°C).

There are two ways to deal with chickpeas. The easiest is to pop them into a bowl, cover them with cold water and leave them overnight or a minimum of 8 hours. But if it slips your mind, what you can do is place them in a saucepan, cover them with cold water and bring them up to the boil for 10 minutes. Then turn off the heat and let them soak for 3 hours. Either way, when you want to start making this recipe, the chickpeas need to be simmered for 20 minutes or until tender.

While they're simmering, place a small frying pan over direct medium heat, add the cumin and coriander seeds and toss them around in a hot pan for about 2–3 minutes or until they start to dance and change colour. Then remove the seeds to a pestle and mortar, crush them coarsely and transfer them to a plate. Next crush the saffron stamens to a powder with the pestle and mortar, then squeeze out the juice of 1 of the lemons and add it to the saffron, stirring well.

Then prepare the chicken by seasoning the joints with salt and pepper, and slice the peppers in half, remove the seeds and pith and cut each half into 4 large pieces. The onions should be sliced roughly the same size as the peppers. Now heat 1

Previous page: Moroccan Baked Chicken with Chickpeas and Rice

74

A Sixties Supper for Six People

First course

Prawn Cocktail 2000

Main course

Beef in Designer Beer (recipe x 1½)
Roasted Roots with Herbs
(recipe x 1½)

Dessert

Classic Crêpes Suzette

———————◇———————

Quick and Easy Supper for Four

First course

Pan-Roasted Italian Onions with San
Daniele Ham and Shaved Pecorino

Main course

Pepper-Crusted Monkfish with Red
Pepper Relish
Pesto Mash

Dessert

Tiramisu

———————◇———————

A Buffet for 18 People

Mini Blinis with Smoked Salmon,
Crème Fraîche and Dill
Baked Eggs in Wild Mushroom
Tartlets (recipe x 2)
Feta, Olive and Sun-Dried Tomato
Scones (recipe x 2)
Rillettes of Duck with Confit of
Cranberries (recipe x 2)
Seared Spiced Salmon Steaks with
Black Bean Salsa (recipe x 2)
Black Bean Chilli with Avocado Salsa
(recipe x 2)
Rice
Gorgonzola Cheese and Apple
Strudel with Spiced Pickled Pears
Green Salad

Desserts

A Return to the Black Forest
Lemon Ricotta Cheesecake with a
Confit of Lemons (recipe x 2)
Mascarpone Creams and Caramel
Sauce with Caramelized Hazelnuts

CHAPTER SEVEN

———————◇———————

A SUNDAY LUNCH REVIVAL *and* OTHER MEAT DISHES

———————◇———————

"*T*hey live well, eat and drink well, clothe warm and lodge soft...in a word the people of England eat the fat, drink the sweet, live better and fare better than the working people of any other nation in Europe. They spend more on back and belly than any other country."

So wrote Daniel Defoe in 1726. Even at the end of the century cartoonists were depicting the gulf between Europeans on a meagre diet and fat, jolly Englishmen consuming huge roast joints and vast puddings. The truth is that two centuries later we may not be seen to be eating better than other European countries but one thing that hasn't changed that much is that in Britain we are geologically geared up to rearing very good meat – the hill country of Wales and Scotland, the Lake District in the Peak District and the pastures of the West Country, where cereals won't grow.

What all this is leading up to is that because we have this special gift and because only 4.3 per cent of the population are vegetarians (from which it follows that 95.7 per cent still enjoy meat), we should celebrate it by keeping up the great British tradition of Sunday lunches. They may not be as vast as they were in the 18th century, thank goodness, but they remain an opportunity to enjoy a large joint, which can feed quite a number of people and still leave some for the next day. Cooked skilfully and lovingly, a roast is something that is unmatched anywhere in the world. I hope in the following pages you will join me in the great revival.

Roast Gammon with Blackened Crackling with
Citrus, Rum and Raisin Sauce (see page 130)

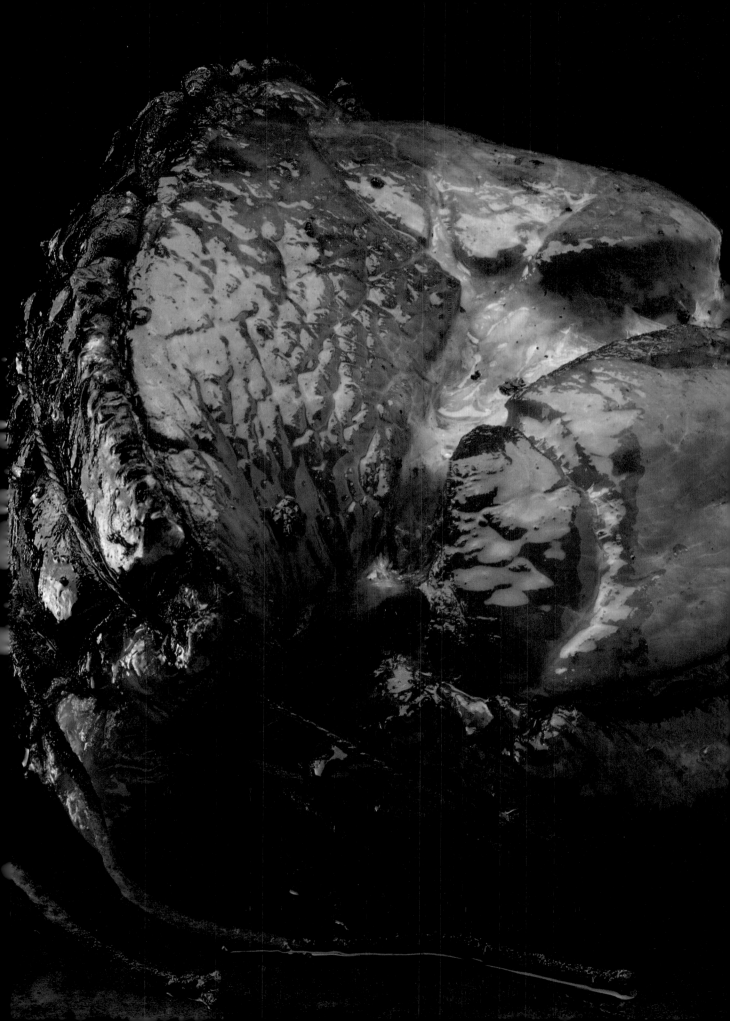

Roast Gammon with Blackened Crackling with Citrus, Rum and Raisin Sauce

SERVES 6

*G*ammon is now much easier to cook than it used to be. Modern curing methods have eliminated the need for pre-soaking, which makes it a perfect joint for roasting. If you leave the skin on, score it and paint it with black treacle, it turns into superb crackling during the cooking. It's then a very easy joint to carve, and serving it with Citrus, Rum and Raisin Sauce is a heavenly combination. If possible, always make this sweet-sharp sauce the day before you need it, so the raisins have plenty of time to absorb all the flavours and become nice and plump. (See photograph on page 129.)

5 lb (2.25 kg) prime gammon joint, smoked or unsmoked	**3 fl oz (75 ml) dark rum**
1 level tablespoon black treacle	**3 oz (75 g) raisins**
Sea salt crystals	**4 oz (110 g) soft dark brown sugar**
	1 slightly rounded teaspoon arrowroot
FOR THE SAUCE:	
1 large juicy orange	
Zest and juice of 1 lime	You will also need a solid shallow roasting tin.

As soon as you buy the gammon remove all the wrapping and dry the skin really well with kitchen paper. After that, using a very sharp pointed knife, score the skin in a criss-cross pattern making little ½-inch (1-cm) diamonds. This is quite easy to do if you insert the tip of the knife only, then holding the skin taut with one hand drag the tip of the knife down in long movements. When you've done this place the gammon on a plate and store uncovered on the bottom of the fridge, if possible for 2 or 3 days before you need it. This means the skin will go on drying, which makes better crackling.

You can make the sauce well in advance too. All you do is remove the outer zest from the orange using a potato peeler so that you don't get any of the pith. Then pile the little strips on top of one another, and using a very sharp knife cut them into really thin needle-sized strips. If you've got the orange peel piled up and your knife is sharp this is a lot easier than it sounds. Next remove the zest from the lime, this time using a fine grater, and squeeze the juice from the lime and orange.

Place all the sauce ingredients except the arrowroot into a saucepan. Whisk the arrowroot into the mixture and place the pan onto a gentle heat, whisking all the time until it starts to simmer. As soon as this happens the sauce will change from opaque to clear, so then remove it from the heat and as soon as it is cool enough pour it into a serving dish, cover with clingfilm and chill until needed.

To cook the gammon pre-heat the oven to gas mark 9, 475°F (240°C). If the treacle is very cold, warm it slightly, then using a pastry brush or a wodge of kitchen paper lightly coat all the little diamonds of skin. After that sprinkle the skin with salt crystals, pressing them well in. Now place the gammon in a roasting tin skin-side upright (if it won't stand up straight use a couple of wedges of foil to keep it in position). Now place the roasting tin in the oven and after 25 minutes turn the heat down to gas mark 4, 350°F (180°C). Then continue to let the gammon cook for 1¾–2 hours – it should feel tender all the way through when tested with a skewer. After it comes out of the oven give it at least 30 minutes' resting time, covered with foil, in a warm place. Remove the sauce from the fridge and serve the gammon carved in slices, giving each person some crackling, and sauce spooned over.

◇

Pork Stroganoff with Three Mustards

SERVES 2

This is what I'd call a five-star supper dish for two people, with the added bonus that it only takes about 20 minutes to prepare from start to finish. Serve it with plain boiled basmati rice and a salad of tossed green leaves.

12 oz (350 g) pork tenderloin	½ oz (10 g) butter
4 oz (110 g) small open cap mushrooms	1 dessertspoon groundnut oil
1 level teaspoon mustard powder	1 small onion, halved and thinly sliced
1 heaped teaspoon wholegrain mustard	3 fl oz (75 ml) dry white wine
1 heaped teaspoon Dijon mustard	Salt and freshly milled
1 x 200 ml tub crème fraîche	black pepper

First of all prepare the pork by trimming it and cutting it into little strips 3 inches (7.5 cm) long and ¼ inch (5 mm) wide. Now prepare the mushrooms by slicing them through the stalk into thin slices. Then in a small bowl mix together the 3 mustards with the crème fraîche.

When you're ready to cook the pork, take a 9-inch (23-cm) solid frying pan then heat the butter and oil together over a medium heat, add the onion slices and fry them gently for about 2–3 minutes until they are soft. Then, using a draining spoon, remove the onion to a plate, turn the heat up to its highest setting and when it's smoking hot add the strips of pork and fry them quickly, keeping them on the move all the time so they cook evenly without burning. After that add the mushrooms and toss these around to cook very briefly until their juices start to run. Next return the onion slices to the pan and stir them in. Season well with salt and pepper then add the wine and let it bubble and reduce slightly before adding the crème fraîche. Now stir the whole lot together and let the sauce bubble and reduce to half its original volume. Then serve the stroganoff immediately spooned over plain basmati rice.

◇

Autumn Lamb Braised in Beaujolais

SERVES 6–8

This is certainly one of the best ways to cook lamb in the autumn or winter months — slowly braising it under a tent of foil keeps it beautifully moist and really seems to develop its full flavour. Adding the root vegetables to cook in the braising juices is also very convenient and makes this an easy main course for entertaining. (See photograph on pages 136–7.)

1 leg of lamb, weighing 5–5½ lb (2.25–2.5 kg)	**A few fresh thyme sprigs**
4 tablespoons olive oil	**1 rosemary sprig**
1 teaspoon each chopped fresh thyme and rosemary leaves	**1 bay leaf**
	1 heaped teaspoon redcurrant jelly
1 bottle Beaujolais	**Rock salt and freshly milled black pepper**
8 small carrots, weighing about 8 oz (225 g)	
2 turnips, weighing about 8 oz (225 g)	
8 small red-skinned potatoes, weighing about 1½ lb (700 g)	TO GARNISH:
4 small parsnips, weighing about 1 lb (450 g)	**2 tablespoons chopped fresh parsley or 1 tablespoon fresh thyme leaves**
8 shallots or small onions, weighing about 8 oz (225 g)	

3 large garlic cloves, unpeeled

You will also need a roasting tin approximately 14½ x 10½ inches (36 x 26 cm) and 2 inches (5cm) deep, and a large shallow roasting tray. Pre-heat the oven to gas mark 8, 450°F (220°C).

First pour 3 tablespoons of the olive oil into the shallow roasting tray and put it into the oven as it pre-heats. Then prepare all the vegetables as follows: scrub the carrots, turnips and potatoes; top and tail the carrots and turnips, leaving the carrots whole but chopping the turnips (with skins left on) into quarters, and cut the potatoes lengthways into 4 pieces (unpeeled). Now peel the parsnips and cut them into halves; and finally peel the shallots but leave them whole.

Now dry the vegetables thoroughly in a clean tea-cloth. When the oven is up to temperature, carefully remove the roasting tray, using an oven glove to protect your hands. Place this over a direct medium heat on the hob and spoon the prepared vegetables and the unpeeled garlic into the fat. Turn them over to make sure they are well coated and return the tray to the top shelf of the oven for 25–30 minutes, turning them over at half time so that they roast evenly.

While they are in the oven, prepare the lamb by placing it in the roasting tin and rubbing the joint all over with the remaining tablespoon of olive oil, some crushed rock salt and coarsely ground black pepper.

When the vegetables are nicely tinged brown at the edges, remove them from the oven and set aside. Place the roasting tin with the lamb in the oven, on the highest shelf that will take it, and let it start to roast for 30 minutes or until it has turned a good golden colour.

Take the lamb out of the oven, then reduce the temperature to gas mark 3, 325°F (170°C) and spoon off any fat to use later. Place the roasting tin over a medium heat on top of the stove, pour in the Beaujolais and baste the meat with it. Then sprinkle with the chopped thyme and rosemary.

As soon as the wine begins to bubble, turn off the heat and cover the whole tin with a tent of foil (without it touching the meat). Fold the foil tight under the rim of the tin and replace it in the oven – on the centre shelf this time – and let it continue cooking for 1½ hours.

When the time is up, remove the roasting tin from the oven and once again transfer it to direct heat. Carefully remove the foil and baste the meat well with the wine. Spoon the browned vegetables all around in the wine, season them with salt and freshly milled black pepper and pop in the sprigs of thyme and rosemary and the bay leaf. When it has come back to simmering point, replace the foil and cook for a further 1½ hours.

After that, remove the meat and vegetables to warmed serving dishes, discarding the sprigs of herbs, then cover to keep warm. Place the roasting tin over direct heat once more and let the sauce reduce. Squeeze the garlic pulp out of the skins into the sauce and whisk this in along with a heaped teaspoon of redcurrant jelly.

Taste and season the sauce with salt and freshly milled black pepper, then pour it into a warm serving jug. Sprinkle the lamb and vegetables with the parsley or thyme and serve.

Classic Roast Pork with Crackling and Roasted Stuffed Apples with Thyme and Parsley

SERVES 8

This recipe is for loin of pork which provides maximum crackling, but the butcher must chine it for you – that is, loosen the bone yet leave it attached, so that it can eventually be cut away to make carving easier.

How to get crisp, crunchy crackling is not a problem if you follow a few simple guidelines. Buy the pork a couple of days before you need to cook it, remove any plastic wrap, put it on a plate immediately and dry it as thoroughly as possible with absorbent kitchen paper. After that, leave it uncovered in the lowest part of the refrigerator, so that the skin can become as dry as possible before you start the cooking.

5 lb (2.25 kg) loin of pork, chined
1 small onion, peeled
1 tablespoon plain flour
10 fl oz (275 ml) dry cider
10 fl oz (275 ml) vegetable stock (or potato water)

Maldon salt and freshly milled black pepper

You will also need a solid roasting tin, approximately 12 x 10 inches (30 x 25.5 cm).

Pre-heat the oven to gas mark 9, 475°F (240°C).

While the oven is pre-heating, score the skin of the pork. It will be scored already, but it's always best to add a few more lines. To do this you can use the point of a very sharp paring knife, or Stanley knife, or you can now even buy a special scalpel from a good quality kitchen shop! What you need to do is score the skin all over into thin strips, bringing the blade of the knife about halfway through the fat beneath the skin.

Now place the pork in a tin, skin-side up, halve the onion and wedge the two pieces in slightly underneath the meat. Now take about 1 tablespoon of crushed salt crystals and sprinkle it evenly over the skin, pressing it in as much as you can. Place the pork on a high shelf in the oven and roast it for 25 minutes. Turn the heat down to gas mark 5, 375°F (190°C) and calculate the total cooking time allowing 35 minutes to the pound. In this case it would be a further $2\frac{1}{2}$ hours.

There's no need to baste pork as there is enough fat to keep the meat moist. The way to tell if the meat is cooked is to insert a skewer in the thickest part and the juices that run out should be absolutely clear without any trace of pinkness. When the pork is cooked remove it from the oven and give it at least 30 minutes' resting time before carving. While that is happening, tilt the tin and spoon all the fat off, leaving only the juices. The onion will probably be black and charred, which gives the gravy a lovely rich colour. Leave the onion in, then place the roasting tin over direct heat, turned to low, sprinkle in the flour and quickly work it into the juices with a wooden spoon.

134

Now turn the heat up to medium and gradually add the cider and the stock, this time using a balloon whisk until it comes up to simmering point and you have a smooth rich gravy. Taste and season with salt and pepper, then discard the onion and pour the gravy into a warmed serving jug.

Serve the pork carved in slices, giving everyone some crackling and one roasted apple.

Roasted Stuffed Apples with Thyme and Parsley

1 lb (450 g) good quality pork sausage meat	**8 small Cox's apples**
	A little melted butter
1 rounded dessertspoon chopped fresh parsley	**8 small thyme sprigs**
	Salt and freshly milled black pepper
2 teaspoons chopped fresh thyme	

About half an hour before the end of the cooking time of the pork, prepare the apples. First of all in a small basin mix the sausage meat, chopped parsley and thyme and add a good seasoning of salt and pepper. Using a potato peeler or an apple corer, remove the core from the apples then cut out a little more apple with a sharp knife to make the cavity slightly larger. Now divide the sausage meat mixture into 8. Then roll each portion into a sausage shape and fit that into the cavity of each apple. There will be some at the top which won't go in. So just pat that into a round neat shape. Now make a small incision around the central circumference of the apple. Brush each one with melted butter and insert a little sprig of thyme on top. Place the apples on a baking tray. Then when the pork comes out of the oven, pop the apples in to roast for about 25 minutes.

NOTE: If you're using the oven for roast potatoes and turning the heat up when the pork is cooked, the apples will cook quite comfortably on a lower shelf at the higher temperature.

Next page: Autumn Lamb Braised in Beaujolais (see page 132)

Steak and Kidney Pudding

SERVES 6

I've subtitled this recipe 'Kate and Sidney make a comeback', after the Cockney slang version of this world-famous recipe. It's certainly time for a revival because it has been shamefully neglected and because it really is the ultimate in comfort food. Home-made is a far superior thing to any factory version and, believe it or not, it's dead simple to make. Once it's on the heat you can forget all about it till suppertime – except for the amazingly appetizing wafts coming out of the kitchen.

FOR THE SUET CRUST PASTRY:	2 level tablespoons well-seasoned flour
12 oz (350 g) self-raising flour	**1 medium onion, sliced**
6 oz (175 g) shredded beef suet	**Cold water**
Salt and freshly milled black pepper	**1 teaspoon Worcestershire sauce**
Cold water to mix	**Salt and freshly milled black pepper**

FOR THE FILLING:

1¼ lb (560 g) chuck steak

8 oz (225 g) ox kidney after trimming, so buy 10 oz (275 g)

You will also need a 2½-pint (1.5-litre) capacity pudding basin and a steamer.

To make the pastry first sift the flour and salt into a large mixing bowl. Add some freshly milled black pepper, then add the suet and mix it into the flour using the blade of a knife. When it's evenly blended, add a few drops of cold water and start to mix with the knife, using curving movements and turning the mixture around. The aim is to bring it together as a dough, so keep adding drops of water until it begins to get really claggy and sticky. Now abandon the knife, go in with your hands and bring it all together until you have a nice smooth elastic dough which leaves the bowl clean. It's worth noting that suet pastry always needs more water than other types, so if it is still a bit dry just go on adding a few drops at a time. After that, take a quarter of the dough for the lid, then roll the rest out fairly thickly. What you need is a round approximately 13 inches (32.5 cm) in diameter. Now line the bowl with the pastry, pressing it well all around. Next chop the steak and kidney into fairly small cubes, toss them in the seasoned flour, then add them to the pastry-lined basin with the slices of onion. Add enough cold water to reach almost the top of the meat and sprinkle in a few drops of Worcestershire sauce and another seasoning of salt and pepper.

Roll out the pastry lid, dampen its edges and put it in position on the pudding. Seal well and cover with a double sheet of foil, pleated in the centre to allow room for expansion while cooking. Now secure it with string, making a little handle so that you can lift it out of the hot steamer. Then place it in a steamer over boiling water. Steam for 5 hours, topping up the boiling water halfway through. You can either serve the pudding by spooning portions straight out of the bowl, or slide a palette knife round the edge and turn the whole thing out on to a serving plate (which is more fun!).

Steak and Kidney Gravy

*A*lthough steak and kidney pudding has a lovely juicy filling, it's always nice to have a little extra gravy – and since there's always some meat trimmings over, this is a good way to use them.

Meat trimmings from the steak and kidney	**1 teaspoon beef dripping**
1 onion, halved	**1 heaped dessertspoon flour**
1 pint (570 ml) water	**A few drops Worcestershire sauce**
	Salt and freshly milled black pepper

Simply place the meat trimmings in a saucepan with half the onion, cover with 1 pint of water, add some seasoning and simmer for approximately 1 hour. Then strain the stock and in the same pan fry the remaining onion, chopped small, in the beef dripping until soft and blackened at the edges. Then stir in the flour, gradually add the stock little by little to make a smooth gravy, adding a spot of gravy browning if it's needed. Taste to check the seasoning and add a few drops of Worcestershire sauce.

◇

Next page: Sunday lunch with Roast Ribs of Traditional Beef and all the trimmings (see page 142)

Roast Ribs of Traditional Beef with Yorkshire Pudding and Horseradish, Crème Fraîche and Mustard Sauce

SERVES 6–8

I still think the roast beef of old England served with meaty gravy, crisp Yorkshire Pudding and crunchy roast potatoes is not only one of the world's greatest meals, it is something the British do better than anyone else. The whole thing can be a bit daunting, so if you've never done it before, for the Sunday lunch novice there is a very easy-to-follow guide on page 146. (See photograph on pages 140–1.)

3-rib joint, wing end or sirloin of beef on the bone (approximately 6 lb/2.7 kg)
1 dessertspoon mustard powder
1 dessertspoon plain flour
1 small onion, peeled and cut in half
Salt and freshly milled black pepper

FOR THE GRAVY:

1 oz (25 g) plain flour (about 1 heaped tablespoon)
Approximately 1¾ pints (1 litre) vegetable stock or water from the potatoes

Salt and freshly milled black pepper

FOR THE HORSERADISH, CREME FRAICHE AND MUSTARD SAUCE:

2 rounded tablespoons hot horseradish
1 heaped tablespoon crème fraîche
2 teaspoons wholegrain mustard
Salt and freshly milled black pepper

You will also need a solid roasting tin.

Pre-heat the oven to gas mark 9, 475°F (240°C).

If you dust the fat surface of the beef with mustard and the flour – just rub them in gently – then season with salt and pepper, it becomes extra crusty during cooking. So do that first, then place the joint in a roasting tin and tuck the two pieces of onion in close to the meat. The onion will caramelize as the beef cooks and give a lovely flavour to the gravy.

Now place the meat just above the centre in the oven and give it 20 minutes' cooking at the initial temperature; after that turn the heat down to gas mark 5, 375°F (190°C) and cook it for 15 minutes to the pound (450 g) for rare, adding another 15 minutes for medium rare and another 30 minutes for well done. While the beef is cooking lift it out of the oven from time to time, tilt the tin and baste the meat really well with its own juices – this ensures that the flavour that is concentrated in the fat keeps permeating the meat, and at the same time the fat keeps everything moist and succulent. While you're basting close the oven door in order not to lose heat. When the beef is cooked, remove it from the oven, transfer it to a board and allow it to stand in a warm place for up to an hour, loosely covered with foil, before carving – to let all the precious juices that have bubbled up to the surface seep back into the flesh. Also, as the meat relaxes it will be easier to carve. Meanwhile, make the gravy.

After removing the meat from the roasting tin, tilt to see how much fat remains – you need about 2 tablespoons for this amount of gravy (the rest should be spooned into a dish and used for the Yorkshire Pudding, see below). Place the roasting tin over a medium heat and sprinkle the flour into the fatty juices. Then, using a wire whisk, blend in the flour using a circular movement.

When you have a smooth paste, slowly add the hot vegetable water, whisking all the time, and scraping the base of the tin to incorporate all the residue from the roast. When the gravy is bubbling, taste to see if it needs a little more seasoning, then let it carry on bubbling and reduce slightly to concentrate the flavour.

You can now pour the gravy into the jug and keep it warm if lunch is imminent or, if not, leave it in the roasting tin and re-heat gently just before serving.

To make the horseradish sauce, simply mix all the ingredients together in the bowl you're going to serve it in.

Traditional Yorkshire Pudding

SERVES 6–8

6 oz (175 g) plain flour	**2 tablespoons beef dripping**
2 x size 1 eggs	**Salt and freshly milled black pepper**
6 fl oz (175 ml) milk (whole or semi-skimmed)	You will also need a solid roasting tin measuring 11 x 9 inches (28 x 23 cm).
4 fl oz (110 ml) water	Pre-heat the oven to gas mark 7, 425°F (220°C).

Begin by placing a sieve over a large mixing bowl, then sift the flour in, holding the sieve up high to give the flour a good airing as it goes down into the bowl. Now, with the back of a tablespoon, make a well in the centre of the flour and break the eggs into it. Add the salt and pepper.

Now measure the milk and water into a measuring jug. Then begin to whisk the eggs with an electric whisk and as you beat them the flour around the edges will be slowly incorporated. When the mixture becomes stiff simply add the milk and water mixture gradually, keeping the whisk going. Stop and scrape the sides of the bowl with a spatula so that any lumps can be pushed down into the batter, then whisk again till all is smooth. Now the batter is ready for use and although it's been rumoured that batter left to stand is better, I have found no foundation for this – so just make it whenever is convenient.

To cook the Yorkshire Pudding, remove the meat from the oven (or if it's not ready place it on a lower shelf) and turn the oven up to the above temperature. Spoon 2 tablespoons of beef fat into the roasting tin and allow it to pre-heat in the oven. When the oven is up to temperature remove the tin, using an oven glove, and place it over direct heat (turned to medium). Then, when the fat begins to shimmer and smoke a little, pour in the batter. Tip it evenly all round and then place the tin on a high shelf in the oven and cook the Yorkshire Pudding for 40 minutes or until golden brown and crisp. Serve it cut into squares *presto pronto*.
NOTE: I remember when I was about five years old, my Yorkshire grandmother giving me slices of hot Yorkshire Pudding with treacle spooned over as a dessert – try it some time, it's really good.

An Authentic Ragù Bolognese

MAKES 8 x 8 oz (225 g) PORTIONS, EACH SERVING 2 PEOPLE

*I*n Britain it's really sad that so often stewed mince with the addition of herbs and tomato purée gets presented as bolognese sauce – even, dare I say it, in lesser Italian restaurants. Yet properly made, an authentic ragù bolognese bears absolutely no resemblance to this travesty. The real thing is a very slowly cooked, thick, concentrated, dark mahogany-coloured sauce, and because of this, very little is needed to coat pasta and give it that unmistakably authentic and evocative flavour of Italy. For me making ragù is something of a ritual; it's not at all difficult, but if you give a little of your time to make it in bulk, then freeze down for the future, you'll always have the basis of a delightful meal ready-prepared when there's no time to cook.

1 lb (450 g) lean minced beef	**2 x 7 oz (200 g) tubes double concentrate tomato purée**
1 lb (450 g) minced pork	
6 tablespoons extra virgin olive oil	**1 x 37.5 cl half bottle red wine or 14 fl oz (400 ml)**
1 x 8 oz (225 g) tub chicken livers	**2 x 15 g packs (or 1 oz) fresh basil**
2 medium onions, finely chopped	**½ whole nutmeg, grated**
4 fat cloves garlic, chopped	**Salt and freshly milled black pepper**
2 x 70 g packs (or 5 oz) pancetta or streaky bacon, finely chopped	
2 x 14 oz (400 g) tins Italian chopped tomatoes	

You will also need a large flameproof casserole of 6-pint (3.5-litre) capacity.

Pre-heat the oven to gas mark 1, 275°F (140°C).

First take a large frying pan, the largest you have, heat 3 tablespoons of the oil and gently fry the onion and garlic over a medium heat for about 10 minutes, moving it around from time to time. While the onion is softening, chop the pancetta: the best way to do this after opening the pack is to roll the contents into a sausage shape, then using a sharp knife slice it lengthways into 4, then slice the lengths across as finely as possible. After 10 minutes, add this to the pan to join the onions and garlic and continue cooking them all for another 5 minutes. Now transfer this mixture to the casserole. Add another tablespoon of oil to the pan, turn the heat up to its highest then add the minced beef and brown it, breaking it up and moving it round in the pan. When the beef is browned tip it into the casserole. Heat another tablespoon of oil and do exactly the same with the minced pork. While the pork is browning, trim the chicken livers, rinse them under cold running water, dry them thoroughly with kitchen paper and chop them minutely small. When the pork is browned, transfer that to the casserole, then heat the remaining tablespoon of oil and brown the pieces of chicken liver. Add these to the casserole.

Now you've finished with the frying pan, so get rid of that and place the casserole over the direct heat, give everything a good stir together, then add the contents of the tins of tomatoes, the tomato purée, red wine and a really good seasoning of salt, pepper and nutmeg.

Allow this to come up to simmering point. Then strip the leaves from half the basil, chop them very finely and add them to the pot. As soon as everything is simmering, place the casserole on the centre shelf of the oven and leave it to cook slowly, without a lid, for 4 hours. It's a good idea to have a look after 3 hours to make sure all is well, but what you should end up with is a thick, concentrated sauce with only a trace of liquid left in it, then remove it from the oven, taste to check the seasoning, strip the leaves off the remaining basil, chop them small and stir them in.

Then when the sauce is absolutely cold, divide it, using scales, by spooning 8 oz (225 g) into polythene freezer bags. Seal them leaving a little bit of air at the top to allow room for expansion. Each 8 oz (225 g) pack, thoroughly defrosted and re-heated, will provide enough ragù for 8 oz (225 g) of pasta, which will serve 2 people.

NOTE: If you don't have a 6-pint (3.5-litre) capacity ovenproof casserole you can use a large baking dish pre-heated in the oven, but make sure everything comes up to simmering point in a large saucepan first.

Pancake Cannelloni with Ragù

SERVES 4

I*n Umbria in Italy they make pancakes for their cannelloni, using these instead of pasta to be stuffed with ragù bolognese then topped with béchamel and Mozzarella before baking. It's a truly inspired version.*

1 quantity pancakes (see page 179).
2 x 8 oz (225 g) ragù bolognese (see opposite)

FOR THE BECHAMEL SAUCE:

3 oz (75 g) grated Mozzarella cheese
1½ oz (40 g) butter
1 oz (25 g) plain flour
15 fl oz (425 ml) cold milk
Freshly grated nutmeg
Salt and freshly milled black pepper

FOR THE TOPPING:

1½ oz (40 g) Parmesan (Parmigiano Reggiano), freshly grated
1 dessertspoon olive oil

You will also need an ovenproof baking dish 10 x 8 inches (25.5 x 20 cm), 2 inches (5 cm) deep or the equivalent, well buttered.

Pre-heat the oven to gas mark 6, 400°F (200°C).

Both the pancakes and the ragù can be made well ahead and chilled or frozen. Make the béchamel sauce by the all-in-one method, that is by adding everything (except the Mozzarella) to a saucepan and whisking over a medium heat till smooth and thickened. Then continue to cook gently for 5 minutes, whisking now and then to prevent it sticking. Now lay the pancakes out and place an equal quantity (about a heaped tablespoon) of cold ragù on each one and roll up, folding in the edges. Next lay the pancakes in the ovenproof dish side by side with the ends tucked up underneath, then sprinkle over the grated Mozzarella. Pour the sauce over the top to give an even covering. Finally sprinkle over the grated Parmesan and oil and place the dish on a high shelf in the oven for 30 minutes or until the surface is golden and the sauce bubbling.

NOTE: If you want to, you could assemble all this well in advance, but make sure everything is completely cold before you cover and chill it until needed. These can also be cooked, 3 pancakes per person, in individual ovenproof dishes – in which case cut the cooking time to 20 minutes.

Timings for One O'Clock Lunches for Eight

Sunday traditional lunches for eight guests with no last-minute panics. Impossible? Not if you follow these straightforward timings.

ROAST RIBS OF BEEF

SEE PAGES 142–3

6 lb (2.7 kg) Rib Joint (or Sirloin)
Timings below are for beef cooked to medium.
9.30 am Place the beef in the oven, lower the oven temperature after 30 minutes, baste three times during roasting.
12 noon Remove the meat from the oven, cover loosely with foil and keep warm. Increase the oven temperature for the roast potatoes.
Meat cooking time: 2½ hours. Adjust cooking times
Rare: 2 hours
Medium rare: 2¼ hours
Well done: 2¾ hours

PERFECT ROAST POTATOES

SEE PAGE 149

12.10 pm Place the prepared potatoes in the oven on a high shelf for 40–50 minutes.

COMPOTE OF GLAZED SHALLOTS

SEE PAGE 160

11.45 am Place the prepared shallots onto a gentle heat for 1 hour 15 minutes.

TRADITIONAL YORKSHIRE PUDDING

SEE PAGE 143

12.20 pm Place the Yorkshire Pudding on the middle shelf for 40 minutes.

GRAVY

Make the gravy at 12.45 pm.

TRADITIONAL ROAST CHICKEN

SEE PAGES 76–7

2 x 4lb (1.8 kg) chickens
10.45 am Place them in the oven, baste every 30 minutes.
12 noon Raise the oven temperature to gas 7, 425°F (220°C).
12.30 pm Remove the chickens from the oven. Keep them warm.
Cooking time: 1¾ hours.

PERFECT ROAST POTATOES

SEE PAGE 149

12.10 pm Place the prepared potatoes on shelf above the chickens for 40–50 minutes.

SAUTEED CARAMELIZED FENNEL

SEE PAGE 158

(1½ times recipe)
12 noon Steam the fennel.
12.10 pm Place the fennel over direct heat for 40–50 minutes.

STEAMED BROCCOLI

Cooking time: 8 minutes.

GIBLET GRAVY

Make at 12.45 pm.

ROAST GAMMON WITH BLACKENED CRACKLING SEE PAGES 130–1 5 lb (2.25 kg) Gammon Joint 9.45 am Place the gammon in the oven, reducing the oven temperature after 25 minutes. 12 noon Raise the oven to gas 7, 425°F (220°C). 12.10 pm Remove the gammon from the oven, keeping it warm and loosely covered with foil. Cooking time: 2½ hours.	**PERFECT ROAST POTATOES** SEE PAGE 149 12.10 Place the prepared potatoes in the oven on a high shelf for 40–50 minutes.	**SPICED SAUTEED RED CABBAGE** SEE PAGE 155 You will need 1½ times the recipe. Pre-cook the cabbage at a convenient time during the morning. 12.50 pm Re-heat gently for 8–10 minutes.	**CITRUS, RUM AND RAISIN SAUCE** SEE PAGE 130 Make at a convenient time in the morning. Chill until needed.
CLASSIC ROAST PORK WITH CRACKLING SEE PAGES 134–5 5 lb (2.25 kg) Loin of Pork (chined). 9.45 am Place the pork in the oven. 12 noon Raise the oven temperature to gas 7, 425°F (220°C). 12.15 pm Remove the pork from the oven and keep warm. Cooking time: 2½ hours.	**PERFECT ROAST POTATOES** SEE PAGE 149 12.10 Place the prepared potatoes in the oven on a high shelf for 40–50 minutes. 12.40 pm Place the stuffed apples on a low shelf for 20 minutes. (They will cook at this slightly higher temperature quite comfortably if you are using the oven for roasted potatoes.)	**COMPOTE OF GLAZED SHALLOTS** SEE PAGE 160 11.45 am Place the prepared shallots onto a gentle heat for 1 hour 15 minutes.	**BRUSSELS SPROUTS** Choose small, tight Brussels, trimmed. Make a cross-like incision at the stalk end. Steam or boil for 5–8 minutes, drain (reserve liquid for gravy). Toss in a little hot, melted butter. 12.50 pm Make the gravy.
AUTUMN LAMB BRAISED IN BEAUJOLAIS SEE PAGES 132–3 5–5½ lb (2.3–2.5 kg) Leg of Lamb 8.45 am Vegetables in oven to brown, 30 minutes, turn them over halfway. 9.15 am Lamb in oven, lower the temperature after 30 minutes.	11.15 am Add the browned vegetables to lamb. 12.45 pm Remove lamb and vegetables, keep warm, finish the sauce. Cooking time: 3½ hours.		

CHAPTER EIGHT

WINTER VEGETABLE SELECTION

───────◇───────

W hile I welcome the new varieties of salad ingredients from around the world that can enliven our winter salads, I have to admit I'm not such a great fan of imported vegetables. I enjoy summer vegetables in the summer and early autumn and after that I'm quite happy to forget about them and look forward to whatever winter has to offer: onions, young leeks, shallots, tiny button Brussels sprouts, crisp squeaky cabbages, fragrant celery. And I love all the roots – celeriac, carrots, swedes, turnips, Jerusalem artichokes and, best of all, parsnips.

First and foremost I think we need to enjoy all these wonderful vegetables simply as they are, especially when they are accompanying dishes with lots of strong, rich flavours. Let us not underestimate simple boiled cabbage, or leeks cooked just in their own juices with a knob of butter, or a dish of carrots steamed then chopped small with a seasoning of black pepper – one of my particular favourites. However, the winter vegetable season does seem to go on for a long time and the limited varieties may get a bit repetitive, so it's also a good time to experiment with new ideas for cooking them, and I hope that's what you'll find on the following pages.

Because of the enormous popularity of oven-roasting vegetables in the *Summer Collection* and seeing how liberating it is when you have to attend to other parts of the meal, I have included here new ideas for oven-roasting winter vegetables along the same lines. This chapter also celebrates the recent revival of mashed potato, which offers all kinds of variations and, when made carefully, is one of the real joys of winter.

───────────────

Perfect Roast Potatoes

SERVES 8

T*he amounts here are not vital because it depends on who's greedy and who is on a diet and so on, but I find that 8 oz (225 g) per person is enough – yielding three each and a few extras for inevitable second helpings! I like Désirée best of all, but my second choice would be Romano.*

4 lb (1.8 kg) Désirée potatoes
4 oz (110 g) dripping or lard
Salt

You will also need a shallow solid roasting tray 16 x 12 inches (40 x 30cm).
Pre-heat the oven to gas mark 7, 425°F (220°C).

First place the roasting tray with the fat in it on the highest shelf of the oven while it pre-heats. Thinly peel the potatoes using a potato peeler, then cut them into fairly even-sized pieces, leaving the small ones whole. Then place them in a saucepan, pour over boiling water from a kettle, just to cover, then add salt and simmer for about 10 minutes. After that lift one out with a skewer and see if the outer edge is fluffy. You can test this by running the point of the skewer along the surface – if it stays smooth, give it a few more minutes.

Then drain off the water, reserving some for the gravy. Place the lid back on the saucepan, and, holding the lid on firmly with your hand protected by a cloth or oven-glove, shake the saucepan vigorously up and down. This shaking roughens up the cooked edges of the potato and makes them floury and fluffy – this is the secret of the crunchy edges.

Now, still using the oven-glove to protect your hands, remove the hot roasting tray containing its sizzling fat and transfer to the direct heat (medium) on the hob. Then use a long-handled spoon and quickly lower the potatoes into the hot fat. When they are all in, tilt the tray and baste each one so it's completely coated with fat. Now place them back on the highest shelf of the oven and leave them unattended for 40–50 minutes or until they are golden brown. There's no need to turn them over at half-time – they will brown evenly by themselves. Sprinkle them with a little crushed salt before serving straight away; they lose their crunch if you keep them waiting. If they're ready before you are, turn the oven off and leave them inside.

◇

Fluffy Mashed Potatoes

SERVES 4

*I*s there anyone anywhere who does not love a fluffy cloud of creamy mashed potatoes – especially if they are carefully and properly made? Grand chefs sometimes make a great deal of complicated techniques but if you have an electric hand whisk it really couldn't be easier.

2 lb (900g) potatoes (Désirée or King Edward)	**4 tablespoons full-cream milk**
	2 tablespoons crème fraîche
2 oz (50g) butter	**Salt and freshly milled black pepper**

Use a potato peeler to pare off the skins as thinly as possible and then cut the potatoes into even-sized chunks, not too small. If they are large, quarter them and if they are small, halve them. Put the potato chunks in a large saucepan then pour boiling water over them, add 1 dessertspoon of salt, put on a lid and simmer gently until they are absolutely tender – they should take approximately 25 minutes. The way to tell whether they are ready is to pierce them with a skewer in the thickest part; the potato should not be hard in the centre. And you need to be careful here, because if they are slightly underdone you do get lumps!

When the potatoes are cooked, drain them. Cover them with a clean tea-cloth to absorb some of the steam for about 5 minutes then add the butter, milk and crème fraîche. When you first go in with the whisk use a slow speed to break the potatoes up, then increase it to high and whip them up to a smooth, creamy, fluffy mass. Taste and season with pepper and more salt if they need it.

Mashed Potato with Garlic-Infused Olive Oil

SERVES 4

*I*f you enjoy the taste of really fine olive oil, you'll know how dipping bread directly into it brings out the full flavour. The same happens with potatoes – a sublime combination.

2 lb (900 g) potatoes (Désirée or King Edward)	**8 tablespoons best quality extra virgin olive oil**
3 fat garlic cloves, halved lengthways	**Salt and freshly milled black pepper**

First place the garlic and olive oil in a small saucepan over the gentlest heat possible – a heat diffuser is good for this – and leave for 1 hour for the garlic to infuse and become really soft. Prepare and cook the potatoes as above, then, using an electric hand whisk on a low speed, begin to break them up using half the garlic and oil. As soon as all that is incorporated, add the rest of the garlic and oil and whisk until smooth, seasoning well with salt and freshly milled black pepper.

Pesto Mash

SERVES 2–3

Not East meets West this time, but Italy meets Britain. Take a classic Italian sauce, add it to some mash (without the bangers) and what you have is a wonderful accompaniment to fish. It's best made with fresh pesto sauce, available from the chill counter in supermarkets (rather than the bottled version, which is not as good).

1 lb (450 g) potatoes (Désirée or King Edward)	**1 x 120 g tub fresh pesto sauce**
	Salt and freshly milled black pepper

Prepare and cook the potatoes as in the basic recipe opposite, then add the pesto and a seasoning of salt and pepper. Using an electric hand whisk, start whisking at a slow speed to break up the potatoes, then increase the speed to fast and whip them up to a smooth purée. Now return the saucepan to a low heat and use a wooden spoon to turn the potatoes round until they become hot – about 1 minute – season, and now they're ready to serve.

Colcannon Potatoes

SERVES 4

Another supremely good version of mashed potato, this is based on the Irish recipe for Colcannon potatoes, which was originally served in a fluffy pile with a sort of well in the centre that was filled with melted butter. The idea was to dip each forkful into the melted butter before eating it! Perhaps our health consciousness and waist-watching would prohibit this today, but even without the melted butter it's extremely good.

1½ lb (700 g) potatoes, Désirée or King Edward, peeled and cut into chunks	**3 fl oz (75 ml) single cream or 5 tablespoons top of the milk**
8 oz (225 g) firm green cabbage, very finely sliced/shredded	**3 oz (75 g) butter**
12 spring onions, trimmed and very finely sliced including the green parts	**Nutmeg, salt and freshly milled black pepper**

Prepare and cook the potatoes as in the basic recipe opposite. Meanwhile melt 1 oz (25 g) butter in a large frying pan and sauté the cabbage for about 3 minutes, keeping it on the move until it's tender and slightly golden at the edges. Then add the chopped spring onions and continue to cook for another minute.

Next drain the potatoes, return them to the pan, cover with a clean tea-cloth and leave them aside for 2 minutes to allow the cloth to absorb the excess steam. Now, using an electric hand whisk, add the nutmeg, cream and remaining butter. Whisk the potatoes to a light fluffy mass before tasting and seasoning. Then finally stir in the contents of the frying pan and serve with or without extra melted butter.

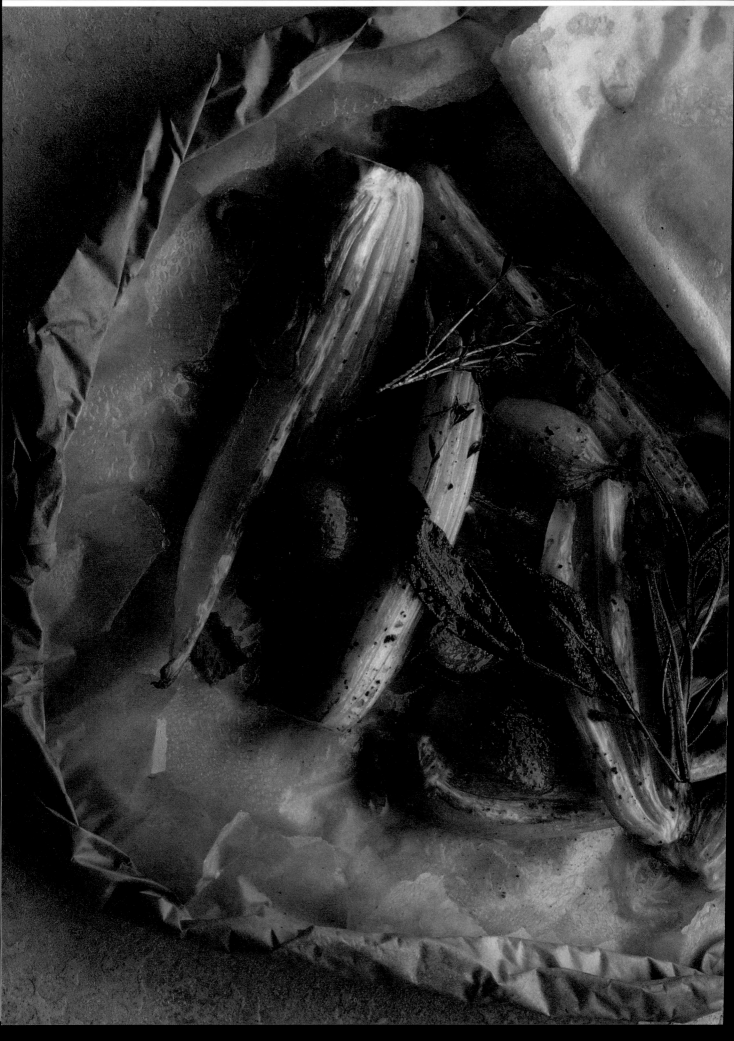

Celery Baked in Vinaigrette with Pancetta and Shallots

SERVES 2

This is a great way to serve celery as a vegetable. I used greaseproof paper for this in the photograph opposite, as it looks very pretty if you take the whole parcel to the table – otherwise foil would do.

1 head celery	**1 dessertspoon white wine vinegar**
6 shallots, peeled (and split if the bulbs are dividing)	**Salt and freshly milled black pepper**
1 or 2 thyme sprigs	
1 rosemary sprig	You will also need a double thickness of
4 sage leaves	greaseproof paper, 15 x 24 inches when folded
3 slices pancetta or smoked streaky bacon	(38 x 60 cm), and a large solid baking tray.
3 tablespoons light olive oil	Pre-heat the oven to gas mark 9, 475°F (240°C).

Begin by removing the tough outer layers of the celery, then pare the outside of the root off, but leave it attached. Now cut across the celery about 3½ inches (9 cm) from the base. Stand the lower half upright and cut vertically through the centre. Then cut each half into 4 to make 8 pieces, keeping them attached to the root. Save a couple of nice leaves (preferably attached to a small stem) and trim the top pieces of celery to a similar length to the base, cutting off any really tough and stringy edges. Now wash all the pieces and dry them on kitchen paper.

Next heat 1 tablespoon of the oil in a frying pan, then lightly brown the celery and shallots, keeping them on the move so they brown evenly. Now transfer them to a plate. Increase the heat under the pan, add the pancetta and fry the slices until they're really crisp – it will take 2–3 minutes and you'll need to keep turning them.

Next lay the greaseproof paper over the baking tray and lightly grease a circle of 9 inches (23 cm) on it. Arrange the celery in an attractive shape on the paper, putting the prettiest pieces on the top, add the shallots, thyme, rosemary and sage leaves in among it, and season with salt and pepper.

Now combine the remaining olive oil and wine vinegar, sprinkle that over the vegetables, followed by the pancetta crumbled into pieces with your hands. Next fold the greaseproof paper over and seal, making pleats, all round – you may find a couple of metal (not plastic) paper clips useful here, as it's essential to keep the steam trapped inside. Place the parcel in the pre-heated oven for 20–25 minutes.

After that carefully unwrap the paper – you may need scissors – and serve the vegetables with the juices spooned over.

NOTE: For 4 to 6 people, double the ingredients and make 2 parcels.

––––––––––––––––– ◇ –––––––––––––––––

Celery Baked in Vinaigrette with Pancetta and Shallots

Sautéed Caramelized Fennel

SERVES 4–6

4 medium-sized heads fennel
1 oz (25 g) butter
1 rounded teaspoon granulated sugar
10 fl oz (275 ml) medium cider
2 fl oz (55 ml) cider vinegar
Salt

You will need a wide saucepan with a lid, about 9–10 inches (23–25.5 cm) in diameter, into which the trimmed fennel will fit snugly.

To prepare the fennel bulbs, first cut off the leafy fronds and reserve them for a garnish. Now trim off the green shoot by cutting diagonally to make a V-shape. Then slice off the root part at the other end, keeping the bulb intact, and remove any tough or brown outer layers, then slice across each bulb to cut it in half.

Then place the fennel in a fan steamer set in the saucepan with 1 inch (2.5 cm) of boiling water under it. Cover and steam for 10 minutes then remove them from the steamer, throw out the water, wipe the inside of the pan with kitchen paper and return it to the heat.

Next melt the butter and sugar in the saucepan and when it starts to foam, stir it around the pan until the sugar dissolves, then add the fennel, cut side down. Keeping the heat fairly high, brown it for 5 minutes then turn the pieces over and brown them on the other side for another 3 minutes.

Now combine the cider, cider vinegar and a little salt and pour this into the pan, then keeping the cut side of the fennel facing upwards, cover with a lid and simmer gently for 20 minutes. After that turn the fennel over again. Then continue to cook for a further 20–25 minutes (this time uncovered). Watch carefully during the last 10 minutes and test to see if it is cooked by inserting a skewer.

When the fennel is tender enough, raise the heat so that the remaining juices reduce to a glaze. Shake the pan carefully to give an even covering of the caramel glaze. Now transfer the whole lot to a warm serving dish with the cut surfaces upwards and scatter with the chopped fennel fronds as a garnish.

Oven-Roasted Cauliflower and Broccoli with Garlic and Coriander

SERVES 4

These two particular vegetables can become a bit repetitive as winter wears on, so here's a deliciously different way to cook them – no water, just in the heat of the oven, which concentrates their flavour wonderfully.

8 oz (225 g) cauliflower	**2 garlic cloves, peeled**
8 oz (225 g) broccoli	**Salt and freshly milled black pepper**
2 tablespoons olive oil	
1 heaped teaspoon whole coriander seeds, coarsely crushed	You will also need a large solid roasting tray.

Pre-heat the oven to gas mark 6, 400°F (200°C).

All you do is trim the cauliflower and broccoli into florets, 1 inch (2.5 cm) in diameter, and place them in a mixing bowl, then sprinkle in the crushed coriander seeds. Crush the cloves of garlic together with ¾ level teaspoon salt in a pestle and mortar until you have a paste. Whisk the oil into this, then pour the whole mixture over the broccoli and cauliflower. Use your hands to toss and mix everything together to get a nice coating of oil and coriander, then arrange the florets on the roasting tray and season with salt and pepper. Bake for 25–35 minutes or until tender when tested with a skewer, and serve straight away.

◇

Compote of Glazed Shallots

SERVES 8

This recipe is dead simple, yet it draws out all the sweet, fragrant flavour of the shallots and at the same time gives them a glazed pink, jewel-like appearance. These make an excellent partner to beef or you can add a bit of sophistication to bangers and mash. Also, cider and cider vinegar can be used instead of wine to make it more economical.

1½ lb (700 g), approximately 24 small, even-sized shallots, peeled and left whole (ones that split into twins count as 2)	2 fl oz (55 ml) red wine vinegar
	14 fl oz (400 ml) dry red wine
	1 teaspoon sugar
	Salt

Use a wide, shallow saucepan which will take the shallots in one layer, then simply place all the above ingredients except the sugar in it and bring everything up to simmering point. Then turn the heat down to its lowest setting and let the shallots simmer (just a few bubbles breaking the surface) for 1–1¼ hours. Turn the shallots over at half-time, and 10 minutes before the end of the cooking time sprinkle in the sugar. You should end up with tender shallots glistening with a lovely glaze. If your heat source is not low enough, you may need to use a diffuser. If it's more convenient you can cook the shallots in advance, and gently re-heat them before serving.

◇

Roasted Roots with Herbs

SERVES 4

S ince oven-roasted vegetables in the 'Summer Collection' were so very popular, I simply had to do a winter version. Here it is and once again it's a winner for entertaining, not least because all the vegetables get cooked together with little or no attention. (See photograph on pages 152–3.)

½ swede (about 5 oz/150 g), cut into 1-inch (2.5-cm) wedges
4 small whole carrots
4 small whole parsnips
1 small turnip, cut in half and then into ¾-inch (2-cm) slices
2 medium red onions, peeled and cut through the root into quarters
2 red potatoes, 5 oz (150 g) each, cut into 6 wedges

1 fat garlic clove, crushed
3 tablespoons olive oil
1 tablespoon chopped mixed herbs (including thyme, rosemary and sage)
Salt and freshly milled black pepper

You will also need a solid baking sheet 16 x 12 inches (40 x 30 cm).

Pre-heat the oven to its highest setting.

First scrub the carrots and parsnips, dry them well and place them in a large bowl with all the other prepared vegetables. Now add the crushed garlic, olive oil and mixed herbs, then using your hands, mix well to make sure they all have a good coating of the oil. You can leave them like this covered with clingfilm for up to 2 hours until you are ready to cook them – in which case the oil will have nicely absorbed the flavour of the garlic and herbs.

Then arrange them on the baking sheet, sprinkle with salt and a good grinding of black pepper and cook in the pre-heated oven on a high shelf for 35–40 minutes or until they are cooked through.

———————◇———————

Roasted Swede with Parmesan

SERVES 4–6

This is another version of a parsnip recipe from my Christmas book. It has been said that even children will eat swede when it tastes this good.

1½ lb (700 g) swede, peeled and cut into large chip-like wedges approximately 2 inches (5 cm) long	A knob of butter
4 oz (110 g) plain flour	Salt and freshly milled black pepper
1½ oz (40 g) Parmesan (Parmigiano Reggiano), freshly grated	You will also need a large solid baking tray 14 x 10 inches (35 x 25.5 cm).
Groundnut oil	Pre-heat the oven to gas mark 6, 400°F (200°C).

Begin by combining the flour, Parmesan and a seasoning of salt and pepper in a mixing bowl. Now pop the swede into a saucepan, cover with boiling water, add some salt, bring back to boiling point then cover and simmer for 3 minutes.

Meanwhile have a kitchen tray ready, then drain the swede and while it is still steaming drop the wedges, using kitchen tongs, a few at a time into the bowl to coat them with the flour and cheese. Do this quickly as the coating will only stick if they're still steamy. Then lay them out on the tray to cool, and refrigerate until you are ready to cook. For this you need to place the baking tray in the oven while it's pre-heating, putting enough oil on the tray to cover the base and adding a knob of butter for flavour.

Then when the oven is up to heat remove the baking tray, place it over direct heat turned to low and arrange the prepared swede wedges on it side by side. Baste the tops with the hot fat then transfer them to the oven, using an oven-glove, to bake for 20 minutes. After that turn them over, remove any excess fat from the tin and continue to bake them for a further 15–20 minutes or until they're crisp and golden.

———————◇———————

Parsnips with a Mustard and Maple Glaze

SERVES 4–6

Peple who normally don't like parsnips like this recipe. It's a very good combination of flavours, and if you get bored with plain roast parsnips at the end of winter, this is just what's needed.

3 lb (1.35 kg) medium-sized parsnips

3 tablespoons groundnut oil

Salt and freshly milled black pepper

You will also need a fan steamer and a good solid baking tray 14 x 10 inches (35 x 25.5 cm).

FOR THE GLAZE:

2 rounded tablespoons wholegrain mustard

2 tablespoons maple syrup

Pre-heat the oven to gas mark 9, 475°F (240°C).

First top, tail and peel the parsnips then cut them in half through the centre. Cut the top half into 4 and the bottom half into 2 so that you have even-sized pieces. Cut out any woody stems from the centre, then place the parsnips in the steamer, sprinkle with salt, cover with a lid and steam over simmering water for 6 minutes. Meanwhile put the baking tray containing the oil on the top shelf of the oven to pre-heat.

When the parsnips are ready, use an oven-glove to remove the baking tray very carefully from the oven so as not to spill the oil, and place it over direct heat turned to low. Add the parsnips, rounded side up, to the sizzling oil. Then tilt the tray and use a large spoon to baste the parsnips to make sure they are evenly coated with the oil. Give them a good grinding of pepper and return the tray to the oven. Bake for 25 minutes, by which time the parsnips should be nicely browned and crispy.

Meanwhile make the glaze – mix the mustard and maple syrup together in a bowl then, using a brush, coat the parsnip pieces with a liberal coating of the glaze and return them to the oven for 8–10 minutes. Serve straight away.

CHAPTER NINE

STARS *of* THE EAST

◇

Since I wrote the *Summer Collection* I have been particularly fortunate in the course of my work for Sainsbury's *The Magazine* to have been able to visit the Far East. On one trip to Tokyo I discovered first-hand how the Japanese make what is undoubtedly the best soy sauce in the world. On another to Bangkok I attended daily classes at the Oriental Cookery School to learn the art of Thai cookery.

An important part of my job is to educate myself about new ingredients, then to share that knowledge and to try to help extend the boundaries. We certainly now live in a most exciting era of cooking. The world has become a smaller place with people zipping about from continent to continent at great speed, and ingredients are on the move too, enabling us to pop into supermarkets and literally shop around the world.

Even so, this can sometimes be frustrating when certain ingredients are not as widely available as we would like them to be. This is where you too can play your part. Be patient and *keep on* asking for ingredients. Between us we have to create a demand, and in doing this all our lives can be enriched by being able to share in new and different cuisines from around the world. You will find details of new ingredients used in this chapter on page 235 and mail order stockists on page 250. But don't forget, keep asking!

Chinese Crispy Beef Stir-Fry

SERVES 2

The good thing about Chinese cooking is that it always manages to make a little meat go a long way. Rump steak is perfect for stir-frying, and for this recipe just 4 oz (110 g) per person is plenty.

4 oz (110 g) rice noodles	1 teaspoon Chinese five-spice powder
8 oz (225 g) rump steak	2 tablespoons groundnut oil
1 stem lemon grass	2 tablespoons soy sauce
1 fat garlic clove	3 tablespoons dry sherry
1½-inch (4-cm) piece fresh ginger	2 tablespoons water
6 spring onions	Salt
1 medium leek	
1 medium carrot	You will also need a wok or a very large
2 rounded teaspoons cornflour	frying pan.

The secret of a successful stir-fry is speed. So what you need to do is have everything prepared before you start. The first item on the list to prepare are the rice noodles. Place these in a large bowl with a little salt, then pour warm water over them and leave them to soak for exactly 15 minutes and no longer.

Now for the vegetables. First the lemon grass – remove the outer tougher leaves, trim off the woody tops, then slice the rest very finely. The garlic should be peeled and also chopped finely. The piece of ginger needs to be peeled, cut into thin slices and then the slices cut into tiny matchstick pieces. Finely slice the white part of the spring onions, then cut the tender green part into 2-inch (5-cm) lengths and then the lengths into little strips. Now the leek: first halve the white part lengthways and cut into similar matchstick-sized strips, then cut the green, tender part of the leek into diagonals to make diamond-shaped pieces. Cut the carrot lengthways and then make this too into matchsticks.

Now for the meat. This is cut into 2-inch (5-cm) pieces and these are then cut lengthways so that the meat, too, is now in thin strips. Next you need to take a small bowl and in it mix the cornflour and the five-spice powder together. Mix the meat in this mixture until it is all well coated. Drain the noodles, shaking off any excess water, and then all is ready to cook.

Now place the wok over a high heat, without adding any oil at first. As soon as it's very hot, add 1 tablespoon of the oil, let it sizzle, then add the meat and toss it and stir-fry it in the hot oil for about 2 minutes. Then remove the meat to a plate. Add the remaining oil, let it sizzle and then add the lemon grass, garlic and ginger. Toss these around for about 30 seconds, then add the carrots, spring onions and leek and toss these around also for 30 seconds. Next add the liquid – soy sauce, sherry and water. Then as soon as the liquid is very hot stir in the noodles, combining them with the vegetables. Finally return the meat to join all the vegetables, and toss everything together a couple of times and serve immediately in hot bowls.

Thai Green Curry
with Chicken

SERVES 4–6

*T*his recipe is inspired by The Oriental's Cookery School in Bangkok. You may have to hunt around for the ingredients, or you can get them by mail order (see page 250). The unique flavours of Thai cooking are so simple and – because you can use a good-quality cooked chicken from the supermarket – this recipe is actually incredibly easy. (See photograph on pages 168–9.)

1 lb (450 g) cooked chicken, sliced into shreds

1½ tins (600 ml) coconut milk

5 Thai shallots, peeled (or normal shallots if not available)

1 teaspoon shrimp paste

FOR THE GREEN CURRY PASTE:

8 green Birdseye chillies (whole)

1 lemon grass stalk, sliced thinly and soaked for 30 minutes in 2 tablespoons lime juice

1 rounded teaspoon kaffir lime peel, pared and thinly shredded

7 thin slices Thai ginger (galangal)

1 heaped teaspoon coriander stalks, chopped

½ teaspoon roasted ground cumin

½ teaspoon roasted ground coriander

3 garlic cloves

FOR THE FINISHED SAUCE:

3–4 dessertspoons Thai fish sauce

1 teaspoon palm sugar

3 dessertspoons fresh green peppercorns (or preserved in brine)

7 kaffir lime leaves

½ mild red chilli, de-seeded and cut into hair-like shreds

1 oz (25 g) Thai basil leaves

You will also need a large flameproof casserole or a wok.

The curry paste can be made well ahead of time and there's absolutely no work involved if you have a food processor or a liquidizer because all you do is simply pop all the curry paste ingredients in and whizz it to a paste (stopping once or twice to push the mixture back down from the sides onto the blades). In Thailand, of course, all these would be pounded by hand with a pestle and mortar, but food processors do cut out all the hard work.

What you need to end up with is a coarse paste but don't worry if it doesn't look very green – that's because I have cut the chilli content; in Thailand they use about 35! If you want yours to be green, then this is the answer! Your next task is to prepare all the rest of the ingredients.

To make the curry, first place the tins of coconut milk on a work surface, upside down. Then open them and inside you will see the whole thing has separated into thick cream and thin watery milk. Divide these by pouring the milk into one bowl and the cream into another. Next place a wok, without any oil in it, over a very high heat and then as soon as it becomes really hot, add three-quarters of the coconut cream and what you do now is literally fry it, stirring all the time so it doesn't catch. What will happen is it will start to separate, the oil will begin to seep out and it will reduce. Ignore the curdled look – this is normal. You may also like to note that when the cream begins to separate you can actually hear it give off a crackling noise. Next add the curry paste and three-quarters of the coconut milk, which should be added a little at a time, keeping the heat high and letting it reduce down slightly. Stay with it and keep stirring to prevent it sticking. Then add the fish sauce and palm sugar, stir these in and then add the chicken pieces and the peppercorns. Stir again and simmer everything for about 4–5 minutes until the chicken is heated through. Then just before serving place the lime leaves one on top of the other, roll them up tightly and slice them into very fine shreds. Then add them along with the red chilli and torn basil leaves. Serve with Thai fragrant rice.

NOTE: You can, if you like, freeze the leftover coconut milk and cream for use later on.

––––––––––––– ◇ –––––––––––––

Next page:
Thai Green Curry with Chicken

Singapore Stir-Fried Noodles

SERVES 2

O*nce again I have to thank Ken Lo for introducing me to this incredibly good recipe, which is a spectacular combination of flavours, textures and colours. If you can't get dried Chinese mushrooms or shrimps (see page 235) use more of the fresh ones and it will still be wonderful.*

4 oz (110 g) rice noodles	½ teaspoon salt
6 Chinese dried mushrooms	2 oz (50 g) cooked chicken or pork, finely shredded
1 heaped tablespoon Chinese dried shrimps	2 oz (50 g) peeled prawns, chopped into thirds
2 tablespoons groundnut oil	2 tablespoons mushroom soaking water
1 medium onion, chopped small	1½ tablespoons soy sauce (Japanese is best)
2 rashers streaky bacon, chopped small	4 spring onions, finely chopped, including green parts
1 large garlic clove, chopped	2 tablespoons dry sherry
1 heaped teaspoon freshly grated ginger	
1 dessertspoon Madras curry powder	You also need a wok or very large frying pan.

First of all you need to soak the dried mushrooms and shrimps – to do this place them in a jug and pour boiling water over them and leave them aside to soak for 30 minutes. Meanwhile you can get on with all the chopping of the other ingredients.

After the mushrooms and shrimps have soaked, drain off the water, reserving it for later. Give the mushrooms a squeeze and chop them into fine shreds. Now place the noodles in a large bowl, cover them with warm water and leave them to soak for 15 minutes.

Next heat the oil in the wok and when it's very hot add the onions, mushrooms, soaked shrimps, chopped bacon, garlic and ginger. Stir them round in the hot oil, then reduce the heat and gently let all the ingredients cook together for about 15 minutes. This initial slow cooking allows all the delicious flavours and aromas to permeate the oil.

After 15 minutes add the curry powder and salt to the cooked ingredients, then drain the noodles in a colander – give them a really good shake to get rid of any excess water. Then turn the heat under the pan up to medium, add the chicken, then the fresh prawns, followed by the chopped spring onion. Next add the drained noodles to the pan, then using either a large fork or some chopsticks toss the ingredients around so that everything is incorporated amongst the noodles. Finally sprinkle in the combined soy sauce, mushroom water and sherry, give everything a good stir and serve immediately on hot plates.

◇

Teriyaki Steak

SERVES 2

*T*eriyaki sauce must be one of the most popular Japanese sauces the world over. The follow-ing recipe is my own interpretation, as I find I like less sugar than the amount the more authentic recipes call for. You don't need the most expensive steak for this, either, because the mari-nade does a wonderful job of tenderizing and mellowing the meat.

2 x 6 oz (175 g) top rump steaks, 1 inch (2.5 cm) thick	1 tablespoon groundnut oil
2 tablespoons soy sauce (Japanese is best)	Sansho pepper, if available
2 tablespoons saké	FOR THE GARNISH:
4 tablespoons mirin	2 garlic cloves, peeled
1 teaspoon sugar	1½ inches daikon radish (mooli), peeled
2 teaspoons grated fresh ginger	½ green chilli, de-seeded
1 fat garlic clove, crushed	Watercress
	Lemon wedges

Allow time for marinating the meat. This can be anything from overnight to a minimum of 1 hour before you cook the steaks. All you do is combine the soy sauce, saké, mirin, sugar, grated ginger and garlic, then place the steaks in a small, shallow dish. Pour the marinade over, cover and leave them in a cool place, turn-ing them once halfway through the marinating time.

Just before you want to cook the steaks, slice the remaining 2 cloves of garlic into rounds. Take the peeled daikon, grate it on the fine side of the grater, then squeeze it tightly in the palm of your hand to get rid of excess juices. Then take the green chilli, grate it and mix it in with the daikon. Now form the mixture into two little cone-shaped mounds (these will be served as a garnish).

To cook the steaks, pre-heat the oil in a good solid frying pan. Brown the gar-lic slices briefly, then remove them to a plate to keep warm. Now turn the heat to its highest setting and, when the pan is very hot, scrape the marinade off the steaks, reserving it, and place them in the pan. Now reduce the heat to medium and cook the steaks for 4 minutes each side if you like them medium rare, 3 min-utes if very rare and 5 minutes for well done. Watch them carefully because the marinade tends to brown them more quickly. Two minutes before the end of your cooking time, pour in the marinade and reduce it by about a third. Now transfer the steaks to a carving board and, using a sharp knife, cut them into slightly diag-onal ½-inch (1-cm) slices. Place these on warm serving plates, season with Sansho pepper, spoon the sauce over, sprinkle the browned garlic on top and garnish with watercress and lemon wedges. Serve with the little mounds of grated daikon and chilli.

NOTE: For information on Japanese ingredients, see page 235.

Thai Prawn Curry with Pineapple

SERVES 2

This lovely recipe from The Oriental's Cookery School in Bangkok has been slightly adjusted to accommodate Western ingredients without, I think, losing its authenticity. It's incredibly simple and easy and it really does taste exotic and unusual. If fresh tiger prawns are not available you can buy them from the freezer cabinet in large supermarkets.

1 lb (450 g) uncooked tiger prawns in their shells	**7 Thai shallots, peeled (or normal shallots if not available)**
2 x 400 ml tins coconut milk	**1 teaspoon shrimp paste (if not available use 2 anchovies)**
1 lb (450 g) fresh pineapple, cut into ¾-inch (2-cm) chunks	**½ teaspoon salt**
	3 tablespoons Thai fish sauce

FOR THE CURRY PASTE:

4 dried red chillies, soaked with the juice and zest of 1 lime for 30 minutes

1 tablespoon lemon grass, finely chopped

1-inch (2.5-cm) cube fresh ginger

5 garlic cloves, peeled

TO GARNISH:

2 kaffir lime leaves (if available)

2 medium-sized red chillies, de-seeded and shredded into hairlike strips

You will also need a wok or a very large frying pan.

If the tiger prawns are frozen, de-frost them by emptying them into a colander and leaving them for about an hour to defrost. Then cook the prawns (either fresh or frozen) in a frying pan or wok placed over direct high heat. Add the prawns in their shells and dry-fry them in the hot pan for about 4–5 minutes, turning and tossing them around whilst you watch their beige and black stripes turn pink.

After that remove them from the heat and when they're cool enough to handle, peel off the skins, then make a slit all along their backs and remove any black thread. Now keep them covered and refrigerated until you need them.

To make the curry paste, all you do is put everything into a food processor or blender then switch on to a high speed and blend until you have a rather coarse, rough-looking paste. Remove the paste and keep it covered in the fridge until you need it.

When you're ready to make the curry, empty the contents of the tins of coconut milk into a wok and stir while you bring it up to the boil, then boil until the fat begins to separate from the solids. This will take approximately 20 minutes, and if you listen carefully you'll hear a sizzle as the fat begins to come out and the whole thing is reduced. Ignore the curdled appearance. Now add the curry paste, give it 3 minutes' cooking time, enough for the flavours to develop, then add the prawns and the pineapple and let them heat through gently for another 2 minutes. During that time shred the lime leaves by placing one on top of the other, then roll them up tightly and cut into very thin shreds. Serve the curry with lime leaves and chilli strips sprinkled over, and some Thai fragrant rice as an accompaniment.

CHAPTER TEN

AUTUMN, WINTER *and* PARTY DESSERTS

◇

Sometimes I get a bit tired of hearing about Chocolate Truffle Torte! It was quite definitely the hit of my *Christmas* collection, and though I still love it myself I really felt that in this book I had to find a comparable chocolate dessert, simply so we can all enjoy a change. Well the good news is I've found it, the best chocolate dessert to date and, yes, even better than the truffle torte. It is called Fallen Chocolate Soufflé (see page 186), and when we filmed it for the television series it got a ten out of ten vote from the entire crew. The secret with this recipe, as with all things chocolatey, is the quality of chocolate you use, so do read the notes on page 233.

Because winter includes the Christmas party season I have been a bit indulgent on the chocolate front. Chocolate Mascarpone Cheesecake (see page 198) is a winner and so is A Return to the Black Forest (see page 222), my sixties revival of a chocolate roulade, filled with bitter cherries, chocolate and cream. And can I also recommend what I think is the definitive recipe for Tiramisu (see page 193), that delightful combination of bitter chocolate, coffee, sponge and mascarpone.

If you are watching your waistline you can skip this chapter or alternatively do what I do: just cook one of them a week, on Sundays!

Grilled Autumn Fruits with Sabayon Cider Sauce

SERVES 4

Than is a very pretty and colourful dessert for the autumn or winter. It can be made well in advance as the fruits are served at room temperature, with a sauce to go with them that can either be warm or cooled.

2 dessert apples	FOR THE SAUCE:
(Cox's or Braeburn)	**3 x size 1 egg yolks**
2 small ripe pears	**2 oz (50 g) caster sugar**
(Packham's or similar)	**5 fl oz (150 ml) dry cider**
10 ripe red plums	**(the reserved juices from the fruits can**
Juice of 1 lemon	**be added to this)**
1 large orange	
2 oz (50g) caster sugar plus	You will also need a large grill tray lined with foil and a shallow plate or dish to put the cooked fruits on.
1 tablespoon	

First prepare the apples and pears. Leave the peel on the fruit but core them and cut the apples into eighths and the pears into quarters. Then halve the plums and remove the stones. Place them in a bowl and toss in lemon juice.

The orange should be cut into double segments, so place it on a board and, using your sharpest knife, pare off all the skin and pith. Then, holding it in one hand over the same bowl to catch the juices, cut out the double segments by slicing the knife in at the line of pith which divides the segments (you need to cut out each wedge with as much of the pithy membrane left behind as possible). As you cut them out, add them to the rest of the fruit.

To cook the fruit, pre-heat the grill to its highest setting about 20 minutes in advance and arrange the fruits in the grill tray (if it's small you might have to cook them in 2 batches). Sprinkle the fruits with the 2 oz (50 g) sugar then place them under the hot grill about 4 inches (10 cm) from the heat. They will take about 15–20 minutes to become caramelized and tinged brown at the edges. Keep an eye on them and turn them over at half-time, sprinkling on the extra tablespoon of sugar. If a lot of juice comes out and creates too much steam, pour it from the corner of the tin into the bowl. The plums will probably cook quickest so remove them first along with the rest of the fruits as they caramelize.

Then make the sauce. Place the egg yolks and sugar in a basin and whisk these with an electric hand whisk until they start to thicken. Now set the basin over a small saucepan of simmering water and add the cider and fruit juice a little at a time, continuing to whisk as you're adding it. When all the juices are in, carry on whisking until the sauce thickens to a fluffy consistency. Draw the whisk across the surface: it is ready when there is no visible liquid left underneath. Pour the sauce into a jug and serve warm along with the fruit.

Spiced Lambrusco Jellies with Brandy Cream and Frosted Black Grapes

SERVES 6

It was in Parma in Italy that I first tasted the dry Lambrusco which is local to that region. Because it's fizzy it makes a lovely bubbly, spicy jelly which slips down coolly at the end of a filling meal. If you can't get hold of a dry Lambrusco a sweet one will be fine, but don't cut the sugar – it still needs it.

FOR THE JELLY:
15 fl oz (425 ml) dry red Lambrusco

Zest and juice of 1 orange

3 oz (75 g) caster sugar

2 x 11 g sachets powdered gelatine

1 cinnamon stick

6 cloves

1 blade mace

1-in (2.5-cm) piece root ginger, peeled and sliced

1 pint (570 ml) water

FOR THE BRANDY CREAM:
5 fl oz (150 ml) double cream

1 tablespoon brandy

1 tablespoon orange juice

1 oz (25 g) caster sugar

1 teaspoon finely grated orange zest

FOR THE FROSTED GRAPES:
6 small clusters of black grapes (3 in each cluster)

1 egg white, very lightly beaten

2 heaped tablespoons caster sugar

You will also need 6 x 7-fl oz (200-ml) stemmed glasses.

To make the jelly, pour the water into a small saucepan and add the orange zest, sugar and spices. Then place it over a medium heat and bring to just below boiling point. At that stage remove from the heat and leave to infuse for about an hour to allow the spices to impart their flavours.

After that strain the spices out, discard them and bring the liquid to just below simmering point again. Take the pan off the heat and sprinkle in the gelatine, whisking the mixture with a balloon whisk at the same time. Now leave it on one side to melt the gelatine, stirring once or twice to ensure it has all dissolved into the liquid.

Next add the orange juice and strain the contents of the pan through a fine sieve lined with kitchen paper. Leave it to cool, then cover and chill in the refrigerator until just on the point of setting (about 1–1½ hours). After that add the wine and stir to blend well, then pour into the glasses. Chill the jellies, covered with clingfilm, for about 4 hours, by which time they should have a lovely soft set.

When the jelly is setting make the brandy cream by simply combining the ingredients in a small bowl, cover with clingfilm and leave in the fridge to chill. Remember to remove the jellies from the fridge 30 minutes before you need to serve them.

For the grapes all you do is dip each cluster in the beaten egg white then coat generously with the caster sugar. Leave them on a sheet of greaseproof paper to dry. Top each jelly with the brandy cream and decorate with frosted grapes.

Basic Pancakes
with Sugar and Lemon

MAKES 12–14 IN A 7-INCH (18-CM) PAN

No winter cookbook would be complete without a pancake recipe – even though Pancake Day usually heralds the end of a long winter and we can look forward again to spring. Every year there are people making pancakes for the first time, and I admit it can be a hazardous affair if you don't know the ropes. So here is my tried and trusted pancake recipe, and once you get into the swing, you can make loads extra for the freezer and try the recipes on pages 89 and 145.

4 oz (110 g) plain flour, sifted
A pinch of salt
2 x size 1 eggs
7 fl oz (200 ml) milk mixed with
3 fl oz (75 ml) water
2 oz (50 g) butter

TO SERVE:

Caster sugar, lemon juice and lemon wedges

You will also need a good solid 7-inch (18-cm) pancake pan or frying pan, some kitchen paper, greaseproof paper, a palette knife or flexible pan slice, and a ladle.

First of all sift the flour and salt into a large mixing bowl with the sieve held high above the bowl so the flour gets an airing. Now make a well in the centre of the flour and break the eggs into it. Then begin whisking the eggs – any sort of whisk or even a fork will do – incorporating any bits of flour from around the edge of the bowl as you do so.

Next, gradually add small quantities of the milk and water mixture, still whisking (don't worry about any lumps as they will eventually disappear as you whisk). When all the liquid has been added, use a rubber spatula to scrape any elusive bits of flour from around the edge into the centre, then whisk once more until the batter is smooth, with the consistency of thin cream. Now melt the 2 oz (50 g) of butter in the pan. Spoon 2 tablespoons of it into the batter and whisk it in, then pour the rest into a bowl and use it to lubricate the pan, using a wodge of kitchen paper to smear it round before you make each pancake.

Now get the pan really hot, then turn the heat down to medium and, to start with, do a test pancake to see if you're using the correct amount of batter. I find 2 tablespoons about right for a 7-inch (18-cm) pan. It's also helpful if you spoon the batter into a ladle so it can be poured into the hot pan in one go. As soon as the batter hits the hot pan, tip it around from side to side to get the base evenly coated with batter. It should take only half a minute or so to cook; you can lift the edge with a palette knife to see if it's tinged gold as it should be. Flip the pancake over with a pan slice or palette knife – the other side will need a few seconds only – then simply slide it out of the pan onto a plate.

Stack the pancakes as you make them between sheets of greaseproof paper on a plate fitted over simmering water, to keep them warm while you make the rest.

To serve, sprinkle each pancake with freshly squeezed lemon juice and caster sugar, fold in half, then in half again to form triangles, or else simply roll them up. Serve sprinkled with a little more sugar and lemon juice and extra sections of lemon.

Pears Baked in Marsala Wine

SERVES 8

The rich, dark flavour of Marsala combined with fragrant pear juices is a quite stunning combination. When you shop for the pears, looks are important: a good pear shape and a long stalk intact are essential, and the fruit needs to be hard and not ripe – which is perhaps fortunate as ripe pears always seem difficult to find.

FOR THE PEARS:	TO SERVE:
8 large hard pears	**1 x 500 ml tub crème fraîche**
1 pint (570 ml) Marsala	
2 oz (50 g) caster sugar	You will also need a large flameproof casserole
2 whole cinnamon sticks	with a tight-fitting lid.
1 vanilla pod	
1 rounded dessertspoon arrowroot	Pre-heat the oven to gas mark ½, 250°F (130°C).

Using a potato peeler thinly pare off the outer skin of the pears, but leave the stalks intact. Then slice off a thin little disc from each pear base so they can sit upright. Now lay the pears on their side in the casserole. Pour in the Marsala then sprinkle over the sugar and add the cinnamon sticks and vanilla pod.

Now bring everything up to simmering point, then cover the casserole and bake the pears on a low shelf in the oven for about 1½ hours. After that remove the casserole from the oven, turn the pears over onto their other side, then replace the lid and return them to the oven for a further 1½ hours.

When the pears are cooked, transfer them to a serving bowl to cool, leaving the liquid in the casserole. Then remove the cinnamon sticks and vanilla pod. Place the casserole over direct heat and then, in a cup, mix the arrowroot with a little cold water until you have a smooth paste. Add this to the casserole, whisking with a balloon whisk as you add it. Bring the syrup just up to simmering point, by which time it will have thickened slightly. Then remove from the heat and when the syrup is cool, spoon it over the pears, basting them well.

Now cover the pears with foil or clingfilm and place them in the fridge to chill thoroughly. Serve the pears sitting upright in individual dishes with the sauce spooned over and the crème fraîche handed round separately.
NOTE: This recipe can also be made, as in the photograph opposite, with red wine or strong dry cider – each version has its own particular charm.

———————◇———————

Pears Baked in Marsala Wine, Red Wine and Dry Cider

Iced Apple Soufflé with Caramelized Apple

SERVES 6

I *first tasted this amazingly good dessert at a meal cooked by a friend, Lesley Nathan, in the summer, when she made it with strawberries. This is her recipe, adapted for winter with apples, and every bit as wonderful.*

4 Granny Smith apples	FOR THE CARAMELIZED APPLE SLICES:
12 fl oz (350 ml) extra strong vintage cider	**1 small 4 oz (110 g) Cox's apple, unpeeled**
Zest and juice 1 large lemon (4 tablespoons juice)	**1 oz (25 g) butter**
6 oz (175 g) caster sugar	**¾ oz (20 g) caster sugar**
1 x 200 ml tub crème fraîche, very well chilled	
4 x size 1 egg whites	

You will also need 6 x 4-fl oz (110-ml) straight-sided ramekins, parchment for making collars and small rubber bands.

First wash the Granny Smith apples and, leaving the skins on, core and chop them roughly. After that place them in a saucepan with the cider, lemon zest, lemon juice and sugar. Now bring it all up to the boil and simmer gently until the apples are mushy, which will take about 15–20 minutes. Then remove them from the heat and allow them to cool slightly before passing them through a fine nylon sieve, pushing the purée through with a ladle. Now discard the skins left in the sieve and leave the apple purée to get completely cold.

Meanwhile prepare the ramekins. First make collars for each of them: cut 6 pieces of parchment measuring 7 x 12 inches (18 x 30 cm), fold each in half along its length to 3½ x 12 inches (9 x 30 cm) then fold one of the long edges over 1 inch (2.5 cm), giving you a thicker piece at the base to stabilize the collar. You will now have collars measuring 2½ x 12 inches (6 x 30 cm), so wrap each collar around the ramekins, keeping the fold to the base and hold them in place with a rubber band.

When the purée is completely cold, remove the crème fraîche from the refrigerator, transfer it to a bowl and whip until it starts to thicken – but be careful not to let it get too stiff. Next put the egg whites in a large bowl and, using an electric hand whisk with squeaky-clean beaters, whisk to the stiff-peak stage. Then fold a third of the egg whites into the apple purée along with the crème fraîche, and when everything is completely amalgamated, very gently fold in the remaining egg whites. Pour the whole lot into a large jug and then into the collared ramekins. The mixture will come right up into the top of the collars. Now stand the ramekins on a tray and freeze for 4–6 hours, making sure they are standing level.

To make the caramelized apple slices, cut the apple into quarters and remove the core, then cut these into slices ⅛ inch (3 mm) thick. You will need 30 thin slices. Next take a large, solid frying pan, 8–9 inches (20–23 cm) in diameter. Melt half the butter. When it starts to foam, sprinkle in half the sugar. Stir it around, keeping the heat high, add the apple slices and cook them 30–40 seconds on each side until golden brown and slightly crisp. You will need to do this in 2 batches. Lay the first lot on baking parchment, then add the remaining butter and sugar, if necessary, and cook the rest. These can be made up to 2 hours in advance.

Take the ramekins out of the freezer and transfer to the fridge 20 minutes before serving. Then just peel away the collars, having removed the rubber bands. Finally arrange the apple slices in circles on top before serving.

———————————— ◇ ————————————

Lime and Mango Ice Cream

MAKES 2 PINTS (1.2 LITRES)

This is a beautiful ice cream, but it is most important that the mangoes are extremely ripe – almost bordering on over-ripe. The way to test this is to hold one and check that it feels heavy when held in the hand and also gives off a powerful and fragrant aroma through the skin. If you can only buy under-ripe mangoes, they should be placed in a brown paper bag and left to ripen in the dark at room temperature.

3–4 limes, to yield 4 fl oz (110 ml) juice
3 large, extremely ripe mangoes
4 oz (110 g) granulated sugar
5 fl oz (150 ml) water

1 x 200 ml tub crème fraîche

You will also need a shallow plastic box measuring 10 x 6 x 2 inches (25.5 x 15 x 5 cm), with lid.

First dissolve the sugar in the water over a low heat until all the grains of sugar have disappeared, then turn the heat up a little bit and simmer gently for 15 minutes, without allowing the liquid to evaporate. Then remove it from the heat and leave on one side for it to cool slightly.

To prepare the mangoes, slice them in half along the length of the stone on either side of it (and have a plate underneath to catch all of the precious juice). Now use a spoon to scrape all the flesh away from the skin, then place this into a liquidizer. Next, using a sharp paring knife, remove the skin from the flesh around the stone then scrape all the flesh from this into the liquidizer, leaving the stone and any fibrous threads behind.

Now liquidize the mangoes until you have a smooth purée. If you don't have a liquidizer or processor, place a plastic sieve over a bowl and push the flesh of the fruit through. Either way, this should yield about 1 pint (570 ml) of purée. Then add the lime juice and the sugar syrup and combine thoroughly.

Next spoon out the crème fraîche into another bowl and whip it lightly till it increases in volume and thickness. Now use a metal spoon to fold the fruit purée into the crème fraîche, and place the mixture in the plastic box and place it in the coldest part of the freezer for about 2 hours or until it is beginning to freeze around the edges. Then, using an electric hand whisk, whisk the frozen edges into the middle, replace the lid and return it to the freezer for another 2–3 hours, then repeat the whole process. After that freeze again until it is quite frozen.

Before serving, place the box in the main body of the fridge for about 1 hour. If you have an ice-cream maker, freeze-churn according to the makers' instructions.

Banoffee Cheesecake with Toffee Pecan Sauce

SERVES 6–8

The magic word 'banoffee' does not, as you might have thought, have exotic origins: it is simply an amalgam of banana and toffee. But it is magic nonetheless – the combination of bananas, cream and toffee is inspired. Here I have incorporated them all into a cheesecake with the addition of one extra star ingredient, toasted pecan nuts.

FOR THE BASE:

4 oz (110 g) sweet oat biscuits

1½ oz (40 g) melted butter

3 oz (75 g) pecan nuts (use half for the base and half for the sauce – see below)

FOR THE FILLING:

3 medium-size ripe bananas, 8 oz (225 g) peeled weight

1 tablespoon lemon juice

3 x size 1 eggs

12 oz (350 g) medium fat curd cheese

1 x 200 g tub fromage frais (8% fat)

6 oz (175 g) caster sugar

FOR THE SAUCE:

2 oz (50 g) butter

3 oz (75 g) soft brown sugar

2 oz (50 g) granulated sugar

5 oz (150 g) golden syrup

5 fl oz (150 ml) double cream

A few drops vanilla extract

FOR THE TOPPING:

3 medium-size ripe bananas

2 tablespoons lemon juice

You will also need a springform cake tin, 8 inches (20 cm) in diameter, lightly buttered. Pre-heat the oven to gas mark 6, 400°F (200°C).

Begin by toasting all the pecan nuts. Place them on a baking tray and bake in the oven for 7 minutes until lightly toasted or, if you watch them like a hawk, you can toast them under a grill. Then chop them quite small.

Place the biscuits in a bowl and crush them with the base of a rolling pin. Add the melted butter and half the nuts, mix them well then press all this into the base of the cake tin and pre-bake the base in the oven for 20 minutes. Then lower the temperature to gas mark 2, 300°F (150°C).

For the filling, first blend the bananas and lemon juice in a food processor until smooth, then simply add all the rest of the filling ingredients. Blend again then pour it all over the biscuit base and bake on the middle shelf of the oven for 1 hour. Turn off the oven and leave the cheesecake inside to cool slowly until completely cold; this slow cooling will stop the cheesecake cracking.

To make the sauce, place the butter, sugars and syrup in a saucepan and, over a very low heat, allow everything to dissolve completely. Let it cook for about 5 minutes. Pour in the cream and vanilla extract and stir until everything is smooth, then add the rest of the chopped pecan nuts. Remove it from the heat and allow it to cool completely before pouring it into a jug ready for serving.

When you are ready to assemble the cheesecake put the 2 tablespoons of lemon juice into a bowl. Slice the remaining bananas at an oblique angle into ¼-inch (5-mm) slices, and gently toss them around to get an even coating of juice. If you like you can spoon a small circle of sauce into the centre, then layer the bananas in overlapping circles all round it. Serve the cheesecake cut into slices with the rest of the sauce handed round separately.

Banoffee Cheesecake with Toffee Pecan Sauce

Fallen Chocolate Soufflé with Armagnac Prunes and Crème Fraîche Sauce

SERVES 8–10

*Y*es, it's really true – this soufflé is supposed to puff like a normal one, but then it is removed from the oven and allowed slowly to subside into a lovely, dark, squidgey chocolate dessert. It is served slightly chilled with a prune and crème fraîche sauce. The only problem I can fore-see with this recipe is that someone will write and tell me that their soufflé wouldn't sink! Let me pre-empt that by saying, don't worry I'm sure it will taste just as good. This also works superbly with prunes in Amaretto or port, so use whichever flavour you like best.

FOR THE PRUNES:
12 oz (350 g) Californian pitted ready-to-eat prunes
5 fl oz (150 ml) water
5 fl oz (150 ml) Armagnac

FOR THE SOUFFLE:
7 oz (200 g) dark continental chocolate, with 75% cocoa solids
4 oz (110 g) unsalted butter
1 tablespoon Armagnac

4 x size 1 eggs, separated
4 oz (110 g) caster sugar
A little sifted cocoa powder for dusting

FOR THE PRUNE AND CREME FRAICHE SAUCE:

The remainder of the soaked prunes
5 fl oz (150 ml) crème fraîche

You will also need an 8-inch (20-cm) springform cake tin, greased and lined with silicone paper.

The prunes need to be soaked overnight, so simply place them in a saucepan with the water, bring them up to simmering point, remove from the heat, then pour the prunes and their cooking liquid into a bowl and stir in the Armagnac while they're still warm. Leave to cool, then cover the bowl with clingfilm and chill in the refrig-erator overnight.

To make the soufflé, pre-heat the oven to gas mark 3, 325°F (170°C). Meanwhile, break the chocolate into squares and place them with the butter into a bowl fitted over a saucepan containing some barely simmering water (making sure the bowl does not touch the water). Leave the chocolate for a few moments to melt, then stir until you have a smooth, glossy mixture. Now remove the bowl from the heat, add the Armagnac and leave to cool.

Next take a large, roomy bowl and combine the egg yolks and caster sugar in it. Then whisk them together for about 5–6 minutes, using an electric hand whisk – when you lift up the whisk and the mixture drops off, making ribbon-like trails, it's ready.

Now count out 18 of the soaked prunes, cut each one in half and combine the halves with the whisked egg mixture along with the melted chocolate.

Next you'll need to wash the whisk thoroughly with hot soapy water to remove all the grease, and dry it well. In another bowl whisk up the egg whites till they form soft peaks. After that, fold them carefully into the chocolate mixture. Spoon this mixture into the prepared tin and bake the soufflé in the centre of the oven for about 30 minutes or until the centre feels springy to the touch. Allow the soufflé to cool in the tin (it's great fun watching it fall very slowly). When it's quite cold, remove it from the tin, peel off the paper, then cover and chill for several hours (or it can be made 2–3 days ahead if more convenient).

To make the sauce, simply liquidize the prunes reserved from above, together with their liquid, place the purée in a serving bowl and lightly stir in the crème fraîche to give a sort of marbled effect. Hand the sauce round separately to serve with the soufflé. Serve the soufflé dusted with cocoa powder and cut into *small* slices (it's very rich).

NOTE: The prunes soaked in Armagnac and served with crème fraîche make an extremely good dessert in their own right. Also, the soufflé and sauce freeze very well for up to a month.

Spiced Cranberry and Orange Jellies

SERVES 4

I like to serve a jelly at a celebration dinner because it is so nice to have something cool, light and refreshing at the end of a meal that has included a lot of rich food. This jelly is incredibly simple to make, but don't be tempted to jazz it up – I've tried that and found this simple version to be best by far.

1 pint (570 ml) cranberry juice
Juice and zest of 2 oranges
2 x 11 g sachets gelatine
½ level teaspoon ground ginger
1 stick cinnamon, broken into pieces
3 oz (75 g) caster sugar

FOR THE FROSTED CRANBERRIES:

Approximately 20 cranberries
1 x size 1 egg white, beaten
1 tablespoon caster sugar

You will also need 4 x 7-fl oz (200-ml) stemmed glasses.

First measure the cranberry juice into a jug and sprinkle in the gelatine. Next use a potato peeler to pare off the outer zest of the oranges, and put the zest in a saucepan with the orange juice, ginger, cinnamon, cranberry juice and sugar. Bring everything up to a gentle simmer, then remove from the heat and leave aside for approximately 2 hours, until the jelly is just on the point of setting.

Now strain the jelly through a nylon sieve into a jug, pour into the stemmed glasses, cover and chill in the fridge until needed.

For the frosted cranberries all you need to do is dip each berry into the beaten egg white and roll it in caster sugar to give a generous coating. Then leave the berries spread out on baking parchment to become crisp.

Remove the jellies from the fridge half an hour before serving and pile about 5 frosted cranberries on top of each glass.

NOTE: If you prefer, you can make the jelly in a 1¼-pint (725-ml) jelly mould.

Lemon Ricotta Cheesecake with a Confit of Lemons

SERVES 6

This is a very light, fluffy lemony cheesecake which, if you serve it with a Confit of Lemons, makes a delightfully refreshing end to a rich meal.

12 oz (350 g) Ricotta
Zest and juice of 3–4 lemons, to yield
5 fl oz (150 ml) juice
1 x 11 g sachet powdered gelatine
2 x size 1 egg yolks
2½ oz (60 g) caster sugar
10 fl oz (275 ml) double cream

Pre-heat the oven to gas mark 6, 400°F (200°C).

FOR THE BASE:

4 oz (110 g) sweet oat biscuits
1 oz (25 g) flaked almonds (these can be bought ready-toasted)
2 oz (50 g) melted butter

You will also need a 7-inch (18-cm) or 8-inch (20-cm) springform cake tin. Line the sides with baking parchment to come 1 inch (2.5 cm) above the rim.

First of all, prepare the base by crushing the biscuits – and the best way to do this is to lay them flat inside a polythene bag then roll them with a rolling pin to crush them coarsely. Then tip them into a bowl along with the flaked almonds and stir the melted butter into them. After that, press this mixture evenly and firmly onto the base of the tin and then place in the oven to pre-bake for 20 minutes. After that remove it from the oven and allow it to get completely cold.

Meanwhile remove the zest from the lemons using a fine grater (it can be grated on to a board and chopped even more finely if required). Then take the juice from the lemons and measure to 5 fl oz (150 ml). Next put 3 tablespoons of the lemon juice into a small bowl, sprinkle the gelatine over, then place the bowl in a small saucepan with 1 inch (2.5 cm) simmering water and leave it for 10 minutes to dissolve, or until it is absolutely clear and transparent.

Now put the egg yolks, sugar and Ricotta into a food processor or liquidizer and blend it all on a high speed for about 1 minute. Then add the lemon rind, the remaining lemon juice and the gelatine, which should be poured through a strainer. Blend everything again now until it's all absolutely smooth. Then take a large bowl and whisk the double cream until you get a floppy consistency then pour this in to join the rest of the cheese mixture and blend again, this time for just a few seconds. Next pour the whole lot over the biscuit base, cover with foil and chill in the refrigerator for a minimum of 3 hours.

To serve the cheesecake, carefully remove it from the tin on to a serving plate, decorate with a circle of lemon confit slices and serve the rest separately.

———————— ◊ ————————

Confit of Lemons

SERVES 6

2 large juicy lemons
(unwaxed if possible)

4 oz (110 g) granulated sugar

12 fl oz (425 ml) water

You will also need a non-aluminium pan approximately 8 inches (20 cm) in diameter and a circle of baking parchment of the same diameter to keep the lemons under the surface of the liquid.

Take one and a half of the lemons and slice them into thin rings about ⅛ inch (3 mm) thick, discarding the end pieces and pips. Place these in a saucepan and cover with sufficient cold water to just cover them, bring to a simmer for 3 minutes, then drain through a sieve and discard the water. Now pour the measured water into the same pan, add the sugar, stir over a gentle heat until all the grains have dissolved then add the lemon slices. Once the liquid has returned to a very gentle simmer lay the circle of baking parchment on the surface of the liquid – this will help the lemon slices to cook evenly.

Now continue to cook them at the very gentlest simmer, without a lid, for 45 minutes – until the skins are tender. Check them at 30 minutes by inserting the tip of a knife just in case they are cooking a little faster. When they are tender remove them with a slotted spoon to a shallow dish. The liquid will be much reduced at this stage, but what we want is about 5 fl oz (150 ml); if you have much more than this increase the heat a little and reduce further. Then squeeze the juice from the remaining half lemon, pour it into the syrup and pour this over the lemon slices. Cover and leave overnight if possible.

───────────── ◇ ─────────────

Mascarpone Creams and Caramel Sauce with Caramelized Hazelnuts

SERVES 6

Rich, luscious Mascarpone lightened by yoghurt makes these little velvety creams cool and soothing after a rich main course. The contrast of the dark flavours of the caramel is an extra delight. People tend to get worried about caramel – so here are two things to remember. First, if it sets too hard, just place it over a gentle heat to soften again, and secondly, to clean the saucepan, place it over a gentle heat, filled with warm soapy water.

FOR THE CREAMS:	FOR THE CARAMELIZED NUTS AND SAUCE:
5 fl oz (150 ml) single cream	9 oz (250 g) granulated sugar
1 x 11 g sachet gelatine	2 tablespoons hot water
3 oz (75 g) caster sugar	5 fl oz (150 ml) whipping cream
1 x 250 g tub Mascarpone (Italian cream cheese)	1 teaspoon vanilla extract
1 x 340 g tub wholemilk organic yoghurt	1 oz (25 g), approximately 30, whole shelled hazelnuts, lightly toasted
2 teaspoons vanilla extract	

You will also need 6 x 6-fl oz (175-ml) aluminium pudding pots and some clingfilm.

First prepare the little pots by lining them with clingfilm, which will make them no problem to turn out later on. The easiest way to do this is as follows – using a piece of kitchen paper dabbed in a flavourless oil (such as groundnut), lightly oil the inside of each pot then take some pieces of clingfilm approximately 10 inches (25 cm) in length and push them inside the pots then, using a clean pastry brush, push it into the sides and base, making sure it overlaps at the rim.

After that you can make the creams. First measure 3 tablespoons of the single cream into a small dish and sprinkle the gelatine into this. Stir it around then leave it for about 10 minutes until it has soaked into the cream. Meanwhile heat the sugar and remaining cream very gently in a small saucepan until all the sugar crystals have dissolved (you can see this quite clearly if you coat the back of a wooden spoon). Now add the soaked gelatine to the pan, remove it from the heat and whisk this until all the gelatine has melted. Then leave it on one side to cool slightly.

Next spoon the Mascarpone into a large bowl and whisk it down to soften it, then add the yoghurt and vanilla. Whisk again, then when everything is smooth pour the cream and gelatine through a sieve into the bowl and mix once more. Now pour the mixture into the little pots, filling them to within ½ inch (1 cm) of the tops. Cover each pot with a little extra clingfilm, place them on a tray and leave in the fridge until well chilled and set – at least 3 hours.

To make the caramel sauce, put the granulated sugar into a medium frying pan over a very gentle heat. When the sugar has melted and the granules have dissolved, turn the heat up to high so the liquid begins to bubble and darken. Stir and simmer until the mixture becomes the colour of dark honey. This will probably take 7–8 minutes but watch it carefully as it only takes a few seconds to change from caramel to burnt sugar! Take the pan off the heat and add the 2 tablespoons of hot water. This will make it bubble and splutter but it *will* die down. Now spoon 2 tablespoons of caramel into a bowl. Add the cream and vanilla to the remaining caramel in the pan and then pour that into a serving jug for later. Dip the hazelnuts in the bowl containing the caramel a few at a time to get them coated, then spread them on a tray lined with silicone paper and leave them to harden.

To serve the creams: remove them from the fridge about half an hour before serving, take the top layer of clingfilm away, turn each pot out onto individual serving plates and gently pull the edges of the clingfilm used to line the pot. Then spoon the sauce over and garnish with the nuts.

Tiramisu

SERVES 6

There isn't a classic recipe for Tiramisu as such, as there are many varying versions both in Italy and around the world, but the following one is I think the nicest I've come across. For lovers of strong coffee, dark chocolate and the rich creaminess of Mascarpone it is one of the nicest, easiest and most popular desserts of the party season.

3 x size 1 egg yolks
2 oz (50 g) caster sugar
1 x 250 g tub Mascarpone (Italian cream cheese)
2 x size 1 egg whites
5 fl oz (150 ml) very strong espresso coffee
3 tablespoons dark rum

About 24 sponge fingers (or boudoir biscuits)
2 oz (50 g) dark continental chocolate, with 75% cocoa solids, chopped
1 level dessertspoon/tablespoon cocoa powder

You will also need 6 stemmed glasses, approximately 7-fl oz (200-ml) capacity.

First put the egg yolks into a medium-sized bowl together with the sugar and beat with an electric hand whisk on high speed for about 3 minutes or until the mixture forms a light, pale mousse. In a separate large bowl stir the Mascarpone with a wooden spoon to soften it, then gradually beat in the egg yolk mixture. Between each addition beat well until the mixture is smooth before adding more. Now wash and dry the beaters of the whisk so they are perfectly clean, then in a third separate bowl whisk the egg whites until they form soft peaks. Now lightly fold this into the Mascarpone mixture and then put the bowl to one side.

Next break the biscuits in half, then pour the coffee and rum into a shallow dish and then dip the sponge fingers briefly into it, turning them over – they will absorb the liquid very quickly. Now simply layer the desserts by putting 3 of the soaked sponge halves into each glass, followed by a tablespoon of Mascarpone mixture and a layer of chopped chocolate. Repeat the whole process, putting 5 halves in next, followed by the Mascarpone, finishing with a layer of chopped chocolate and a final dusting of cocoa powder. Cover the glasses with clingfilm then chill in the refrigerator for several hours and serve straight from the fridge – I think it tastes better very cold.

───────◇───────

Tiramisu

Apple Crêpes with Calvados

SERVES 6

Calvados has all the concentrated flavour and aroma of an apple loft and it is a wonderful store-cupboard cooking ingredient, but if you don't have any Calvados you can make this recipe using strong cider. Either way you end up with a mouthwatering combination of apples, pancakes and cinnamon – made even more special if served with some well-chilled cream laced with Calvados (or cider).

2 oz (50 g) plain flour
1 oz (25 g) buckwheat flour
1 level teaspoon ground cinnamon
2 x size 1 eggs
1 x 200 ml tub crème fraîche
1 large Granny Smith apple
2 tablespoons Calvados

TO MAKE THE PANCAKES:
2 oz (50 g) melted butter

TO SERVE:
Caster sugar
2 tablespoons Calvados
Double cream, well chilled

You will also need a small, solid frying pan.

Begin by peeling and coring the apple then cut it into quarters and grate it on the coarse side of the grater into a bowl. Then toss the grated apple around in 2 table-spoons of Calvados and leave it aside for 10 minutes. Meanwhile sift the flour, buckwheat flour and cinnamon into a bowl. Then in a separate bowl or jug, whisk the eggs and crème fraîche together, then gradually whisk this into the flour mixture using an electric hand whisk until you have a smooth, lump-free batter. Then stir in the apple and Calvados.

Before you make the pancakes put a large plate in a warm oven or a warming-drawer so that as you make them they can be kept warm, covered with some foil.

To make the pancakes, melt the butter in the frying pan, then tip it into a cup. To make your first pancake, heat the pan over a medium heat until it is really hot then use 1 tablespoon of the batter to make each pancake, cook until it becomes crisp at the edges and is a lovely golden colour underneath, then, using a palette knife or spatula, turn the crêpe over and cook the other side until crisp and gold-en (this should take about 45 seconds on each side). Remove the crêpe to a warm plate. Use a wodge of kitchen paper to lubricate the pan again with melted but-ter, then continue cooking the pancakes until the batter is all used up. When you are ready to serve the pancakes, transfer them to warmed serving plates, giving each person three or four, lightly dusted with caster sugar. Then combine the cream and Calvados, put a little on each serving and hand the rest round sepa-rately. For a special occasion you could flame these by leaving them piled on a large plate, dusting with caster sugar, then warming 3 tablespoons of Calvados in a small pan – light it with a match and pour the flaming Calvados over the pan-cakes. When the flame has died down serve each person three or four pancakes with pouring cream, served separately.

Classic Crêpes Suzette

SERVES 6

This is another qualifier for my sixties recipe revival. There was a time when this recipe was certainly overexposed, but now that it has become a forgotten rarity, we can all re-appreciate its undoubted charm which remains in spite of changes in fashion.

FOR THE CREPES:

1 quantity basic pancake batter (see page 179), with the addition of the grated zest of 1 medium orange and 1 tablespoon caster sugar mixed into the batter

FOR THE SAUCE:

5 fl oz (150 ml) orange juice (from 3–4 medium oranges)

Grated zest of 1 medium orange

Grated rind and juice of 1 small lemon

1 tablespoon caster sugar

3 tablespoons Grand Marnier, Cointreau or brandy

2 oz (50 g) unsalted butter

A little extra Grand Marnier for flaming

You will also need a solid-based 10-inch (25-cm) frying pan.

These little crêpes should be thinner than the basic pancakes, so when you're making them as described on page 179 with the above additions to the batter, use only 1½ tablespoons of batter at a time in a 7-inch (18-cm) pan. If they look a bit ragged in the pan, no matter because they are going to be folded anyway. You should end up with 15–16 crêpes.

For the sauce, mix all the ingredients – with the exception of the butter – in a bowl. At the same time warm the plates on which the crêpes are going to be served. Now melt the butter in the frying pan, pour in the sauce and allow it to heat very gently. Then place the first crêpe in the pan and give it time to warm through before folding it in half and then half again to make a triangular shape. Slide this onto the very edge of the pan, tilt the pan slightly so the sauce runs back into the centre, then add the next crêpe. Continue like this until they're all re-heated, folded and well soaked with the sauce.

You can flame them at this point if you like. Heat a ladle by holding it over a gas flame or by resting it on the edge of a hotplate, then, away from the heat, pour a little liqueur or brandy into it, return it to the heat to warm the spirit, then set light to it. Carry the flaming ladle to the table over the pan and pour the flames over the crêpes before serving on the warmed plates.

———————◇———————

Chocolate Mascarpone Cheesecake with Fruit and Nuts served with Crème Fraîche

SERVES 6–8

This is quite simply a chocolate cheesecake to die for. If you like chocolate, if you like dark chocolate with fruit and nuts and if you like luscious, velvet-textured Mascarpone...need I say more? (See photograph on pages 196–7.)

FOR THE BASE:

4 oz (110 g) sweet oat biscuits

1 oz (25 g) butter, melted

1 x 2 oz (50 g) pack chopped toasted hazelnuts

FOR THE FILLING:

1 x 250 g tub Mascarpone (Italian cream cheese)

1 x 200 g tub fromage frais (8% fat)

3½ oz (100 g) dark continental chocolate, with 75% cocoa solids

2 x size 1 eggs

1½ oz (40 g) caster sugar

2 oz (50 g) raisins

4 oz (110 g) whole hazelnuts

FOR THE CHOCOLATE CURLS TO DECORATE:

3½ oz (100 g) dark continental chocolate with 75% cocoa solids

TO SERVE:

1 teaspoon cocoa powder

Crème fraîche or pouring cream

You will also need a 7-inch (18-cm) cake tin, preferably springform, with a depth of 3 inches (7.5 cm); if shallower than this, line the sides with baking parchment.

Pre-heat the oven to gas mark 6, 400°F (200°C).

Before embarking on a baked cheesecake remember that, to prevent cracking, it's best cooled slowly in a switched-off oven. So you also need to make it well ahead.

First of all place the whole hazelnuts into the oven and toast to a golden brown; use a timer and have a look after 5 minutes, giving them 5 extra if they need it. Then remove them from the hot tray to cool. Meanwhile, make the base of the cheesecake by crushing the biscuits with a rolling pin – not too finely, though, as it's nice to have a fairly uneven texture. Scoop all the crushed biscuit crumbs into a bowl then add the chopped nuts and melted butter and mix everything very thoroughly before packing into the base of the cake tin, pressing it very firmly all over. Now place the tin in the oven and pre-bake the crust for 20 minutes. Then remove it and let it cool while you make the filling. Reduce the oven temperature to gas mark 2, 300°F (150°C).

Previous page: Chocolate Mascarpone Cheesecake with Fruit and Nuts served with Crème Fraîche

To make the filling, first place 2 inches (5 cm) of water into a saucepan, then put the saucepan on to heat and meanwhile break the chocolate into small squares and place this into a basin. As soon as the water is boiling remove the pan from the heat and place the bowl on top until everything melts. Don't be tempted to put the bowl on top of the saucepan while the water is still boiling – because of the high cocoa solid content this chocolate mustn't get overheated or it will separate. Now spoon the Mascarpone and fromage frais into a large bowl and whisk them together until smooth, preferably with an electric hand whisk. Then add the eggs and sugar and give it another good whisking before adding the melted chocolate – use a rubber spatula so that you get every last bit of chocolate from the basin – and then lightly fold the chocolate into the egg mixture. Finally add the raisins and toasted hazelnuts.

Now pour the mixture into the tin, smoothing it out with the back of a spoon, then place it on the centre shelf of the oven and bake for 1¼ hours. After that turn the oven off, but leave the cheesecake inside until it's completely cold.

FOR THE CHOCOLATE CURLS

Melt the chocolate as before, then pour it onto a flat, smooth surface. The underside of a large plate will do. It should form a circle of about 6 inches (15 cm) diameter and ¼ inch (5 mm) thick. Place the plate into the fridge to chill for 45 minutes. What you want is the chocolate to be set hard enough so that if you press the surface of the chocolate it doesn't leave an indentation.

Now take it from the fridge, and if you want curls like those in our photograph use a cheese slicer, otherwise a sharp knife will do if you hold the blade in both hands. Just pull it all along the chocolate towards you and it should curl up. What is very important to know here is that if it doesn't curl and you end up with a pile of chocolate shavings they'll look just as nice – either way, place them in a rigid plastic container and then put this in the fridge until you need them.

To serve the cheesecake, sprinkle the surface with chocolate curls, dust with a sprinkling of cocoa powder and serve in slices with crème fraîche or cream handed round separately.

CHAPTER ELEVEN

———————————◇———————————

PROPER PUDDINGS

---◇---

*I*n my attempt to revive Sunday lunch I am including proper, old-fashioned British puddings here. Whatever your views on health and diet, Sunday *is* a feast day, and the joy of cooking and eating a proper pudding must increase our sense of well-being, and that surely has to be a healthy thing.

If you enjoyed the little Sticky Toffee Puddings in the *Christmas* book, I can promise you will love the little Sticky Gingerbread Puddings with Ginger Wine and Brandy Sauce in this chapter (see page 202), which can also be made well in advance and frozen. And if you really want to spoil your family and friends, do get the hang of making proper custard: it isn't difficult and with the addition of a little cornflour to stabilize it, it will never curdle.

I doubt if anyone anywhere does not love bread and butter pudding, and I've included two here – one made with dark chunky marmalade on page 211 and the other a very sophisticated chocolate version on page 208. Both are to die for.

Steamed Treacle Sponge Pudding

SERVES 6–8

If the winter weather is getting you down or you're feeling grey or sad, I'm certain a steamed treacle sponge will put you right in no time at all. It takes moments to prepare, will steam away happily all by itself without needing attention, and is the ultimate in comfort foods.

3 tablespoons golden syrup
6 oz (175 g) self-raising flour
1 rounded teaspoon baking powder
6 oz (175 g) softened butter
3 x size 1 eggs
6 oz (175 g) soft light brown sugar
1 tablespoon black treacle

TO SERVE:

3 extra tablespoons golden syrup
Custard or crème fraîche

You will also need a well-buttered 2-pint (1.2-litre) pudding basin, and a double sheet of foil measuring 16 x 12 inches (40 x 30 cm).

First of all butter the basin then measure 3 tablespoons of golden syrup into it (grease the spoon first). Now take a large mixing bowl, sift the flour and baking powder into it, add the softened butter, eggs, sugar and black treacle. Then use an electric hand whisk (or a large fork and a lot of elbow grease) and beat the mixture for about 2 minutes until it's thoroughly blended.

Now spoon the mixture into the basin, use the back of a spoon to level the top, then place the foil over, making a pleat in the centre. Then pull it down the outside of the basin and tie the string round the rim, taking it over the top and tying it on the other side to make yourself a handle for lifting. Then trim off the excess foil all the way round. Now place the pudding in a steamer fitted over a saucepan of boiling water and steam the pudding for 2 hours, checking the water level halfway through.

To serve, loosen the pudding all round using a palette knife, invert it onto a warmed plate and pour another 3 tablespoons of extra syrup (warmed if you like) over the top before taking it to the table. Serve with custard or some well-chilled crème fraîche.

———————◇———————

Sticky Gingerbread Puddings with Ginger Wine and Brandy Sauce

SERVES 8

For quite a long time now I've been trying to come up with an idea that matches the charm and popularity of the Sticky Toffee Pudding in the 'Christmas' book. This is quite definitely it – it has the same degree of lightness and this time the fragrance and spiciness of preserved ginger, which takes the edge off the sweetness beautifully. (See photograph on pages 204–5.)

4 oz (110 g) preserved ginger in syrup (8 pieces)
6 oz (175 g) self-raising flour
⅓ teaspoon ground cinnamon
⅓ teaspoon ground cloves
¼ teaspoon ground ginger
½ level teaspoon baking powder
¾ level teaspoon bicarbonate of soda
2 x size 1 eggs
3 oz (75 g) soft butter
4 oz (110 g) molasses sugar
1 tablespoon black treacle
1 heaped teaspoon freshly grated ginger
6 oz (175 g) Bramley apple, peeled, cored and chopped small
6 fl oz (175 ml) warm water

FOR THE GINGER WINE AND BRANDY SAUCE:

6 oz (175 g) soft dark brown sugar
4 oz (110 g) unsalted butter
4 tablespoons ginger wine
2 tablespoons brandy
2 pieces preserved ginger, chopped small

TO SERVE:

Chilled pouring cream

You will also need 8 x 6-fl oz (175-ml) pudding basins, well buttered, and a solid baking sheet.

Pre-heat the oven to gas mark 4, 350°F (180°C).

First of all place the pieces of preserved ginger in a food processor and turn the motor on for about 7–10 seconds. Be careful not to process for too long – the ginger should be chopped small, but not puréed! After that sift the flour, spices, baking powder and bicarbonate into a mixing bowl. Then add the eggs, butter and sugar. The way to deal with the treacle is to grease the spoon first and, using a spatula or another spoon, push it into the bowl to join the rest of the ingredients. Now add the freshly grated ginger, then using an electric hand whisk, whisk everything together gradually, adding the water until you have a smooth mixture. Finally fold in the apple and preserved ginger.

Now divide the mixture between the buttered pudding basins, stand them on a baking sheet and bake in the centre of the oven for 35 minutes or until they feel firm and springy to the touch. After that remove them from the oven and let them stand for about 5 minutes, then run a small palette knife around the edges of the tins and turn them out. Allow the puddings to get completely cold and keep them wrapped in clingfilm until you need them.

To make the sauce, all you do is gently melt together the sugar and butter until all the granules of sugar have completely dissolved, then whisk in the ginger wine and brandy, add the chopped ginger and the sauce is then ready to serve.

To serve the puddings: pre-heat the grill to its highest setting and arrange the puddings on a heatproof dish or tray. Spoon the sauce over, making sure that no little bits of ginger are actually on the top of the puddings, then place the whole thing under the grill so that the tops of the puddings are about 5 inches (13 cm) from the source of heat. Now allow them to heat through – this will take about 8 minutes, by which time the tops will be slightly crunchy and the sauce will be hot and bubbly. Serve with chilled pouring cream.

NOTE: If you want to make these puddings in advance, they freeze beautifully, and after de-frosting should be re-heated as above.

———————————— ◇ ————————————

*Next page: Sticky Gingerbread Puddings
with Ginger Wine and Brandy Sauce*

Apple Sponge Puddings with Mincemeat Topping and Real Custard

SERVES 6

*S*omehow it's more elegant to serve little individual puddings if you are entertaining. These are incredibly light and fluffy with chunks of apple in them that become soft and squidgey during the steaming. My thanks to Sister Lucy at St. Joseph's Rearsby for giving me the original recipe.

5 oz (150 g) self-raising flour
4 oz (110 g) softened butter
4 oz (110 g) caster sugar
1 level teaspoon baking powder
A pinch of salt
1 medium Bramley apple, left unpeeled and chopped small
Zest of 1 lemon, grated
2 x size 1 eggs

3 heaped tablespoons mincemeat, preferably home-made
1 tablespoon brandy

You will also need 6 x 6-fl oz (175-ml) capacity aluminium pudding basins or a 1¾-pint (1-litre) capacity pudding basin, well buttered, and a steamer, plus 6 pieces of aluminium foil measuring 6 x 8 inches (15 x 20 cm).

First of all sift the flour, salt and baking powder into a large bowl, then simply add the softened butter, caster sugar and eggs, and whisk, preferably with an electric hand whisk, until you have a soft, smooth, creamy mixture (about 2 minutes). After that, lightly fold in the chopped apple and half the lemon zest.

Next spoon the mincemeat into a small bowl and add the brandy and the other half of the lemon zest. Stir them together then divide the mincemeat equally between the little pots and spoon the pudding mixture on top, smoothing it out with the back of a spoon. You'll need to leave a space of about ½ inch (1 cm) to allow the puddings to rise. Now place a square of foil onto each pudding, making a pleat in the centre, then fold in the edges of the foil all the way around the edge of the basin. Now place the steamer over a saucepan filled with boiling water. Put three puddings in, then loosely place a piece of crumpled foil on top, and put the other three puddings on top of that. Now place a well-fitting lid on the steamer and let the puddings steam for 1 hour, topping up with more boiling water if it needs it. Before serving allow the puddings to stand for 15 minutes before turning them out on to warm serving plates. Serve with real custard sauce.

NOTE: If you want you can make this as one large pudding and steam for 2½ hours, using a 1¾-pint (1-litre) pudding basin.

Real Custard Sauce

MAKES 1½ PINTS, 850 ML (ENOUGH FOR 6 PEOPLE)

*P**roper custard is a treat for special occasions, and if you really want to push the boat out you can use double or whipping cream in place of single.*

1 pint (570 ml) single cream	**5 x size 1 egg yolks**
8 fl oz (225 ml) milk	**1½ oz (40 g) caster sugar**
1 vanilla pod	**2 level teaspoons cornflour**

First of all take a saucepan and slowly heat the cream and milk together, with the vanilla pod added, until the liquid just reaches simmering point. Then take it off the heat and allow the vanilla to infuse for about 15 minutes.

Meanwhile, whisk the egg yolks, sugar and cornflour together in a large bowl. After 15 minutes remove the vanilla pod (you can wipe it dry and use it again), then whisk the milk and cream gradually into the egg mixture. Now pour everything back into the pan and over a gentle heat, still whisking the whole time, allow the mixture gently to come back to a simmer – by which time it will have thickened. If it looks at all grainy, don't worry, it will always regain its smoothness when cooled and whisked. Serve the custard either warm or well chilled.

If you want to make it in advance and keep it hot, just put the custard in a bowl and place it over a pan of hot water with clingfilm resting on the surface until you are ready to serve it.

◇

Chocolate Bread and Butter Pudding

SERVES 6

I have to thank Larkin Warren for her original recipe from her restaurant, Martha's Vineyard, which I have adapted. It is quite simply one of the most brilliant hot puddings ever invented. It's so simple but so good – and even better prepared two days in advance. Serve in small portions because it is very rich. Though I doubt if there will be any left over, it's also wonderful cold.

9 slices, each ¼ inch (5 mm) thick, good quality white bread, 1 day old, taken from a large loaf

5 oz (150 g) dark continental chocolate with 75% cocoa solids

15 fl oz (425 ml) whipping cream

4 tablespoons dark rum

4 oz (110 g) caster sugar

3 oz (75 g) butter

A good pinch cinnamon

3 x size 1 eggs

TO SERVE:
Double cream, well chilled

You will also need a shallow ovenproof dish 7 x 9 inches (18 x 23 cm) base x 2 inches (5 cm) deep, lightly buttered.

Begin by removing the crusts from the slices of bread, which should leave you with approximately 9 x 4-inch (10-cm) squares. So now cut each slice into 4 triangles. Next place the chocolate, whipping cream, rum, sugar, butter and cinnamon in a bowl set over a saucepan of barely simmering water, being careful not to let the bowl touch the water, then wait until the butter and chocolate have melted and the sugar has completely dissolved. Next remove the bowl from the heat and give it a really good stir to amalgamate all the ingredients.

Now in a separate bowl, whisk the eggs and then pour the chocolate mixture over them and whisk again very thoroughly to blend them together.

Then spoon about a ½-inch (1-cm) layer of the chocolate mixture into the base of the dish and arrange half the bread triangles over the chocolate in overlapping rows. Now pour half the remaining chocolate mixture all over the bread as evenly as possible then arrange the rest of the triangles over that, finishing off with a layer of chocolate. Use a fork to press the bread gently down so that it gets covered very evenly with the liquid as it cools.

Cover the dish with clingfilm and allow to stand at room temperature for 2 hours before transferring it to the fridge for a minimum of 24 (but preferably 48) hours before cooking. When you're ready to cook the pudding, pre-heat the oven to gas mark 4, 350°F (180°C). Remove the clingfilm and bake in the oven on a high shelf for 30-35 minutes, by which time the top will be crunchy and the inside soft and squidgey. Leave it to stand for 10 minutes before serving with well-chilled double cream poured over.

◇

Chocolate Bread and Butter Pudding

Hot Citrus Pudding in its own Juices

SERVES 6

*T*his *delightful hot pudding full of fresh citrus flavours is very light and fluffy and has the advantage of emerging from the oven in a pool of its own sauce. Then all it needs is some chilled pouring cream.*

3 oz (75 g) softened butter	**Grated zest and juice of 2 limes**
6 oz (175 g) caster sugar	**7 fl oz (200 ml) milk**
3 x size 1 eggs, separated	You will also need a deep baking dish of 3-pint
3 oz (75 g) self-raising flour	(1.75-litre) capacity, well buttered.
Grated zest and juice of 1 orange	
Grated zest and juice of 1 lemon	Pre-heat the oven to gas mark 4, 350°F (180°C).

First take a large bowl and in it whisk the butter and sugar together until pale in colour – it won't go light and fluffy, but don't worry, it's because there is more sugar than butter. After that beat the egg yolks and whisk them into the mixture a little at a time. Next sift the flour and lightly fold it into the mixture, alternating it with the combined citrus juices, zests and lastly the milk.

Now in a clean bowl and using a washed and dried spanking-clean whisk, whisk the egg whites to the soft-peak stage and lightly fold those into the mixture. Don't worry that it might look a little curdled at this stage – it's supposed to. Now pour the mixture into the prepared dish and bake it on the middle shelf of the pre-heated oven for 50 minutes, by which time the top should be a nice golden brown colour.

Although this pudding is served hot, it is just as nice cold. Mind you, I doubt if there will be any left over.

———————◇———————

Chunky Marmalade Bread and Butter Pudding

SERVES 4–6

Is there anyone, anywhere who doesn't like bread and butter pudding? If you're a devoted fan, then this is bread and butter pudding as you've always known it but with the added extra of Seville orange marmalade, chunky candied peel and grated orange zest – a delightfully different combination, which produces another winning version of an old-time favourite. Bread and butter pudding is served a lot in restaurants nowadays, but none is as good as the home-made version, which for me has to have a crunchy top to contrast with a soft fluffiness inside. (See photograph on pages 240–1.)

6 slices white bread, from a good-quality large loaf, ½ inch (1 cm) thick with crusts left on
2 oz (50 g) softened butter
2 rounded tablespoons Seville orange marmalade (see page 242)
10 fl oz (275 ml) whole milk
2½ fl oz (60 ml) double cream
3 x size 1 eggs
3 oz (75 g) sugar
Grated zest of 1 large orange
1 level tablespoon demerara sugar

1 oz (25 g) candied peel, finely chopped

TO SERVE:
Crème fraîche or chilled pouring cream

You will also need a baking dish, base 7 x 9 inches (18 x 23 cm) and 2 inches (5 cm) deep, lightly buttered.

Pre-heat the oven to gas mark 4, 350°F (180°C).

First generously butter the slices of bread on one side, then spread the marmalade on 3 of these slices, and put the other 3 slices on top (buttered-side down) so you've got 3 rounds of sandwiches. Now spread some butter over the top slice of each sandwich and cut each one into quarters to make little triangles or squares.

Then arrange the sandwiches, butter-side up, overlapping each other in the baking dish and standing almost upright. After that whisk the milk, cream, eggs and sugar together and pour this all over the bread. Scatter the surface of the bread with the grated orange zest, demerara sugar and candied peel, then place the pudding on a high shelf and bake it for 35–40 minutes until it's puffy and golden and the top crust is crunchy.

Serve the pudding straight from the oven while it's still puffy, with either crème fraîche or chilled pouring cream.

CHAPTER TWELVE

◇

Back *to* HOME BAKING

———◇———

I well remember both my grandmother and mother having weekly 'baking days', an entire day spent in the kitchen producing cakes, apple pies and all sorts of tarts. All these would be cooled, then stored in large air-tight tins and each day at tea-time out would come something like a piece of jam sponge, an almond or jam tart or some fluffy butterfly cakes.

Now this tradition has died out; we count calories one minute and eat snack bars the next. So here I want to indulge a little in the pleasures of my childhood and suggest that, although batch-baking might be ruled out by the pressures of our modern lives, you can still take just one free Saturday afternoon, closet your-self in the kitchen and immerse yourself in some very rewarding home baking. If there's no rush and no pressure it can actually be very relaxing – put on some music, listen to the radio, or just be silent with your thoughts. Then watch the smiles of pleasure as the house is filled with a delicious aroma and everyone gets a tea-time treat.

American One-Crust Pie with Spiced Apples and Raisins

SERVES 6–8

*T*his is without doubt the easiest apple pie in the world. No special pie tins needed, no lids to be cut and fitted, no tiresome fluting of edges. It's also a beginner's dream because, somehow, the more haphazard the whole thing looks, the better.

FOR THE SHORTCRUST PASTRY:	¼ teaspoon ground cloves
8 oz (225 g) plain flour	1 level teaspoon ground cinnamon
2 oz (50 g) pure lard, at room temperature	3 oz (75 g) raisins
2 oz (50 g) butter, at room temperature	¼ whole nutmeg, grated
Cold water	2 oz (50 g) soft brown sugar
	FOR THE GLAZE:
FOR THE FILLING:	1 small egg, separated
1 lb (450 g) Bramley apples, peeled, cored and sliced	6 demerara sugar cubes, crushed
8 oz (225 g) Cox's apples, peeled, cored and sliced	

You will also need a solid baking sheet.

Make up the pastry by sifting the flour into a large mixing bowl then rubbing the fats into it lightly with your fingertips, lifting everything up and letting it fall back into the bowl to give it a good airing. When the mixture reaches the crumb stage, sprinkle in enough cold water to bring it together to a smooth dough that leaves the bowl absolutely clean. Give it a little light knead to bring it fully together, then place the pastry in a polythene bag in the fridge to rest for 30 minutes.

Meanwhile prepare the apples and all the other filling ingredients and mix them together in a bowl. After that, pre-heat the oven to gas mark 6, 400°F (200°C).

Then roll the pastry out on a flat surface to a round of about 14 inches (35 cm) in diameter: as you roll it, give it quarter-turns so that it ends up as round as you can make it. (Don't worry about ragged edges – they're fine.) Now carefully roll the pastry round the rolling pin and transfer it to the centre of a lightly greased baking sheet. To prevent the pastry getting soggy from the juice of the apples, paint it with the egg yolk over roughly a 10-inch (25.5-cm) inner circle – this forms a kind of waterproof coating.

Now simply pile the prepared fruit mixture in the centre of the pastry, then turn in the edges of the pastry. If any breaks, just patch it back again – it's meant to look ragged and interesting. Brush the pastry surface all round with the egg white, then crush the sugar cubes with a rolling pin and sprinkle over the pastry (the idea of using cubes is to get a less uniform look than with granulated).

Pop the pie on the highest shelf of the oven and bake for approximately 35 minutes, or until the crust turns golden brown. Remove from the oven and serve warm with chilled crème fraîche or ice cream.

Traditional Apple Pie with a Cheddar Crust and Mascarpone Nutmeg Ice Cream

SERVES 8

This is a huge family apple pie, which I often call 'More Apple Than Pie' as it has four pounds of apples in it. Putting Cheddar cheese in the crust gives it a lovely crisp, flaky texture without a strong cheese flavour. If you serve it still warm from the oven with some Mascarpone Nutmeg Ice Cream (see opposite) it tastes heavenly. (See photograph on pages 216–17.)

FOR THE PASTRY:

8 oz (225 g) plain flour

2 oz (50 g) butter, softened

2 oz (50 g) pure lard, softened

3 oz (75 g) mild Cheddar, coarsely grated

3 tablespoons cold water

FOR THE FILLING:

2 lb (900 g) Bramley apples

2 lb (900 g) Cox's apples

1 level tablespoon fine semolina

3 oz (75 g) caster sugar

12 whole cloves

1 x size 1 egg, beaten, to glaze

You will also need a rimmed metal pie dish, 9 inches (23 cm) in diameter and 1¼ inches (3 cm) deep, with sloping sides, and a solid baking sheet.

Pre-heat the oven to gas mark 7, 425°F (220°C).

First make the pastry. Sift the flour into a roomy bowl, holding the sieve up high to give it a good airing, then add the butter and lard cut into small pieces, rubbing the fat into the flour with your fingertips until it reaches the crumbly stage. Now add the grated Cheddar and enough of the water to make a soft dough that leaves the bowl clean. Then turn it out onto a board, knead it briefly and lightly, then wrap it in clingfilm and leave it to rest in the fridge for about 30 minutes.

Meanwhile peel, quarter and core the apples and then cut them into very thin slices straight into a bowl, mixing the two varieties together. Now is a good time to switch the oven on to pre-heat.

Next take a little less than half of the pastry and roll it out very thinly to approximately 12 inches (30 cm) in diameter to line the base and sides of the pie dish. Trim the edges and leave unused pastry aside for the trimming. Then scatter the semolina over the base of the pastry and after that pile in the apple slices, building up the layers closely and scattering in the sugar and cloves as you go. Then press and pack the apples tightly.

Now roll the remaining pastry out, again very thinly, to make the lid, this time 16 inches (40 cm) in diameter. Brush the rim of the base pastry with a little beaten egg and carefully lift the lid over the top. Press the edges together to get a good seal all round, then trim using a knife. Finally gather up the trimmings and re-roll them to cut out into leaf shapes. Make a small hole in the centre the size of a 10p piece (to allow the steam to escape) and arrange the leaves on top. Now using the back of a small knife 'knock up' the edges then flute them using your thumb and the back of a knife.

Finally brush the whole lot with beaten egg then place the pie on the baking sheet and bake on a high shelf for 10 minutes. After that reduce the temperature to gas mark 5, 375°F (190°C) and cook for a further 45 minutes or until it has turned a deep golden brown. Then remove the pie and allow it to stand for at least 20 minutes before serving.

Mascarpone Nutmeg Ice Cream

MAKES 1 PINT (0.5 LITRE)

This very easy ice cream is made with Mascarpone and has a rich, velvety texture. The freezing process seems to draw out the aromatic flavour of the nutmeg superbly, making it an absolute winner with apple pie.

3 fl oz (75 ml) whole milk	**1 x 250 g tub Mascarpone**
½ whole nutmeg	**(Italian cream cheese)**
2 x size 1 egg yolks	**1 x 200 g tub fromage frais (8% fat)**
1 level teaspoon cornflour	You will also need a shallow plastic freezer box
3 oz (75 g) caster sugar	of approximately 2 pints or 1 litre capacity.

Begin by placing the milk in a small saucepan, then, using either a nutmeg grater or the fine side of an ordinary grater, grate the nutmeg into the milk. Then place it on a low heat and let it come up to a gentle simmer. Meanwhile put the egg yolks, cornflour and sugar in a large bowl and whisk these together until light and creamy.

Now pour the hot milk over the egg mixture, still whisking away, then return the whole lot to the pan and bring it back to a gentle simmer, continuing to whisk the whole time to keep the mixture smooth. Then cover the pan and put on one side to cool.

After that whisk the Mascarpone and fromage frais together in another bowl, then combine this with the egg custard mixture, and whisk again to combine thoroughly. Now pour the mixture into the freezer box, put a lid on and place in the coldest part of the freezer for 2 hours or until the edges are frozen. Then remove and, using an electric hand whisk, blend the edges into the softer middle. Put the lid on and return to the freezer until completely frozen (about 6 hours). If you're using an ice-cream maker, freeze-churn according to the instructions. In either case, about 1½ hours before serving, remember to remove the ice cream to the main body of the fridge to soften enough to scoop easily.

Next page: Traditional Apple Pie
with a Cheddar Crust

Hot Cross Buns

MAKES 12

Hot cross buns cannot be dashed off quickly – they are best made when you have set aside some time to lock yourself in the kitchen, switch on the radio and lose yourself in a rewarding session of yeast cookery. Kneading the dough and watching it rise is all very satisfying, and then your family can enjoy all that fruity, spicy stickiness! Hot cross buns are a special occasion in themselves, so serve them still slightly warm from the oven and spread with best butter.

1 lb (450 g) strong plain white flour	**2 oz (50 g) butter, melted**
1 level teaspoon salt	
1 level teaspoon mixed spice	FOR THE CROSSES:
½ teaspoon cinnamon	**2 oz (50 g) plain flour**
½ teaspoon freshly grated nutmeg	**1½ tablespoons water**
2 x 6 g sachets easy-blend yeast	
2 oz (50 g) caster sugar	FOR THE GLAZE:
4 oz (110 g) currants	**2 tablespoons granulated sugar**
2 oz (50 g) chopped mixed peel	**2 tablespoons water**
5 fl oz (150 ml) hand-hot milk	
1½–2 fl oz (40–55 ml) warmed water	You will also need a greased baking sheet and a large polythene bag, lightly oiled.
1 x size 1 egg, beaten	

First of all sift the flour, salt, mixed spice, cinnamon and nutmeg into a mixing bowl. Then sprinkle in the yeast and caster sugar, followed by the currants and mixed peel. Mix everything together evenly. Then make a well in the centre and pour in the milk and water, followed by the beaten egg and melted butter.

Now mix everything to a dough, starting off with a wooden spoon and then using your hands when the mixture becomes less sticky. Because it is never possible to be exact with the liquid, as flour can vary, if you need to add a spot more water, do so – or if you find the mixture is getting too sticky, sprinkle in a bit more flour.

Then transfer the dough to a clean surface and knead it until it feels smooth and elastic – this will take about 6 minutes. After that place the dough back in the bowl and cover the bowl with clingfilm. Leave it in a warm place to rise – it will take about 1½ hours to double in size. If it takes longer than that, don't worry, just wait until the dough is double its original volume. Then, pressing the air out of it, reshape the dough.

Now divide it into 12 round portions and place them on the greased baking sheet, leaving plenty of room around each one. Use a sharp knife to make a cross on the top of each bun. Then leave them to rise again, covering them with an oiled polythene bag. This time they will take about 30 minutes.

While that's happening, pre-heat the oven to gas mark 7, 425°F (220°C) and make the crosses. Form a paste with the flour and water, then roll this out and cut it into ¼-inch (5-mm) strips. When the second rising time is up, brush the strips with water to make them stick and place them on top of the buns along the indentations you made earlier. Put the buns on a high shelf in the oven and bake them for about 15 minutes.

While they are cooking, make the glaze by slowly melting together the sugar and water over a gentle heat until all the sugar grains have dissolved and you have a clear syrup. As soon as the buns come out of the oven, brush them immediately with the glaze while they are still warm. If you want to make them ahead of time, it's quite nice just to warm them through again in the oven before eating. If you want to freeze them, they do freeze well – just remember to put on the glaze after defrosting and then warm the buns through in the oven.

———————————◇———————————

Cranberry and Orange One-Crust Pies

SERVES 6

I seem to have a craze at the moment for cooking everything in individual portions. I love individual steamed puddings and now I'm into making individual pies as well. These are dead simple to make, easy to serve and the rich, luscious flavour of the cranberries is extremely good.

FOR THE PASTRY:
6 oz (175 g) plain flour
3 oz (75 g) butter
Cold water

FOR THE FILLING:
1½ lb (700 g) cranberries
4 oz (110 g) sugar
Zest and juice of 1 orange
¼ teaspoon ground cloves
¾ teaspoon ground cinnamon
¾ teaspoon ground ginger
½ whole nutmeg, freshly grated

1 x size 1 egg yolk
9 teaspoons semolina

FOR THE GLAZE:
1 x size 1 egg white, lightly beaten
6 sugar cubes, crushed

TO SERVE:
Sifted icing sugar and crème fraîche

You will also need a solid baking sheet, lightly greased.

Pre-heat the oven to gas mark 6, 400°F (200°C).

First of all prepare the cranberries by placing them in a saucepan with the sugar, zest and juice of the orange and the spices. Bring everything up to simmering point then reduce the heat, cook for about 10 minutes or until the cranberries are soft. Then remove them from the heat and leave them aside to get cold.

If you are feeling lazy, make the pastry in a food processor, placing the flour and butter in the bowl and process until you have fine crumbs. Then add 3 tablespoons of cold water and process until the pastry just comes together, then gather it up into a ball and place it in a polythene bag in the fridge for 30 minutes to rest.

After that remove the pastry and divide it into 6 equal-sized pieces. Roll each piece into roughly a 7-inch (18-cm) circle – it doesn't matter how uneven it is. Then paint a 3½-inch (9-cm) circle in the centre with egg yolk and sprinkle 1½ teaspoons of semolina onto this circle. (The semolina is there to soak up any excess juices.)

Now divide the cranberries between the pastry circles, spooning them over the semolina and leaving a couple of tablespoons left over. Fold the edges of the pastry over them, leaving an uncovered area in the centre. Now pop the leftover cranberries in to fill any gaps. Next brush the pastry all over with the beaten egg white and sprinkle with the crushed sugar cubes. Then very gently place the pies (a fish slice is good for this) on a greased baking sheet and bake in the oven for about 15–20 minutes or until the pastry is golden brown.

Serve the pies warm from the oven with a dusting of icing sugar – and I like to serve them with large quantities of crème fraîche.

Quick Apricot, Apple and Pecan Loaf Cake

*I*f you've never made a cake in your life before, I promise you that you can make this one – whether you're male, female, age 6 or 106, it really is dead simple, but tastes so divine you would think it took oodles of skill. The only important thing to remember (as with all cakes) is to use the right-sized tin.

6 oz (175 g) no-soak apricots, each chopped in half	**2 x size 1 eggs, beaten**
	3 tablespoons milk
6 oz (175 g) cooking apple (1 medium apple), cut into ½-inch (1-cm) chunks with skins on	FOR THE TOPPING:
6 oz (175 g) pecan nuts	**4 cubes demerara sugar, roughly crushed**
A pinch of salt	**¼ teaspoon ground cinnamon**
1½ level teaspoons baking powder	
2 rounded teaspoons cinnamon	
4 oz (110 g) wholewheat flour	You will also need 1 x 2-lb (900-g) bread loaf
4 oz (110 g) plain flour	tin with a base measurement of 3½ x 6½ inches
4 oz (110 g) butter, at room temperature	(9 x 16 cm), lightly buttered.
6 oz (175 g) soft brown sugar	Pre-heat the oven to gas mark 4, 350°F (180°C)

First of all when the oven has pre-heated, spread the nuts out on a baking sheet and toast them lightly for about 8 minutes, using a timer so that you don't forget them. After that remove them from the oven to a chopping board, let them cool a bit, then chop them roughly.

Meanwhile, take a large mixing bowl, sift the salt, baking powder, cinnamon and both flours into it, holding the sieve up high to give the flour a good airing and adding the bran from the sieve to the bowl as well. Then simply add all the rest of the ingredients except the fruit and nuts. Take an electric hand whisk, begin to beat the mixture on a slow speed, then increase the speed to mix everything thoroughly till smooth before lightly folding in the apricots, apple and pecans.

When it's all folded in add a drop more milk if necessary to give a mixture that drops easily off the spoon when you give it a sharp tap, then pile the mixture into the tin, level the top and sprinkle on the crushed sugar cubes and cinnamon. Bake in the centre of the oven for 1¼–1½ hours or until the cake feels springy in the centre.

After that remove it from the oven, let it cool for about 5 minutes before turning it out onto a wire tray. Let it get completely cold before transferring it to a cake tin, which may not be needed if there are people around, as this cake tends to vanish very quickly!

◇

A Return to the Black Forest

SERVES 10–12

Though much debased by many frozen versions, the original Black Forest gâteau, way back in the sixties, was a delight: a soft, light concoction made with seriously dark chocolate and Morello cherries. So, here it is – still using the lightest base (no flour), baked flat, then rolled round a luscious filling and decorated with chocolate curls.

FOR THE BASE:
6 x size 1 eggs, separated
5 oz (150 g) caster sugar
2 oz (50 g) cocoa powder, sifted

FOR THE FILLING:
8 oz (225 g) dark continental chocolate with 75% cocoa solids
2 tablespoons water
2 x size 1 eggs, separated
1 x 1½ lb (680 g) jar pitted Morello cherries
2 tablespoons cherry brandy
8 fl oz (225 ml) double cream

FOR THE TOPPING:
3½ oz (100 g) dark dessert chocolate with 75% cocoa solids
1 tablespoon Morello cherry jam
A little cocoa powder

You will also need a Swiss roll tin 13 x 9 x ½ inch (32 x 23 x 1 cm), lined with baking parchment, cut and folded to give a depth of at least 1½ inches (4 cm).

Pre-heat the oven to gas mark 4, 350°F (180°C).

You can make the chocolate filling well ahead of time. To do this, break the pieces of chocolate into a basin and add the water. Now place the basin over a saucepan of barely simmering water, making quite sure the basin isn't actually touching the water. Then remove the pan from the heat and wait for the chocolate to melt before beating it with a wooden spoon until smooth.

Next beat the egg yolks, first on their own and then into the warm chocolate mixture. As soon as the mixture has cooled, whisk the egg whites to the soft-peak stage then gently cut and fold them into the chocolate mixture. Cover the bowl with clingfilm and leave it in the fridge until you're ready to use it, but for a minimum of an hour.

Drain the cherries in a sieve, discard the syrup, then place them in a shallow dish, spoon over the cherry brandy and leave aside till needed.

To make the base: first place the egg yolks in a bowl and whisk them with an electric hand whisk until they begin to thicken. Then add the caster sugar and continue to whisk, but be careful not to overdo this, as it can eventually become too thick – stop when it falls off the whisk in ribbons. Now fold in the sifted cocoa powder. Then, using a spanking-clean bowl and carefully washed and dried beaters, whisk the egg whites to the soft-peak stage. Then take 1 large spoonful, fold it into the chocolatey mixture to slacken it, and gently cut and fold in the rest of the egg whites.

Now pour the mixture into the prepared tin and bake the cake on the middle shelf of the oven for about 20 minutes or until it's springy in the centre. It will

look very puffy, but a little finger gently pressed into the centre should reveal that it is cooked. It's important not to overcook it, otherwise it will be difficult to roll.

Remove it from the oven and don't panic as it sinks down, because this is quite normal. Leave it until it's absolutely cold, then turn it out on a sheet of grease-proof paper which has been lightly dusted with sieved cocoa powder. Then carefully peel away the baking parchment.

Drain the cherries again in a sieve placed over a bowl to catch the liqueur and sprinkle all but 1 tablespoon of the liqueur all over the base. Next remove the chocolate filling from the fridge and, using a small palette knife, spread it carefully and evenly all over the surface of the base. Next whip the double cream softly, and spread this all over the chocolate filling, leaving a good 1-inch (2.5-cm) border all round to allow for it spreading, then lightly press the cherries into the cream.

Rolling this cake up is going to be a lot easier that you think. All you do is take hold of one edge of the greaseproof paper beneath it, lift it and, as you lift, the cake will begin to come up. Just gently roll it over, pulling the paper away as it rolls. If the cake itself cracks as you roll it, this is not a problem – it's all going to get covered in chocolate anyway!

Now to make the chocolate curls for the topping – don't worry, it's much easier than it sounds – all you do is melt the chocolate as before, taking great care not to overheat it, then pour it onto an upturned plate 6 inches (15 cm) in diameter. Then place in the fridge for about 45 minutes until it's set. The chocolate should be firm when you touch it. If it's too soft it won't make nice curls.

To make the curls use a cheese slicer, or a very sharp knife will do if you hold the blade with both hands. Start at one end and just pull the slicer or knife along the surface of the chocolate towards you until curls form. As you make the curls, place them in a plastic container, as they're much easier to handle later on if they're well chilled. Put the container in the fridge.

Now you can decorate the cake: spoon the cherry jam into a small saucepan, add the reserved tablespoon of liqueur from the cherries, warm it gently and then brush it all over the surface. Place the chocolate curls all over that. Finally, sift over a little cocoa powder to dust the surface lightly.

––––––––––––––––– ◇ –––––––––––––––––

Four Nut Chocolate Brownies

*I*f *you've never made brownies before, you first need to get into the brownie mode, and to do this stop thinking 'cakes'. Brownies are slightly crisp on the outside but soft, damp and squidgey within. I'm always getting letters from people who think their brownies are not cooked, so once you've accepted the description above, try and forget all about cakes.*

2 oz (50 g) dark continental chocolate, with 75% cocoa solids
4 oz (110 g) butter
2 x size 1 eggs, beaten
8 oz (225 g) granulated sugar
2 oz (50 g) plain flour
1 level teaspoon baking powder
¼ teaspoon salt

1 oz (25 g) each macadamia, brazil, pecan and hazelnuts

You will also need a well-greased oblong tin measuring 7 x 11 inches (18 x 28 cm), lined with baking parchment, allowing the paper to come 1 inch (2.5 cm) above the tin. Pre-heat the oven to gas mark 4, 350°F (180°C).

Begin by chopping the nuts roughly, not too small, then place them on a baking sheet and toast them in a pre-heated oven for 8 minutes exactly. Please use a timer here otherwise you'll be throwing burned nuts away all day! While the nuts are cooking, put the chocolate and butter together in a large mixing bowl fitted over a saucepan of barely simmering water, making sure the bowl doesn't touch the water. Allow the chocolate to melt, then beat it until smooth, remove it from the heat and simply stir in all the other ingredients until thoroughly blended.

Now spread the mixture evenly into the prepared tin and bake on the centre shelf of the oven for 30 minutes or until it's slightly springy in the centre. Remove the tin from the oven and leave it to cool for 10 minutes before cutting into roughly 15 squares. Then, using a palette knife, transfer the squares onto a wire rack to finish cooling.

———————◇———————

Four Nut Chocolate Brownies

Deep Lemon Tart

SERVES 6–8

I once spent a great deal of time trying every sort of lemon tart imaginable in order to come up with the definitive version. And here it is – thicker than is usual which, quite rightly I think, includes much more filling than pastry. If you want to serve it warm you can prepare everything in advance – and pour the filling in just before you bake it.

FOR THE PASTRY BASE:

6 oz (175 g) plain flour

1½ oz (40 g) icing sugar

3 oz (75 g) softened butter

A pinch of salt

1 x size 1 egg yolk
(reserve the white for later)

1 tablespoon water

FOR THE FILLING:

Zest of 6 lemons and 10 fl oz (275 ml) juice (about 6–8 lemons)

6 x size 1 eggs

6 oz (175 g) caster sugar

7 fl oz (200 ml) whipping cream

TO SERVE:

A little icing sugar and crème fraîche

You will also need a deep, fluted quiche tin with a loose base 9 inches (23 cm) round and 1½ inches (4 cm) deep, lightly oiled.

The best way to make the pastry is in a food processor. To do this add all the pastry ingredients (except the egg white) to the bowl and process until it forms a firm dough. Then turn it out and knead lightly before placing in a polythene bag and leaving in the fridge for 30 minutes to rest. To cook the pastry base, pre-heat the oven to gas mark 6, 400°F (200°C) and place a solid baking sheet inside to pre-heat as well. Now roll out the pastry as thinly as possible and carefully line the flan tin, pressing the pastry around the base and sides so that it comes about ¼ inch (5 mm) above the edge of the tin. Then prick the base with a fork and brush it all over with the spare egg white, which you should lightly beat first.

Bake on the baking sheet on the middle shelf for 20 minutes, then, as you remove it, turn the temperature down to gas mark 4, 350°F (180°C).

To make the filling, grate the zest from 6 of the lemons, and squeeze enough juice to give 10 fl oz (275 ml). Now break the eggs into a bowl, add the sugar and whisk to combine, but don't overdo it or the eggs will thicken. Next add the lemon juice and zest followed by the cream, and whisk lightly. Now pour it all into a 2-pint (1.2-litre) jug.

The easiest way to fill the tart is to place the pastry case on the baking sheet in the oven, and then pour the filling straight into the pastry (this avoids having to carry the tart to the oven and spilling it). Bake for about 30 minutes or until the tart is set and feels springy in the centre. Let it cool for about half an hour if you want to serve it warm. It's also extremely good served chilled. Either way, dust it with icing sugar just before serving and serve with well-chilled crème fraîche.

◇

Prune, Apple and Armagnac Cake with Almond Streusel Topping

*T*his is a cake that borders on being a dessert, and would be my choice for a celebration winter supper party, served warm with crème fraîche or whipped cream. If you are not a lover of Armagnac, the prunes also taste good soaked in port or Amaretto liqueur.

FOR THE PRUNES:

12 oz (350 g) ready-to-eat prunes (the ones without stones)

3 oz (75 g) caster sugar

5 fl oz (150 ml) water

3 fl oz (75 ml) port or Armagnac

FOR THE STREUSEL TOPPING:

3 oz (75 g) self-raising flour

1 oz (25 g) butter, at room temperature

3 oz (75 g) demerara sugar

2 oz (50 g) whole untoasted almonds, halved lengthways and shredded very finely

FOR THE CAKE:

3 oz (75 g) self-raising flour

½ teaspoon baking powder

2 oz (50 g) soft butter

1 oz (25 g) ground almonds

2 oz (50 g) caster sugar

1 x size 1 egg

2 tablespoons milk

2 oz (50 g) diced Bramley apple

TO FINISH:

Icing sugar

You will also need an 8-inch (20-cm) tin with a loose base, greased and lined with greaseproof paper.

Pre-heat the oven to gas mark 4, 350°F (180°C).

Although the ready-to-eat prunes are not supposed to need soaking, I prefer to soak them just the same (the advantage is having them ready-stoned). Start the recipe the night before you want to serve the cake by placing the prunes in a saucepan along with the sugar and water, and simmer them very gently for 15 minutes. After that drain them, discarding the cooking liquid, then place them in a bowl, add the Armagnac, stir well, cover and leave overnight.

When you're ready to make the cake, begin with the streusel topping: place the sifted flour and butter in a bowl and rub the butter in until the mixture becomes crumbly. Then add the sugar, mixing it in evenly, and after that sprinkle in 1 dessert-spoon of cold water and fork the mixture until it is coarse and lumpy. Now leave it to one side with the almonds.

The cake mixture is very simple indeed – all you do is sift the flour and baking powder into a bowl, add the rest of the ingredients (except for the apple), then, using an electric hand whisk or a wooden spoon and some old-fashioned elbow grease, beat the mixture together until smooth. After that, fold in the apple, then spoon the mixture into the prepared tin.

Now arrange the prunes all over the mixture, then fork the streusel topping over them and finally sprinkle the shredded almonds evenly over the surface. Place the cake on the centre shelf of the oven, bake it for 1 hour, and remove it from the oven. Then leave it in the tin for 30 minutes before turning it out to cool on a wire rack. Just before serving sift the icing sugar over the surface.

Iced Lemon Curd Layer Cake

*Y*ou couldn't get a more lemony recipe than this: layers of lemon-flavoured sponge, filled with home-made lemon curd and then a lemon icing for the finishing touch. It's wonderful.

6 oz (175 g) self-raising flour, sifted
1 level teaspoon baking powder
6 oz (175 g) butter at room temperature
6 oz (175 g) caster sugar
3 x size 1 eggs
Grated rind of 1 lemon
1 tablespoon lemon juice

FOR THE LEMON CURD:

3 oz (75 g) caster sugar

Grated zest and juice of 1 large juicy lemon

2 x size 1 eggs

2 oz (50 g) unsalted butter

FOR THE ICING:

2 oz (50 g) sifted icing sugar

Zest of 1 large lemon

2–3 teaspoons lemon juice

Prepare 2 x 7-inch (18-cm) sandwich tins, 1½ inches (4 cm) deep, by greasing them, lining the bases with greaseproof or silicone paper and greasing the paper too.

Pre-heat the oven to gas mark 3, 325°F (170°C).

Just measure all the cake ingredients into a mixing bowl and beat – ideally with an electric hand whisk – till you have a smooth, creamy consistency. Then divide the mixture evenly between the two tins and bake them on the centre shelf of the oven for about 35 minutes or until the centres feel springy when lightly touched with a little finger.

While the cakes are cooking, make the lemon curd. Place the sugar and grated lemon rind in a bowl, whisk the lemon juice together with the eggs, then pour this over the sugar. Then add the butter cut into little pieces, and place the bowl over a pan of barely simmering water. Stir frequently till thickened – about 20 minutes. You don't have to stay with it – just come back from time to time to give it a stir.

When the cakes are cooked, remove them from the oven and after about 30 seconds turn them out onto a wire rack. When they are absolutely cold – and not before – carefully cut each one horizontally into 2, using a sharp serrated knife. Now spread the curd thickly to sandwich the sponges together.

Then to make the icing, begin by removing the zest from the lemon – it's best to use a zester to get long, curly strips. Then sift the icing sugar into a bowl and gradually stir in the lemon juice until you have a soft, runny consistency. Allow the icing to stand for 5 minutes before spreading it on top of the cake with a knife, almost to the edges, and don't worry if it runs a little down the sides of the cake. Then scatter the lemon zest over the top and leave it for half an hour for the icing to firm up before serving.

———————————◇———————————

Iced Lemon Curd Layer Cake

Polenta and Ricotta Cake with Dates and Pecans

This is a very unusual cake, quite different in flavour and texture from anything else. It's Italian in origin and polenta (maize flour) gives it a sandy texture, while at the same time Ricotta cheese and Amaretto liqueur give a wonderful moistness. It also freezes very well, but as you won't have any left over you might as well make two – it's so dead easy!

6 oz (175 g) chopped dates	**8 oz (225 g) caster sugar**
2 oz (50 g) pecan nuts, roughly chopped	**4 oz (110 g) butter, melted**
3 tablespoons Amaretto	**7 fl oz (200 ml) tepid water**
1 x 250 g tub Ricotta	**1 level tablespoon demerara sugar**
7 oz (200 g) polenta (maize flour)	
7 oz (200 g) self-raising flour	You will also need an 8-inch (20-cm) loose-based tin lined with baking parchment.
1 rounded teaspoon baking powder	
1 heaped teaspoon ground cinnamon	Pre-heat the oven to gas mark 3, 325°F (170°C).

First of all place the dates in a small bowl, pour the liqueur over them and leave them to soak for 15 minutes. Then place the pecans on a baking tray and toast them for 8 minutes – use a timer so they don't get over-cooked. Now to make the cake, take a large mixing bowl and first sift in the two flours, baking powder and cinnamon. Keep the sieve held high to give the flour a good airing then tip the grains from the maize flour in to join the rest.

Next add the caster sugar, Ricotta, melted butter and water and whisk with an electric hand whisk until everything is thoroughly blended (about 1 minute). After that fold in the nuts, dates and the liqueur in which they were soaking.

Fold everything in thoroughly, spoon the mixture into the prepared tin and smooth the top with the back of a spoon. Now scatter the demerara sugar evenly over the surface, then pop the cake into a pre-heated oven on the middle shelf, where it will take between 1¾ and 2 hours to cook. When it's cooked it will feel springy in the centre when you make a very light depression with your little finger. If it's not cooked give it another 10 minutes and then do another test.

When the cake is ready remove it from the oven, allow it to cool in the tin for 15 minutes then remove it from the tin and leave it to cool completely on a wire rack. Store in an airtight tin.

———————◇———————

Rich Fruit Buttermilk Scones

MAKES 12 SCONES

These tempting little scones are so quick and easy to make that you can have them on the table in less than half an hour after you'd first thought about making them. Don't worry if you can't get buttermilk, just use ordinary milk.

8 oz (225 g) self-raising flour
1½ oz (40 g) caster sugar
A pinch of salt
3 oz (75 g) butter at room temperature
2 oz (50 g) mixed dried fruit
1 x size 1 egg, beaten

3–4 tablespoons buttermilk to mix
A little extra flour for dusting tops

You will also need a lightly greased baking sheet and a 2-inch (5-cm) cutter.

Pre-heat the oven to gas mark 7, 425°F (220°C).

Begin by sifting the flour and salt into a bowl and sprinkling in the sugar, then rub the butter in lightly until the mixture looks crumbly. Now sprinkle in the dried fruit, pour in the beaten egg and add 3 tablespoons of the buttermilk. Start to mix the dough with a knife and finish off with your hands – it should be soft but not sticky, so add more milk, a teaspoon at a time, if the dough seems too dry.

Next form the dough into a ball and turn it out onto a lightly floured working surface. Now roll it out very lightly to a round at least 1 inch (2.5 cm) thick, then cut the scones out by placing the cutter on the dough and giving it a sharp tap. Don't twist the cutter, just push the dough out, then carry on until you are left only with trimmings – roll these and cut an extra scone. Then place the scones on the lightly greased baking sheet and dust lightly with the extra flour.

Bake the scones in the top half of the oven for 10–12 minutes or until they are well risen and golden brown. After that remove them to a cooling tray and serve very fresh, split and spread with butter.

NOTE: Scones do not keep well so are best eaten on the day they're made. Any left over, however, will freeze perfectly well.

———————◇———————

Feta, Olive and Sun-Dried Tomato Scones

MAKES 12

These are lovely served as a snack or savoury at tea-time. They also go very well as a companion to any of the soups in the first chapter for lunch.

3 oz (75 g) Feta cheese, cubed small	**1½ teaspoons chopped fresh thyme**
10 pitted black olives, roughly chopped	**1 x size 1 egg**
2 oz (50 g) sun-dried tomatoes, drained of oil and chopped (reserve oil)	**2 tablespoons milk**
6 oz (175 g) self-raising flour	FOR THE TOPPING:
2 oz (50 g) wholewheat flour	**Milk for brushing**
¼ teaspoon baking powder	**2 oz (50 g) Feta cheese, crumbled**
¼ teaspoon cayenne pepper	
¼ teaspoon mustard powder	You will also need a 2-inch (5-cm) cutter and a small baking tray.
2 tablespoons extra virgin olive oil	
1 tablespoon oil from sun-dried tomatoes	Pre-heat the oven to gas mark 7, 425°F (220°C).

First sift the flours and baking powder into a large, roomy bowl, tip in any bran left in the sieve, then add the cayenne and mustard powder and, using a knife, work in the 2 tablespoons of oil, plus the oil from the sun-dried tomatoes. When the mixture looks like lumpy breadcrumbs stir in the chopped thyme, cubed Feta, sun-dried tomatoes and olives.

Now in a separate bowl beat the egg with 2 tablespoons of milk and add half this mixture to the other ingredients. Using your hands, gradually bring the mixture together to form a dough, adding more of the egg and milk as it needs it – what you should end up with is a dough that is soft but not sticky.

Now on a floured board, roll the dough out to a depth of 1 inch (2.5 cm). Then stamp out the scones using a 2-inch (5-cm) cutter, either plain or fluted. Put the cut-out pieces on a baking tray and brush them with the milk. Finally top each scone with crumbled Feta, and put the tray on the highest shelf of the oven to bake for 12–15 minutes or until they've turned a golden colour. Then remove them to a wire rack until they are cool enough to eat.

———————— ◇ ————————

INGREDIENTS UPDATE

One of the tasks of the cookery writer is to keep up to date with new ingredients and then pass on the information so that hopefully everyone everywhere will be able to get hold of them and be able to use them. This does initially cause disappointment because when a new ingredient is mentioned on television there can be such a rush for it and it can sell out, or it may not be widely available anyway. I feel it's worth the initial problem because eventually the more we ask for things, the more they will become available. The following is a list of ingredients in this book that you may particularly want to look out for.

PUY LENTILS

Unlike other pulses, lentils do not need pre-soaking. We have included these tiny grey slate-like lentils in quite a few recipes as they retain their shape and texture when they're cooked, without going mushy. Add them to a little sautéed onion and garlic, braise with wine or cider and serve as an accompaniment to meat or fish, or they're also very good in a salad. (See Warm Lentil Salad with Walnuts and Goats' Cheese, page 33; and Grilled Chicken with Lemon, Garlic and Rosemary, served with Puy Lentils, page 82.)

FLAGEOLET AND CANNELLINI BEANS

These tiny green unripe flageolets and the fully grown cannellini have a wonderful flavour. They are cheap, they help to bulk out meat and they are also very nutritious and filling. The other advantage is they are very good at absorbing the flavours of the dish (see Braised Lamb with Flageolet Beans, page 110, or Oxtail Braised in Guinness with Cannellini Beans, page 119). If you're serving these, there's no need to serve either rice or potatoes.

DRIED PORCINI MUSHROOMS

They may seem a little expensive but these Italian dried mushrooms have a wonderfully intense concentrated flavour, and you'll find very little goes a long way. They are always soaked first in a little boiling water, which itself becomes infused with the flavour so this can either be used in the recipe or kept aside for stock. Because we can rarely get hold of wild mushrooms, porcini are a must for every store cupboard.

PANCETTA

Pancetta is Italian cured streaky bacon, smoked or green, with a very fine concentrated bacon flavour. Pancetta Coppata is unsmoked and rolled up with a bit of shoulder ham giving the round slices. I use this a lot as it gives a much deeper flavour than bacon – it's fantastic in Spaghetti alla Carbonara (see page 31). Supermarkets now sell the sliced pancetta and also small cubes. In an Italian deli you can buy it in one piece.

CHOCOLATE

If you want to make the best chocolate dessert in the world, I've got the recipes, but you need to get the best chocolate. Look out for dark continental deluxe chocolate and check the amount of cocoa solids – 75% is the best as this gives all the concentrated flavour of chocolate, so it's really worth trying to hunt this down. Once you've used it you'll never go back to the normal chocolate with only 51%.

RICOTTA

Ricotta is Italian wheyed cheese, mostly used in fresh unripe form. It's white and creamy, with a slightly acidic dairy flavour that has a sweet edge. We've used it in Polenta and Ricotta Cake with Dates and Pecans, page 230; Lemon Ricotta Cheesecake with a Confit of Lemons, page 188; Vegetarian Moussaka with Ricotta Topping, page 102; and in Pancake Cannelloni with Spinach and Four Cheeses, page 89.

FONTINA

This is a beautiful cheese for cooking – it comes from the Alpine meadows of Valle d'Aosta in Italy. It's made from unpasteurized cows' milk and has all the melting quality of Mozzarella but with a richer, creamier flavour. The texture is rather like Swiss Gruyère, glossy and springy with random holes. We really need to keep asking for this one. We have used this in Roasted Pumpkin Soup with Melting Cheese, page 14.

CRANBERRIES

If I was teased about limes in the *Summer Collection*, I'm probably in for the same here, as I really don't feel we pay enough attention to cranberries. When the last of the autumn fruits have disappeared, November brings in a fresh crop of these dazzling scarlet berries with their rich juice and sharp flavour. So instead of just confining them to the Christmas turkey I have included them in several recipes for

you to try. We've also had great fun testing their freshness – to do this you bounce them, and the higher they bounce the fresher they are!

POLENTA

This is a very fine golden cornmeal from Italy which can be used on its own to make a type of maize porridge – a popular Italian staple. We have used it in a Polenta and Ricotta Cake with Dates and Pecans, page 230, which really does give a *different* texture. Polenta also makes a great alternative to flour both for cooking and as a coating instead of breadcrumbs.

MORELLO CHERRIES

In Britain it's hard to find fresh Morello cherries, but now thankfully they're available in dried form.. Because these cherries are sour they can be used with sugar without becoming too sweet and they give a lovely concentrated flavour. Look out too for some very high quality Morello cherry jam, as this again is not too sweet and can be used in a sauce for Roast Duck with Sour Cherry Sauce, see page 69. The third way to buy Morello cherries is in a jar and we have used these in A Return to the Black Forest on page 222.

SUN-DRIED TOMATO PASTE

This has all the deep concentrated flavour of sun-dried tomatoes in a dense textured paste which adds a lovely tomatoey flavour when added to recipes. I now use it quite often instead of the regular tomato paste. It should be becoming more widely available but again we need to keep asking.

ORIENTAL INGREDIENTS

JAPANESE

• Mirin is a sweet rice cooking wine, quite mild.

• Saké is a fortified rice wine, stronger and more powerful.

• Japanese rice vinegar is much softer and mellower than Chinese.

• Daikon, known as mooli radish, has twice the vitamin content of red radishes with a fresh peppery taste. It's long and white and is mostly grated. (See Teriyaki Steak on page 174.)

• Sansho pepper spice comes from the jacket of the prickly ash seed.

• Kikkoman soy sauce is a traditionally matured soy sauce, containing only roasted wheat soy beans, water and salt.

CHINESE

• Five-spice powder is a combination of star anise, fagara, cassia, fennel seed and cloves.

• Dried shrimps, available from oriental food shops, are tiny dried pink shrimps with a lovely concentrated shrimp flavour.

• Rice noodles are transparent noodles made from rice and need no cooking, just soaking.

• Star anise is a pretty star-shaped spice which has a very pungent aniseed flavour, so a little goes a long way.

THAI

• Fish sauce looks like medium sherry and is now becoming more widely available.

• Shrimp paste, available from Thai shops, is not pleasant to look at or to smell, but a little gives all the authentic flavour of Thai cooking.

• Kaffir lime leaves are small shiny leaves that come in twos like twins. These are now available in supermarkets and also in speciality supermarkets.

• Birdseye chillies: extremely hot! So for non-Thais only a few are needed.

• Palm sugar is a soft mellow sugar, but our light brown sugar can be used to replace it.

• Galangal is a first cousin of ginger and has a mild peppery flavour. It is also known as Thai ginger.

MORE CREME FRAICHE

No, I haven't got shares in it, but because it's such a wonderful ingredient and has slightly less fat than double cream, more flavour and a longer shelf life, I tend to use it most of the time. But if you prefer you can replace it with double cream in recipes.

For specialist ingredients in general Sainsbury's *Special Selection* has an exceptionally wide range for cooks. Stores that include this are listed on page 249.

CHAPTER THIRTEEN

MARMALADES *and* OTHER PRESERVES

———————◇———————

*E*very Sunday begins for me with a small but very significant luxury: really good marmalade on bread or toast. It makes a very cheery start to the day. And I emphasize really good marmalade, by which I mean proper home-made marmalade, which really is one of the world's great luxury foods. For, however good the shop-bought versions are, they can never match what can be made at home from just three simple ingredients – Seville oranges, water and sugar.

Why Seville oranges? Because they are bitter. If you cook sweet oranges with an equal amount of sugar, what you get is overpowering sweetness with only a background of orange flavour. On the other hand, when you combine the bitter ones with sugar, the predominant flavour is that of oranges. The Seville orange season is short, from December to February, so it's best to make enough marmalade for the whole year while they're available. But if you don't have the time, you can still put some by, as Sevilles do freeze perfectly well.

I have included two other marmalade recipes in this chapter, to ring the changes. I've also discovered three exciting new chutneys and a variation on Christmas mincemeat, using cranberries, which has now become my standard recipe.

———————————————

Spiced Cranberry Chutney

MAKES 2 x 0.5-LITRE JARS

*B*ecause the cranberry season is so short, it is a good idea to preserve some for later, and this cranberry and orange chutney makes a wonderful store-cupboard ingredient to use with pork, gammon or other cold cuts. It also has a fantastic colour, which adds a bit of brightness to a dull January day.

1 lb (450 g) fresh cranberries
14 oz (400 g) granulated sugar
1 teaspoon coriander seeds
10 fl oz (275 ml) red wine vinegar
7 fl oz (200 ml) cider vinegar

6 whole cloves
Zest and juice of 1 medium orange

You will also need 2 x 0.5 litre preserving jars, sterilized as described below.

First heat a large saucepan until it gets really hot at the base, then tip in the coriander seeds, shaking them around and watching them carefully. When they get hot and slightly brown they will start to 'jump' and dance and this will draw out their flavour. Then transfer them to a pestle and mortar and crush them coarsely. Now turn the heat to low, pour the wine vinegar and cider vinegar into the pan and stir, then add the sugar and cook, stirring with a wooden spoon until all the sugar crystals have dissolved. While that is happening, pare off the outer zest of the orange with a potato peeler and then cut into fine shreds, squeeze the juice from the orange and reserve it.

Now test to see if the sugar has dissolved by coating the back of a wooden spoon and if it has, bring the liquid back to a simmer and add the orange zest and juice, cloves, coriander and cranberries. Stir well, then simmer gently without a lid for 1 hour, stirring occasionally to prevent the mixture catching on the base. Be gentle with the stirring to avoid bursting berries – some will burst during the cooking but the chutney looks more attractive if the majority of berries remain whole in the jars.

When the cooking time is up remove the pan from the heat and leave the contents to stand for half an hour. By this time it will be cool enough to handle and the chutney can be ladled into sterilized jars, sealed and, when completely cold, labelled. Don't be tempted to eat the chutney for at least a month as it takes this long for it to mellow and develop.

NOTE: To prepare the jars, wash them thoroughly in warm soapy water, rinse and dry them, then place in a medium oven for 5 minutes to sterilize.

◇

Mango Chutney

MAKES 3 x 0.5-LITRE JARS

*I*t *gets more and more difficult to find mango chutney which has really visible chunks of mango all through it. So, since it is very easy to make, here is a recipe which includes large luscious chunks of mango. It is really good served with cold ham, poultry or game – or, of course, any kind of curry.*

8 mangoes, slightly under-ripe (total weight about 6 lb, 2.7 kg)
1½ lb (700 g) soft light brown sugar
1 teaspoon cumin seeds
2 heaped teaspoons coriander seeds
12 cardamom pods
1 teaspoon cayenne pepper
1 teaspoon ground turmeric
4 oz (110 g) fresh root ginger, grated

1 teaspoon ground cloves
32 fl oz (800 ml) malt vinegar
8 cloves garlic, crushed with 2 heaped teaspoons salt in a pestle and mortar
2 Spanish onions, finely chopped

You will also need a preserving pan or large wide saucepan, and 3 x 0.5-litre preserving jars, sterilized as described on page 237.

Begin this recipe a day ahead by preparing the mangoes. The easiest way to do this is to peel them using a potato peeler, then with a small sharp paring knife, cut wedges out of them, each about ½ inch (1 cm) thick. This is very easy – cut through to the large stone as if you were segmenting oranges, do it over a large bowl and let the pieces drop into it. If any of the flesh remains clinging to the stone, scrape it off to join the rest of the mangoes. Then sprinkle the sugar over the fruit in the bowl, turning it lightly to distribute the sugar evenly, then cover with clingfilm and leave it in a cool place overnight.

Next day begin by pre-heating a small frying pan then dry-roast the cumin, coriander and cardamom pods for a couple of minutes to draw out their full flavour. Then crush them with a pestle and mortar – the cardamom pods will separate from the seeds, but put the whole lot (pods as well) into the preserving pan together with all the other ingredients, including the mangoes and their syrup. Now bring everything up to a gentle simmer and let it simmer for about 3 hours, stirring from time to time, until the mango becomes translucent and the liquid has almost evaporated, leaving behind a thick syrup. You will need to do a bit more stirring from time to time at the end to prevent it catching.

After that remove the chutney from the heat, let it cool for 15 minutes then ladle it into warm sterilized jars, using a funnel. Seal whilst the chutney is still hot and label when cold. Now you're going to have to forget all about it for 8 weeks so that it can mellow and mature.

◇

Lemon and Lime Marmalade

MAKES 5 x 0.5-LITRE JARS

This is a very refreshing marmalade, good wake-up food on a dull morning. Its other advantage is that it can be made at any time of the year. Although this does need fast-boiling, the quantity is small enough for a modern hob (see page 242).

6 large thin-skinned lemons
6 limes
3 pints (1.75 litres) water
3 lb (1.35 kg) granulated sugar

You will also need a large lidded saucepan or preserving pan of 9-pint (5-litre) capacity; a piece of string, and a piece of muslin or gauze 12 inches (30 cm) square. Jars should be sterilized as described on page 237. You will need about 4 saucers to test for setting point.

Begin by measuring the water into a preserving pan, then cut the lemon and limes in half and squeeze the juice out of them. Add the juice to the water, and place the pips and any bits of pith that cling to the squeezer on the square of muslin (laid over a dish or cereal bowl first). Now cut the lemon and lime peel into quarters with a sharp knife, and then cut each quarter into thinnish shreds. As you cut, add the shreds to the water and any pips or spare pith you come across should go onto the muslin. The pith contains a lot of pectin so don't discard any, and don't worry about any pith and skin that clings to the shreds – it all gets dissolved in the boiling.

Now tie the pips, etc up loosely in the muslin to form a little bag, and tie this onto the handle of the pan so that the bag is suspended in the water. Then bring the liquid up to simmering point and simmer gently, uncovered, for 2 hours or thereabouts until the peel is completely soft – test a piece carefully by pressing it between your finger and thumb. Towards the end of the simmering time pre-heat the oven to gas mark 3, 325°F (170°C). Pour the sugar into a roasting tin lined with foil and place it in the oven to warm gently for 10 minutes. At this point pop the saucers into the freezing compartment of the fridge.

Next remove the bag of pips and leave it to cool on a saucer. Then pour the sugar into the pan and stir it now and then over a low heat until all the crystals have dissolved (check this carefully, it's important). Now increase the heat to very high, and squeeze the bag of pips over the pan to extract all of the sticky, jelly-like substance that contains the pectin. As you squeeze you'll see it ooze out. You can do this by placing the bag between two saucers or using your hands. Then stir or whisk it into the rest.

As soon as the mixture reaches a really fast boil, start timing. Then after 15 minutes take the pan off the heat and spoon a little of the marmalade onto one of the cold saucers from the fridge, and let it cool, back in the fridge. You can tell – when it has cooled – if you have a 'set' by pushing the mixture with your little finger: if it has a really crinkly skin, it is set. If not, continue to boil the marmalade and give it the same test at about 10-minute intervals until it does set.

After that remove the pan from the heat (if there's a lot of scum, most of it can be dispersed by stirring in half a teaspoon of butter, and the rest can be spooned off). Leave the marmalade to settle for 20 minutes before potting into jars. Label when completely cold.

Dark Chunky Marmalade

MAKES 7 x 0.5-LITRE JARS

*T*he problem with 20th-century marmalade-making is that today's hobs don't always oblige when it comes to getting large amounts of marmalade up to what old-fashioned cooks called a rolling boil, without which traditional marmalade stubbornly refuses to set. So when, in 1994, I tasted one of the best marmalades ever, I was thrilled to learn that the friend who had made it had cooked it long and slow – which solves the dilemma completely. Here is my version of Mary McDermot's original recipe, and it's the best I've ever tasted.

3 lb (1.35 kg) Seville oranges
2 lemons
5 pints (3 litres) water
6 lb (2.7 kg) granulated sugar

You will also need a preserving pan, a 15-inch (38-cm) piece of muslin or double gauze, a nylon sieve, some foil and 7 x 0.5-litre preserving jars, sterilized as described on page 237, and some small flat plates.

This recipe is extremely easy as long as you remember that it happens in *two* stages. So ideally begin the recipe one afternoon or evening and finish it the following morning.

So for stage 1: lightly scrub the fruit then place it in the preserving pan, add the water and bring it all up to a gentle simmer. Now take a large piece of double foil, place it over the top of the pan and fold the edges firmly over the rim. What needs to happen is for the fruit to very gently poach without any of the liquid evaporating. This initial simmering will take 3 hours.

After this remove the preserving pan from the heat and allow everything to get cool enough to handle. Then place a large colander over a bowl and, using a draining spoon, lift the fruit out of the liquid and into this. Now cut the oranges in half and scoop out all the inside flesh and pips as well, straight into a medium-sized saucepan. Next do the same with the lemons but discard the peel. Now add 1 pint (570 ml) of the poaching liquid to the fruit pulp, then place the saucepan over a medium heat and simmer for 10 minutes. Have ready a large nylon sieve, lined with gauze, and place it over a bowl, then strain the contents of the saucepan through the sieve. Leave it all like this while it cools and drips through.

While you are waiting for it to cool is a good time to deal with the orange peel. Cut the halves of peel into quarters then cut them into chunky strips – the thickness is up to you – according to how you like your marmalade. Add these back into the preserving pan.

When the pulp is cool what you need to do next is gather up the corners of the muslin and twist it into a ball, then, using your hands, squeeze all of the pectin-rich juices into the preserving pan. Don't be faint-hearted here – squeeze like mad so that every last bit of stickiness is extracted and you're left only with the pithy membranes of the fruit, which you can now discard. When you have added the strained pectin, just leave all of this overnight, loosely covered with a clean tea-cloth.

Previous page: Chunky Marmalade Bread and Butter Pudding
(see page 211) made with Dark Chunky Marmalade

Stage 2: the following day, empty the sugar into a large roasting tin lined with foil then place it in a warm oven, gas mark 3, 325°F (170°C), and allow it to warm gently for 10 minutes. Then place the preserving pan and its contents over a gentle heat and as soon as it starts to warm through tip the warmed sugar into the pan to join the rest.

Now, using a large wooden spoon, stir the marmalade, keeping the heat gentle, until all the sugar crystals have fully dissolved. What you must *not* do is let the marmalade boil until all the sugar is completely dissolved. Keep looking at the back of the wooden spoon as you stir and when you are sure there are no more crystals left turn up the heat and let the marmalade bubble away gently – it can take 3–4 hours for it to darken and develop its lovely rich flavour.

When the marmalade has been cooking for 2½ hours place some small flat plates in the fridge. Then to test for a set, after 3 hours draw the pan from the heat and spoon a teaspoonful of marmalade onto a chilled plate. Allow it to cool for a minute back in the fridge, then push it with your little finger – if a crinkly skin forms, it has reached setting point. If not, continue cooking and do more testing at 15-minute intervals. When it has set, leave the marmalade to cool for 30 minutes before ladling through a funnel into warm sterilized jars (see footnote on page 237). Seal the jars while they are hot, then label the next day when cold. Then, as soon as possible, make the Chunky Marmalade Bread and Butter Pudding on page 211. It's utterly divine!

––––––––––––––– ◇ –––––––––––––––

Suntina Marmalade

MAKES 2 x 1-LITRE OR 4 x 0.5-LITRE JARS

*S*untinas are available from mid-December to the end of February and have a charming tangerine flavour which makes a delightfully different marmalade, and I think the nice thing about having a choice of marmalades is you never get bored.

2¼ lb (1 kg) Suntina oranges
2 thin-skinned lemons
3 lb (1.35 kg) granulated sugar
3½ pints (2.1 litres) water

You will also need a large preserving pan, 2 x 1-litre or 4 x 0.5-litre preserving jars, sterilized as described on page 237, a 10-inch (25-cm) square of muslin and 3 small flat plates.

Begin by measuring the water into a preserving pan, scrub the fruit, then cut the oranges and lemons in half and squeeze the juice out of them. Add the juice to the water, then place the pips and any bits of pith that cling to the squeezer on the square of muslin (laid over a dish or cereal bowl). Now cut the peel into quarters with a sharp knife, and then cut each quarter into thinnish shreds. As you cut, add the shreds to the water, and any pips or spare pith you come across should go on the muslin. The pith contains a lot of pectin, so don't discard any and don't worry about any pith and skin that clings to the shreds – it all gets dissolved in the boiling.

Now tie up the pips and pith loosely in the muslin to form a little bag, and tie this onto the handle of the pan so that the bag is suspended in the water. Then bring the liquid up to simmering point and gently simmer, uncovered, for 2 hours or thereabouts until the peel is completely soft – test a piece by squashing it against the side of the pan. At this point pop the plates into the freezing compartment of the fridge.

Next remove the bag of pips and leave it to cool on a saucer. Then warm the sugar, as in the recipe on page 239, pour it into the pan and stir it now and then over a low heat until all the crystals have dissolved (check this carefully, it's important). Now increase the heat to very high and squeeze the bag of pips over the pan (you'll see the pectin ooze out). You can do this by placing the bag between two saucers or using your hands. Then stir or whisk it into the rest.

As soon as the mixture reaches a really fast boil, start timing. Then after 15 minutes remove the pan from the heat, spoon a little of the marmalade onto one of the cold plates from the fridge, and let it cool, back in the fridge. When it has cooled you can tell if you have a 'set' by pushing the mixture with your little finger – if it has a really crinkly skin, it is set. If not, continue to boil the marmalade and give it the same test at about 10-minute intervals until it does set. (If there's a lot of scum, most of it can be dispersed by stirring in half a teaspoon of butter, and the rest can be spooned off.) Leave the marmalade to settle for 20 minutes.

Finally pour the marmalade, using a funnel or a ladle, into the sterilized jars and cover with waxed discs and seal while still hot. Label the jars when quite cold.

———————— ◇ ————————

Home-made Christmas Mincemeat with Cranberries

MAKES 5 x 0.5-LITRE JARS

This is my own traditional recipe, but by replacing some of the apple with cranberries it is sharper and slightly different. This recipe always comes with a warning: once you have tasted home-made mincemeat you will never buy it again. In the past people used to have problems storing mincemeat because the high proportion of fruit oozed too much juice, and the juice started to ferment. In this recipe the mincemeat is placed in a barely warmed oven to let the suet melt gradually and, as this happens, it coats all the fruits and seals in all the juices.

1 lb (450 g) fresh cranberries	**Grated zest and juice of 2 lemons**
8 oz (225 g) Bramley apples, cored and chopped small (no need to peel them)	**2 oz (50 g) whole almonds, cut into slivers**
8 oz (225 g) shredded suet	**4 teaspoons ground mixed spice**
12 oz (350 g) raisins	**½ teaspoon ground cinnamon**
8 oz (225 g) sultanas	**A good grinding of fresh nutmeg**
8 oz (225 g) currants	**6 tablespoons brandy**
8 oz (225 g) whole mixed candied peel, finely chopped	
12 oz (350 g) soft dark brown sugar	You will also need 5 x 0.5-litre preserving jars,
Grated zest and juice of 2 oranges	sterilized as described on page 237.

All you do is combine the above ingredients, except for the brandy, in a large ceramic mixing bowl, stirring them and mixing them together very thoroughly indeed. Then cover the bowl with a clean tea-cloth and leave the mixture in a cool place overnight or for 12 hours, so the flavours have a chance to mingle and develop. After that pre-heat the oven to gas mark ½, 225°F (120°C), cover the bowl loosely with foil and place in the oven for 3 hours.

Then remove the bowl from the oven and don't worry about the appearance of the mincemeat, which will look positively swimming in fat – that's how it should look. As it cools, stir it from time to time so that everything gets a coating of melted suet. When the mincemeat is quite cold, stir in the brandy, then pack in sterilized jars (see footnote on page 237), cover with waxed discs and seal. It will keep in a cool, dark cupboard indefinitely, but I think it is best eaten within a year of making.

NOTE: Vegetarians can make this mincemeat happily, using vegetarian suet.

◇

Fresh and Sun-Dried Tomato Chutney

MAKES 4 x 0.5-LITRE OR 8 x 0.25-LITRE JARS

One of the delights of the winter months is being able to taste some of the fruits of summer. So it's good to find a little bit of space for pickling and chutney-making in the autumn. This one's an absolute winner, great for jazzing up sausages or hamburgers, and we love it spread on top of cheese for sandwiches – it also has a great affinity with any kind of toasted cheese.

8 oz (225 g) sun-dried tomatoes (not preserved in oil)

4 lb (1.8 kg) fresh tomatoes, halved, but no need to skin or de-seed

1 rounded dessertspoon whole coriander seeds

1 dessertspoon whole mustard seeds

4 fat garlic cloves, peeled

4 fresh red chillies, halved lengthways with seeds left in

4 large onions, quartered

2 large red peppers, de-seeded

8 oz (225 g) soft dark brown sugar

1 pint (570 ml) cider vinegar

1 rounded dessertspoon salt

You will also need a small preserving pan and jars as above, sterilized as described on page 237.

First of all rinse the dried tomatoes under running water to remove any dust or grit, then put them in a bowl and cover them with hot, not boiling, water and leave them to soak for about 20 minutes. Then heat a small heavy-based frying pan and dry-roast the coriander and mustard seeds over a medium heat, turning and stirring them round for 2 minutes to draw out their flavour. Then crush them together with a pestle and mortar, not very much – they just need to be broken up.

Now making the chutney is going to be a lot easier if you have a processor. In the past an old-fashioned mincer was used for chutneys; now a processor is even faster, but if you have neither then you just need to chop everything uniformly small.

First drain the dried tomatoes, add these to the processor, switch on and chop till roughly ¼ inch (5 mm) in size. Then add the fresh tomatoes and process briefly until they too are the same size. Now pour the whole lot into the preserving pan and reposition the processing bowl and blade. Then add the garlic, chillies, onions and red pepper and process these to approximately the same size. Then transfer them to join the tomatoes and add the spices, sugar, cider vinegar and salt.

Bring everything up to simmering point, stirring all the time, then when you have a gentle simmer, turn the heat low and let it simmer uncovered very gently for about 3–3½ hours. It doesn't need a great deal of attention – just come back now and then and give it a stir to prevent it sticking.

The chutney is ready when all the liquid has been absorbed and the mixture has thickened to a nice soft consistency. The way to test for the right moment is by using a wooden spoon to make a trail all the way across the top of the chutney – if the trail fills with juice, it's not ready. When the spoon leaves a trail that does not fill with the vinegary juices, the chutney is ready.

You need to watch this carefully at the end because undercooking will make the chutney too sloppy and over-cooking will make it dry. When the chutney is ready, allow it to cool a little and spoon it into hot sterilized jars. Cover with a waxed disc, seal it down when hot, but don't put the label on until it's cold. Store the chutney in a cool dark place for 6–8 weeks before using.

———————————— ◇ ————————————

Equipment Update

After every TV series I always get inundated with letters from people wanting to know about the various items of equipment used. So the following notes may be useful:

REALLY SOLID ROASTING TRAYS AND TINS

The really solid roasting tray campaign is still underway. Since the *Summer Collection* more and more of them are being sold and hopefully extinguishing forever the flimsy, buckling, poor quality varieties which are useless. When you buy a roasting tin or tray check that it can be put onto direct heat (this will cancel out the majority of them). If you invest in the right one it will last you a lifetime and prove in the end to be less expensive. We have therefore persuaded one supplier – Mermaid – to manufacture a solid Yorkshire Pudding tin (see page 143).

QUALITY FRYING PANS

The very best solid frying pans available now are made by a firm called Morso. They are black with wooden handles, are superb quality and there's no lining which means no nasty peeling and flaking if the heat is too high. Morso also make ovenproof frying pans (skillets) which are perfect for things like Red Onion Tarte Tatin.

MINI SAUCE WHISK

This is very good for making emulsions and for whisking vinaigrettes just before serving. Also brilliant for getting lumps out of sauces.

WIRE ROASTING RACKS

Wire roasting racks to fit in roasting tins. Especially good for duck recipes, so the bird doesn't sit in its own fat.

PANCAKE PAN

This is inexpensive and worth keeping just for making pancakes. There is also a pancake pan handle holder available, to protect your hands from the heat.

PALETTE KNIFE

Serrated palette knife. I have been using one made by Victorinox for years and it is still my favourite knife – it spreads, it slices, it lifts, all you want in life.

MULTIMIX

A Multimix is an electric hand whisk by Braun and a very useful piece of equipment with attachments for chopping, blending and whisking. A real winner.

MANDOLIN

The one I use is a Japanese invention and is great for slicing things very thinly in a lot less time than it takes trying to do it with a knife.

COPPER PANS

Copper pans with stainless steel linings are simply wonderful for sauces. There is also now an excellent aluminium version. I used both in the TV series.

The best mail order kitchen suppliers in the country are as follows:

Hogarth and Dwyer
240 High Street
Guildford
Surrey GU1 3JF
01483 456251

Lakeland Plastics
Alexandra Buildings
Windermere
Cumbria LA23 1BQ
015394 88100

Cookshops are in the following Sainsbury's stores:
*Apsley Mills
 Badger Farm
*Blackhall
*Brookwood
*Burpham
*Bury St Edmunds
*Camden
 Chase Lane
 Chichester
*Chippenham
*Coldhams Lane
*Cromwell Road
*Dulwich
*Durham
*Farlington
*Fosse Park
*Fulham
*Harrogate
*Hendon
 Hornchurch

*Hedge End
*Horsham
*Islington
*Kempshott
*Kidlington
 Kingsway
*Ladbroke Grove
*Locksbottom
*Marshall Lake
*Mere Green
*Nine Elms
*Purley Way
 Salford
*Sevenoaks
*Springfield
*St. Clares
*Stanway
*Streatham Common
*Tewkesbury Road
*Torquay
*Tunbridge Wells
*Wandsworth
*New Watford
*Winchmore Hill

*denotes Sainsbury's stores with both cookshop and Special Selection

Special Selection store without cookshop
Beaconsfield
Calcot
Chester
Chiswick
Cobham
Haywards Heath
Kiln Lane
London Colney
Low Hall
Queens Road
St. Albans
Staines
Taplow
Upton
Watchmoor Park

Stockists and Suppliers of Oriental Ingredients

LONDON

Bushwacker Wholefoods
132 King Street
Hammersmith
London W6 0QU
0181 748 2061

Cornucopia
64 St Mary's Road
South Ealing
London W5 5EX
0181 579 9431

Freshlands
196 Old Street
London EC1V 9FR
0171 250 1708
Mail order: 0171 490 3170

A large macrobiotic store selling wholefood products, organic where possible.

Habitat
All branches.

Japanese utensils: tempura pans and suribachis.

Loon Fung Supermarket Ltd
42-44 Gerrard Street
London W1
0171 437 7332

The biggest London Chinese supermarket, with Japanese food as well. Fresh tofu and exotic vegetables; also Chinese dried beancurd skin, dried mushrooms, Japanese sauces and vinegar.

Neal Street East
7 Neal Street
London WC2H 9PU
0171 240 0135

Japanese utensils and crockery. Mail order available.

Ninjin Food Shop
244 Great Portland Street
London W1
0171 388 2511

A large Japanese supermarket with a very wide range of Japanese foods, including fresh tofu.

Panzer's
13-19 Circus Road
St John's Wood
London NW8 6PB
0171 722 8162/8596

Yaohan
Yaohan Plaza
299 Edgware Road
Colindale
London NW9 0JJ
0181 200 0009

Sri Thai
56 Shepherds Bush Road
London W6 7LT
0171 602 0621

Talad Thai
320 Upper Richmond Road
London SW15 6TL
0181 789 8084

OUTSIDE LONDON

BATH

Harvest Wholefoods
37 Walcot Street
Bath
Avon
BA1 5BN
01225 465519

Japanese wholefoods, including nigari.

BRIGHTON

Infinity Foods
25 North Road
Brighton
BN1 1YA
01273 603563

The basic range of Japanese wholefoods, including nigari and koji; a wide range of utensils.

BRISTOL

Wild Oats
11 Lower Redland Road
Redland
Bristol
01272 731967

All the basic Japanese wholefoods, including koji and nigari; some utensils.

HEREFORD

Fodders Wholefoods
Church Street
Hereford
01432 358171

KINGSTON

Miura Foods
44 Coombe Road
Norbiton
Kingston
Surrey
0181 549 8076

Japanese food shop.

LEEDS

Wing Lee Hong
Hereford House
6 Edward Street
Leeds
LN2 7NN
01532 457203

Basic Japanese ingredients, fresh tofu, oriental vegetables.

LINCOLN

Pulse
25 Corporation Street
Lincoln
LN2 1HL
01522 528666

MANCHESTER

On the Eighth Day
111 Oxford Road
Manchester
M1 7DU
0161 273 4878

Japanese wholefoods, including nigari; also sells utensils.

NEWCASTLE-UPON-TYNE

Mandala Wholefoods Ltd
43 Manor House Road
Newcastle-upon-Tyne
0191 281 0045

Wing Hong Company
45–51 Stowell Street
Newcastle-upon-Tyne
0191 233 1800

Some Japanese foods, including seaweed, Japanese tea and tinned burdock root.

NOTTINGHAM

The Natural Food Co
37a Mansfield Road
Nottingham
0115 9559914

TRURO

Carley and Co
34–36 St. Austell Street
Truro
Cornwall
TR1 1SE
01872 77686

Japanese wholefoods, including nigari; utensils.

TWICKENHAM

Gaia Wholefoods
123 St. Margaret's Road
Twickenham
Middlesex
0181 892 2262

Stockists of fresh oriental herbs, also offering a mail order service.

SCOTLAND

Scotherbs
Kingswell
Castle Huntly Road
Longforgon
Dundee
DD2 5HJ
01382 360642

Index

Page numbers in *italic* refer to the photographs